A biographical dictionary of

THE BYZANTINE EMPIRE

Donald Nicol

Seaby

LONDON

SEABY'S BIOGRAPHICAL DICTIONARIES

A Biographical Dictionary of Dark Age Britain Williams, Smyth and Kirby
(in preparation)
A Biographical Dictionary of Dark Age Europe James (forthcoming)
A Biographical Dictionary of Ancient Egypt David and David (forthcoming)

Typeset by Setrite Typesetters
Printed by Biddles Ltd, Guildford, England

for the publishers
B A Seaby Ltd
7 Davies Street
London W1Y 1LL

Distributed by
B T Batsford Ltd
PO Box 4, Braintree, Essex CM7 7QY

A CIP Catalogue record for this book is available from the British Library

ISBN 1 85264 048 0

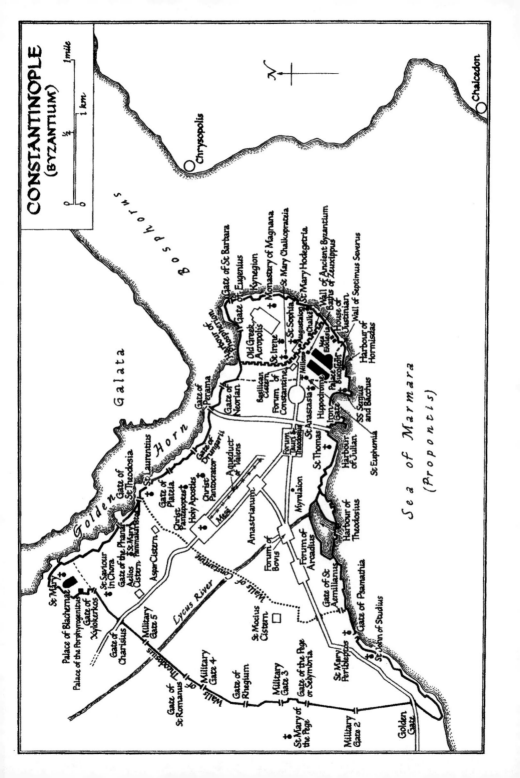

CONSTANTINOPLE
(BYZANTIUM)

1 mile
1 km.

N

Bosphorus

Chrysopolis

Chalcedon

Galata

Golden Horn

Gate of St. Barbara
Gate of Eugenius
Kynegion
Monastery of Magnana
St. Mary Chalkoprazia
St. Mary Hodegeria
Wall of Ancient Byzantium
Baths of Zeuxippus
House of Justinian
Wall of Septimus Severus
Harbour of Hormisdas
Harbour of Prosphorion
Old Greek Acropolis
St. Irene
St. Sophia
Augustaion
Milion
Chalke
Mese
Bucoleon
Palace
Iron Gate
SS. Sergius and Bacchus
Gate of Perama
Gate of Neorion
Basilican Cistern
Forum of Constantine
St. Anastasia
Hippodrome
Forum of Theodosius
St. Thomas
Harbour of Julian
St. Euphemia
Gate of Drungarii
Aqueduct of Valens
Christ Pantocrator
Christ Pantopoptes
Holy Apostles
Mese
Amastrianum
Mynelaion
Forum Tauri
Forum of Bovus
Forum of Arcadius
Gate of St. Aemillianus
Harbour of Theodosius
St. Laurentius
Gate of St. Theodosia
Gate of the Phanar
St. Mary Pammakaristos
Aetios Cistern
Aspar Cistern
St. Saviour In Chora
Lycus River
Mese to Thrace
St. Mocius Cistern
St. Mary Peribleptos
Gate of Psamathia
St. John of Studius
St. Mary
Palace of Blachernae
Palace of the Porphyrogenitus
Gate of Xylokerkos
Gate of Charisius
Military Gate 5
Gate of Rhegium
Military Gate 4
Military Gate 3
Gate of the Page or Selymbria
Gate of St. Romanus
St. Mary of the Page
Military Gate 2
Wall of Theodosius
Golden Gate

Sea of Marmara
(Propontis)

Contents

Preface

This is a work of reference listing in alphabetical order most of the persons of note and influence in the Byzantine Empire from the foundation of Constantinople in AD 330 to its conquest by the Turks in 1453. Only those who were native to the Byzantine world based on Constantinople are listed, with short biographies of each person. There are thus no entries for popes, emperors, kings and princes of western Europe in the Middle Ages; nor for caliphs, sultans and luminaries of the Arab and Turkish worlds; nor for the tsars and princes of the Slavs. Included are all the Byzantine Emperors, many of the Empresses, most of the Patriarchs of Constantinople, as well as writers, philosophers, theologians, scientists, teachers, soldiers, and notable members of the ecclesiastical and political hierarchy in the Byzantine Empire. The Byzantines would probably have approved of a compilation of this nature. Historiography, the writing of narrative history after the manner of the ancient Greek historians, was one of the arts at which they excelled. But they saw their past almost entirely in terms of top people. Narrative biography was more to their taste than structures or mentalities; though many of them were obsessed with theology. They were snobs as well as being xenophobic and suspicious or contemptuous of foreigners whether Christian or pagan. Their emperors were God's regents on earth. The deeds and misdeeds of ruling families, their wars against the unbeliever and the heretic, their intrigues, their marriages, their mistresses and their murders were of far greater interest than the state of the market, the misery of the poor and the peasantry, or the antics of western Christians and eastern Muslims.

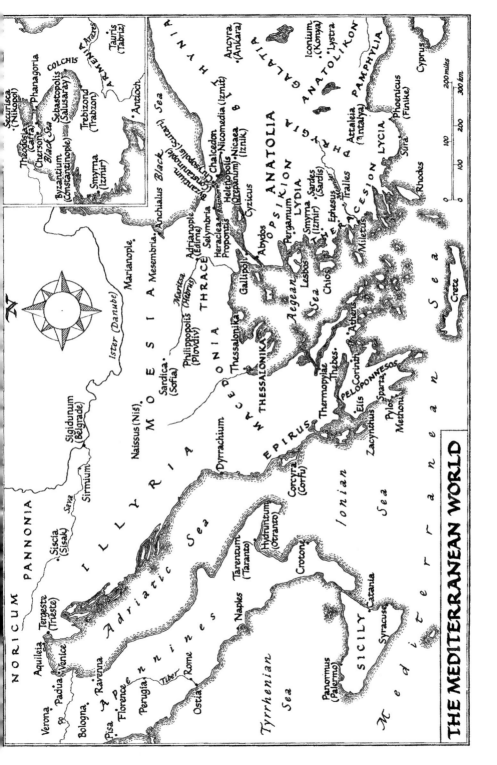

THE MEDITERRANEAN WORLD

Introduction

The Byzantine Empire was the continuation in Christian form of the ancient Roman Empire. Its long history began in AD 330 with the foundation of the second capital of that Empire at Constantinople by its Emperor, Constantine the Great. Its boundaries were those of the Roman Empire of old at least until the fifth century, when its western provinces were overrun by the 'barbarians' from the north. Thereafter its dominions were mainly confined to the Greek-speaking areas of the ancient world; and in the seventh century Greek replaced Latin as its official language. Yet its citizens continued to call themselves Romans (*Romaioi*) down to the fifteenth century. 'Byzantine' is a relatively modern term of convenience coined to describe the civilization that emanated from the ancient Greek city of Byzantium. For it was on the site of that city that Constantine built his New Rome in the fourth century.

Without Constantinople and its founder Constantine there would have been no Byzantine civilization. He was the first Christian Emperor of the Romans and the city to which he gave his name was the first purely Christian city. These two facts determined the course and the character of the Byzantine world for the next millennium and more. It was a world dominated by the letter if not always the spirit of the Christian faith, permeated by Roman concepts of law and order, and heir to the legacy of ancient Greek literature and thought. The Byzantine character was an amalgam of these three ingredients. It is well illustrated by Byzantine art, a style of art for which no other epithet will serve. It is part Greek, part Roman, and predominantly Christian. It may therefore seem odd that no names of Byzantine artists are listed in this biographical dictionary of their Empire. The reason is that Byzantine artists, mosaicists and icon-painters were usually anonymous, either because they were merely the humble media of God's purposes or because they were no more than modest artisans paid to serve their imperial masters.

The mortal remains of the Byzantine Empire today are to be seen in churches and monuments from Ravenna to Venice, from Rome to Sicily, all over the Slav countries of eastern Europe, in Greece, in Turkey, in Syria and Egypt and North Africa. The Greek language lives on. But the most evident survival of Byzantium now is the Orthodox church in its various communions. Orthodoxy or right belief as opposed to heresy was a necessary condition of Byzantine citizenship. The cultural revolution begun by Constantine's conversion to Christianity was legally enshrined in the canons of the early Councils of the Christian church over which he and his successors presided. It was the duty of a Roman Emperor to enforce law and order among his subjects. The emperors before Constantine had been tolerant of religious sects which posed no challenge to the prevailing order. The Christians had been persecuted because they were disorderly. After Constantine, when the miracle had happened, it was the turn of the Christians to be intolerant of Jews and pagans and also of each other; for they were a contentious and disputatious lot, seldom of one mind on the fundamental

tenets of their faith. To bring them to order the Christian Emperors period-
ically summoned councils of the church so that the doctrines of Orthodoxy
could, so far as possible, be defined and unanimously accepted by all right-
thinking Christians. Orthodoxy became the law. The heterodox or deviationists were condemned as outlaws.

After Constantine's death in 337, eighty-two Emperors of the Romans
reigned at Constantinople, until the last of them fell fighting his enemies at
its walls in 1453. Only one of them, Julian the Apostate, tried to put the
clock back and revert to paganism. Constantine started something permanent.
The Empire had no written constitution. In theory an Emperor became the
elect of God when he was proclaimed by the army, the senate and the
people and, perhaps most important, was in possession of Constantinople.
Emperors such as Basil I or Alexios I showed that the way to the throne was
a *carrière ouverte aux talents*. In practice, however, most Emperors strove to
secure and perpetuate their power and influence by creating a dynasty of
hereditary successors. There were nine such dynasties in the years between
Heraclius in 610 and Constantine XI in 1453.

In the fifth century, the Christian Roman Empire centred on Constantinople became the only Roman Empire when the western provinces, Italy,
France, Spain and North Africa, were barbarized by the Germanic invasions.
The city of Rome ceased to be in any sense a world capital, for all that it
remained the seat of the senior bishop of the church. The evident capital of
the Christian world was the New Rome at Constantinople. In the sixth
century the Emperor Justinian determined to win back what had been lost in
the west. The operation was directed from Constantinople and for a time
Roman rule was reasserted over Italy, from Ravenna, and over North
Africa, from Carthage. Justinian believed that God was on his side, for the
Goths in Italy were heretics as well as barbarians. But the cost of doing
God's work was more than the Empire could bear. Its resources had been
stretched too far for it to contain its older enemies, the Persians in the east,
and its nearer enemies, the Avars and the Slavs in the north.

It was left to Justinian's great successor Heraclius to save the New Rome
from a combined assault of Persians and Avars in 626–7 and then to deal
the final blow to the Persians on their home ground. The vacuum left in the
east was, however, promptly filled by the Arabs. The richest provinces of
the Empire, Egypt, Syria, Palestine, were rapidly overrun by Arab conquerors and lost for ever to Christian rule. Constantinople itself was besieged
by Arab armies and navies for months on end in the late seventh and early
eighth centuries. At the same time the Slavs descended on the Balkans and
on Greece, driving a wedge down the middle of the map of the ancient
Greco-Roman world. The Slavs, like the Arabs, were newcomers, with no
respect for the Roman concept of law and order nor for Christianity. The
historic urban centres of civilisation and of the Christian church, such as
Alexandria, Antioch or Corinth, were in the hands of infidels and pagans, or
in ruins. Only the cities of Thessalonica in the north of Greece and Constantinople were left to maintain and defend the Greco-Roman tradition and
the Christian faith.

So long as the Arabs could be kept out of the great land mass of Asia
Minor there was hope. For Asia Minor was the recruiting ground for the

Byzantine army. In the seventh century the Emperors began the battle for survival by imposing a form of martial law. They divided what remained of their eastern provinces into military and administrative regions known as Themes, each under a governor (*strategos*) appointed by and answerable to the Emperor. The consequence of this innovation was that the Byzantine army was transformed. So also, in the long term, was the structure of Byzantine society, its economy and its agriculture. Gone were the landed estates and the hereditary aristocracy. The village communes with their free-holding peasantry in the Themes were the units of taxation payable to the central government and of recruitment for the army. The Theme system was extended to cover the European provinces in the eighth and ninth centuries. It set Byzantine society on a course different from that of western Europe. The Slav settlements in the Balkans and in Greece effectively cut Constantinople off from the Christians of the west. The Byzantines became more isolated and more introspective. Theirs had always been a multi-racial society. Many of their greatest Emperors were Armenians. Yet Greek was their vernacular and their literary language; and they could converse with Latins of the west only through interpreters. At the same time, the loss of the eastern provinces made their Empire a smaller, more compact and more manageable unit. They became dedicated to the jealous preservation of their unique characteristics and to fighting to win the battle for survival against their enemies.

The first conclusive victories in that battle were achieved by the Emperor Leo III who, in 717–18, thwarted the second great siege of Constantinople by the Arabs and then defeated their army in the east in 740. He was also, however, the prime mover of a religious controversy that divided Byzantium for more than a hundred years. The rights and wrongs of icons or holy images as visual aids to Christian worship may seem to us a matter of taste. But in a world where the Emperor's word was law, religion was the only form of politics. The Byzantines found it hard to draw the line between things spiritual and things temporal. The theological and political storm aroused by iconoclasm or the enforced destruction of icons was not finally abated until 843. It was the most serious, if not the last, conflict of its kind. But even their detractors had to admit that the iconoclast Emperors had been remarkably successful soldiers; and when the religious storm had blown itself out the tide of war was turning in favour of Byzantium. Light was dawning at the end of the dark age.

The golden age of Byzantium was to last from about 850 to 1050. Those were the centuries in which the Emperors and their people were at their most self-confident and most assured of their superiority over other races, not least the Latins of the west. They became convinced that their Empire was meant to endure until the Second Coming. It was a time of recovery and then of expansion. Much lost territory was reconquered from the Arabs and from the Slavs. Christianity in its Orthodox form was carried by Byzantine missionaries into the Slav Kingdom of Moravia, into Bulgaria, into Russia; and the message of salvation was conveyed not in Greek or Latin but translated into the Slavonic languages through the invention of the Cyrillic script. Since church and state went hand in hand, the spread of Orthodoxy meant also the spread of Byzantine political ideas, law, art and literature.

The wealth of Byzantium was plain for all to see. There was a booming monetary economy. The Byzantine gold coin (*solidus* or *nomisma*), first minted by Constantine the Great, and known in the west as the Bezant, was the standard of international currency. It was the age in which some of the finest works of Byzantine art, architecture, craftsmanship, literature and scholarship were produced.

It came to its lingering end after the death of Basil II and his heirs of the Macedonian family, the longest-lived of all Byzantine dynasties, in 1056. Basil's immediate successors were content to live off the capital of prestige and prosperity which he bequeathed to them. They were oblivious of the internal and external dangers that threatened their complacency. The reconquest of lost territory and the extension of the frontiers brought unforeseen problems. A new social class of military aristocracy emerged in the eastern provinces, men who had made their family fortunes from the spoils of war. They invested their wealth in landed property and they bought out the peasant farmers who went with it, thus subverting the Theme system on which the defence and the economy depended. Successful soldiers and landed gentry were no longer prepared to live under a form of martial law that had been designed for an emergency, especially when it was imposed and perpetuated by a huge civilian bureaucracy in Constantinople. Men of wealth and local influence began to take pride in their independence from the bonds that tied them and their families to a faraway government. The use of family names was a late development in Byzantium. Emperors like Heraclius, Leo III, or Basil I had not troubled to advertise their clans or affinities by adopting surnames. Their successors wanted to identify themselves as the progeny of such proud and wealthy families as Phokas, Komnenos, Doukas, or Palaiologos. By so doing they marked the change in social structure, from a firmly centralized autocracy in Constantinople to a less integrated aristocracy based on family kinship, riches and property, in which public office could be acquired by influence. The great military families of the new landed aristocracy despised the bureaucracy in Constantinople and looked to the day when a soldier and not a civil servant would become Emperor.

Being provincials they were also more aware of the growing danger from the east after the Seljuq Turks took over the Arab caliphate at Baghdad and began to infiltrate into Byzantine territory in Asia Minor. There were new and unexpected perils also in the west. The Normans invaded the Byzantine protectorate in the south of Italy in the eleventh century. They met little opposition. In 1071 they captured Bari, the last remaining Byzantine possession in Italy. In the very same year the Emperor Romanos IV, the first soldier Emperor for many years, was overwhelmingly defeated by the Seljuq Turks at Manzikert in Armenia. Ten years later the Turks had occupied most of Asia Minor and reached Nicaea, within striking distance of Constantinople.

Once again the Empire had to fight for survival. This time, however, it had to contend with competition from western Christendom. When Charlemagne had been crowned as Emperor in the west in 800 the Byzantines had been deeply offended. When Otto I of Germany was crowned as Emperor of the Romans in 962 they had been at the height of their glory and confident enough to hold his presumption in contempt. A hundred years later the balance of power was changing between the eastern and western claimants to the imperial title. The Byzantines could no longer comfort themselves that they were the greatest Christian power on earth. Latin Christians began to go on pilgrimages to the Holy Land. Inevitably they passed through Constantinople. They were not welcome. There was mutual incomprehension and dislike between Greeks and Latins. The schism between the churches of Rome and Constantinople in 1054 had been a symptom of differences in ideology and culture far deeper than those aired in the celebrated clash between the Patriarch and the Pope's legate.

After the disaster at Manzikert in 1071 there was no shortage of pretenders to the throne at Constantinople. In 1081 one of the military aristocracy at last came to the top in the person of Alexios I Komnenos. It was he who saved the day; and the dynasty that he founded reigned until 1185, giving much-needed stability and tenacity to the Empire. As his daughter, the historian Anna observed, Alexios took over an Empire beset by enemies on all sides. The Normans had invaded the mainland opposite Italy. The barbarous Pechenegs threatened the frontier on the north. The Seljuq Turks were victorious in the east. With a little help from western Christendom Alexios could have weathered these storms. What he least expected was the descent on his Empire of hordes of western pilgrims in arms, committed not to the defence of Constantinople and eastern Christendom but to the liberation of distant Jerusalem from the infidel. In 1096 the knights and soldiers of the First Crusade burst upon Byzantium in unmanageable numbers. They came and they stayed, carving out their own estates and principalities in what had once been Byzantine territory. They were followed by traders from Genoa and from Venice, eager to make money out of the new markets in the Levant. The Venetians had helped Alexios in his war against the Normans. He rewarded them with trading concessions in Byzantium and a commercial quarter in Constantinople. The more they got the more they wanted. The Byzantine government charged them with being disorderly. The Byzantine people found them rude and arrogant. There were violent incidents and murders in the streets.

In the twelfth century the Emperor Manuel I, grandson of Alexios, sank his imperial pride to the point of recognizing that the other Christian powers in the world had a right to exist and might even be appeased or befriended by diplomatic measures. It was a policy that cut no ice with the western Emperor Frederick Barbarossa and alienated Manuel's own subjects. Barbarossa called him simply King of the Greeks. The Byzantines called him a Latinophile. The Venetians thirsted for revenge after he had arrested all their merchants in his dominions; and his final humiliation came in a catastrophic defeat by the Turks at Myriokephalon in 1176.

It was a pity that the good intentions of Manuel I were thwarted. By the end of the twelfth century it was too late to avoid a confrontation between the Christians of east and west. The crusades had magnified the incomprehension and ill-feeling between them. The greed of the Italian merchants had begun to sap the economy of Byzantium. There were those in the western world who believed that there were sound moral and commercial reasons for putting Constantinople under western management. It was commonly said that the Byzantines had sabotaged the sacred cause of the crusade and that their obstinate refusal to join the fold of the Roman church merited a crusade against them for their own salvation. The Venetians would seize any opportunity to monopolize the markets of Constantinople. The opportunity offered itself with the Fourth Crusade. In April 1204 the crusaders, who had been ferried there on Venetian warships, stormed and captured the city in the name of God and Mammon. A Frenchman, Baldwin of Flanders, became Emperor of Constantinople. A Venetian became Patriarch. The crusaders invaded and conquered much of the mainland of Greece, while the Venetians commandeered the ports and islands of the Empire.

The Byzantines never fully recovered from the shock of the Fourth Crusade. Those who escaped from Constantinople gathered together three fragments of their Empire in exile, one in Epiros in the north-west of Greece, one at Trebizond on the south coast of the Black Sea, the third at Nicaea in Asia Minor. It was from Nicaea that the last of the Emperors in exile, Michael VIII Palaiologos, expelled the Latin intruders and restored Constantinople to its rightful owners in 1261. The Latins did not give in gracefully. For twenty years the new Emperor had to be constantly on his guard against a repetition of the Fourth Crusade, advocated by the French who had been dispossessed, with the support of Venice and the papacy. While his armies were poised to defend the western approaches to his Empire, new bands of Turkish raiders, dislodged by the Mongols, were penetrating the neglected eastern frontiers. By 1300 Constantinople was crowded with Christian refugees from Asia Minor. The defences had broken down. The Byzantine army was mainly composed of unreliable and expensive mercenaries. In 1302 a Turkish warrior chieftain called Osman fought and won a battle with them in Bithynia. He was the founder of the Osmanli or Ottoman people. Within a few years Nicaea and the other Greek cities in the area had fallen into his hands.

The events of the fourteenth century demonstrated that the Byzantine Empire had been not only shocked but shattered by the Fourth Crusade. Much of mainland Greece remained under foreign occupation; the Greek islands were Italian colonies; the wealth of Crete went to Venice; that of Chios to Genoa. The economy was beyond repair. The Byzantine gold coin, hopelessly devalued, gave place to the Venetian ducat. The fragmentation of the Empire's territory was mirrored by the disintegration of its government. A series of civil wars for possession of the throne advertised its weakness. The Empire of the Romans had degenerated into a petty kingdom fought over by princes who were the victims and the puppets of the Italians and the Ottoman Turks. In the two cities of Thessalonica and Constantinople, however, there was still much wealth in private hands. There was also a remarkable revival of artistic, cultural and spiritual activity. Scholars took to rediscovering the heritage of ancient Greek literature and philosophy; monks took to re-exploring the inner meaning of the Christian life and of man's relationship with God. As in the years of iconoclasm, the political conflicts of the mid-fourteenth century were partly expressed in religious differences in the so-called Hesychast controversy. While the authority of the state declined, that of the church increased. The latterday

Patriarchs of Constantinople commanded more universal respect than the Emperors among all Orthodox Christians, Slavs as well as Greeks; and they preached that God would not forsake his chosen people if they held fast to their inherited faith.

By 1400 Constantinople was almost all that was left of the Empire. It had become a shabby and depopulated city. Yet it was still a magnet drawing to it merchants and exploiters and even scholars from Italy. Above all it attracted the Ottoman Turks, whose warriors had already overrun most of eastern Europe. Their prophets foretold that Constantinople was destined to become a Muslim city. Their Sultans threatened and bullied the Emperors while they sheltered behind their city walls. The Emperors in despair travelled to the west to put their pitiful case in Venice, in Paris and in London, appealing to western Christendom to come to their aid. In 1438 the Emperor John VIII Palaiologos led a delegation to the Council of Ferrara-Florence to declare the submission of his church to Rome. The Orthodox abjured their alleged heresies and were accepted as fellow Christians, which made it easier for the Pope to preach a crusade for their rescue. To most of the Byzantines, however, it seemed like the ultimate betrayal of their Orthodox faith. They had lost the last round in the battle of wits with the Latins which had begun with the Fourth Crusade; and they wept no tears when the promised relief army from the west, the reward for their Emperor's treachery, came to grief at the hands of the Turks at Varna in 1444.

Nine years later the conquering Sultan Mehmed II conducted the final siege of Constantinople. The great land walls of the city, which had deterred every enemy since the fifth century, could not withstand weeks of bombardment by the new weapons of heavy artillery. On the dawn of Tuesday, 29 May 1453, the Ottoman troops broke in. The last Byzantine Emperor, Constantine XI Palaiologos, died in the defence of his city. The Byzantine Empire as an institution also died on that Tuesday. It was at once transmogrified into the Ottoman Empire, with a Muslim Sultan in place of a Christian Emperor. But the Byzantine tradition and spirit lived on in the Orthodox church, to keep the Greeks in mind of past glories and to foster in them the hope that one day the Ottoman Empire too would take to its bed as the sick man of Europe.

Note on Transliteration

Consistency in the transliteration of Greek personal and place names is notoriously problematical. Most English and American Byzantinists render them in latinized form. The French prefer to gallicize the Greek. This has always seemed to me to be insulting to the Byzantines who were deeply conscious and proud of their linguistic and ethnic differences from the Latins of western Christendom. I therefore prefer, in company with German historians, to present their names in a form as near to the Greek spelling as can be contrived: e.g., Nikephoros and not Nicephorus; Komnenos and not Comnenus; Doukas and not Ducas. However, it was not until the seventh century that Greek replaced Latin as the official language of the Byzantine Empire. I have therefore adhered, so far as possible, to Latin forms of personal names until about 650. This is no doubt pedantic. But it would be carrying pedantry too far to offer the forms Konstantinos for Constantine, or Johannes for John; and where there is an accepted English version of a Greek Christian name I have generally adopted it. Total consistency is, however, probably impossible.

Abbreviations

The following abbreviations have been adopted in the bibliographic references for each entry:

DHGE = Ed A Baudrillart *et al.* 1912− (in progress) *Dictionnaire d'histoire et de géographie ecclésiastiques*. Paris

MPG = Migne, J-P 1857−66 *Patrologiae cursus completus: series Graeco-Latina* 161 vols, Paris

PLP = Ed E Trapp *et al.* 1976− (in progress) *Prosopographisches Lexikon der Palaiologenzeit*. Vienna

All other references are given by author and date; a full list of references may be found at p. 149.

Chronological Table of Events

324	Accession of *Constantine I
325	1st Oecumenical Council at Nicaea
330	Foundation of Constantinople
378	Defeat of *Valens by Visigoths at Adrianople
381	2nd Oecumenical Council at Constantinople
410	Capture of Rome by Alaric
431	3rd Oecumenical Council at Ephesos
438–9	Theodosian Code; building of walls of Constantinople
451	4th Oecumenical Council at Chalcedon (*Marcian)
476	Fall of Roman Empire in west
482–518	Acacian schism between churches (*Acacius)
529	Code of *Justinian
532	Nika riot in Constantinople
533	Digest and Institutes of *Justinian
533–52	Reconquest of Italy from Goths (*Belisarius, *Narses)
542	Outbreak of plague
553	5th Oecumenical Council at Constantinople
c. 580	Avars and Slavs begin to settle in Balkans and Greece
c. 582	Exarchates of Ravenna and Carthage created by *Maurice
610	Overthrow of *Phokas by *Heraclius
622–7	Defeat of Persians by *Heraclius
626–7	Constantinople besieged by Persians and Avars
638	Arab conquest of Jerusalem
640–2	Arab conquest of Egypt
674–8	Arab siege of Constantinople (*Constantine IV)
680–1	6th Oecumenical Council at Constantinople
691	Quinisextum Council at Constantinople (*Justinian II)
697–8	Arabs capture Carthage
717–18	Arab siege of Constantinople (*Leo III)
730	Edict of Iconoclasm by *Leo III
741	*Ecloga* of *Leo III
751	Lombards capture Ravenna
754	Iconoclast Council of *Constantine V
787	7th Oecumenical Council at Nicaea restores icons (*Eirene)
800	Coronation of Charlemagne as Emperor in west
c. 805	Recovery of Greece from Slavs
811	*Nikephoros I defeated and killed by Krum of Bulgars
815	Iconoclasm revived by Council at Constantinople (*Leo V)
820–3	Revolt of *Thomas the Slav against *Michael II
826–7	Arab conquest of Crete and Sicily
843	Final restoration of icons (*Theophano)
863	Missions of *Constantine-Cyril and *Methodios to Moravia

867	Accession of *Basil I
867–97	Photian Schism between Rome and Constantinople (*Photios)
887–93	Basilika of *Leo VI
896	Symeon of Bulgaria defeats Byzantine army (*Leo VI)
904	Arabs plunder Thessalonica
919	Usurpation of *Romanos I Lakapenos
927	Death of Symeon of Bulgaria
934–44	Campaigns against Arabs (John *Kourkouas)
961	Reconquest of Crete from Arabs (*Nikephoros II)
965–9	Campaigns against Arabs (*Nikephoros II)
971	Defeat of Russians by *John I Tzimiskes
972–6	Campaigns against Arabs (*John I)
988–9	Conversion of Russians
1000–19	Conquest and annexation of Bulgaria (*Basil II)
1054	Schism between churches (*Michael Keroullarios)
1056	End of Macedonian dynasty (*Theodora)
1071	Norman conquest of Bari; Battle of Manzikert (*Romanos IV)
1081–91	Wars against Normans and Pechenegs (*Alexios I Komnenos)
1082	Byzantine treaty with Venice; trial and condemnation of John *Italos
1096	First Crusade (*Alexios I)
1147	Second Crusade (*Manuel I)
1171	Arrest of all Venetian merchants (*Manuel I)
1176	Battle of Myriokephalon; defeat of *Manuel I by Seljuq Turks
1185	Norman capture of Thessalonica; downfall of *Andronikos I
1203–4	Fourth Crusade captures Constantinople; Byzantine Empire in exile at Nicaea (1204–61) (*Theodore I Laskaris); foundation of Empire at Trebizond (*Alexios I Komnenos)
1224	Byzantines of Epiros capture Thessalonica and set up rival Empire in exile (*Michael I and *Theodore Komnenos Doukas)
1244–6	Thessalonica incorporated into Empire of Nicaea (*John III Doukas Batatzes)
1259	Battle of Pelagonia; *Michael II of Epiros defeated by armies of Nicaea
1261	Recapture of Constantinople (*Michael VIII Palaiologos)
1266–82	Attempts by Charles of Anjou to reconquer Constantinople
1274	2nd Council of Lyons; union of eastern and western churches
1281	Byzantine victory over Charles of Anjou (*Michael VIII)
1282	Sicilian Vespers; death of *Michael VIII
1321–8	Civil war between *Andronikos II and *Andronikos III

1341−7	Civil war between *John VI Kantakouzenos and *John V Palaiologos
1347−54	*John VI Emperor
1341−51	Hesychast controversy (Gregory *Palamas)
1349	Establishment of Despotate of Morea at Mistra (*Manuel Kantakouzenos)
1354−91	*John V Palaiologos Emperor
1354	Turkish occupation of Gallipoli
1369	*John V visits Rome and submits to Pope
1371	Battle of the Marica; Serbians defeated by Ottoman Turks
1376−9	Revolt of *Andronikos IV
1389	Battle of Kossovo
1390	Revolt of *John VII
1394−1402	Turkish blockade of Constantinople (*Manuel II)
1399−1403	*Manuel II visits western Europe
1402	Battle of Ankara; Ottoman Turks defeated by Mongols
1430	Turkish conquest of Thessalonica
1438−9	Council of Ferrara-Florence; union of churches again proclaimed (*John VIII)
1444	Crusade of Varna
1453	Fall of Constantinople (29 May); death of *Constantine XI
1454	*Gennadios II invested as first Patriarch under Turkish rule
1460	Fall of Mistra (*Thomas Palaiologos)
1461	Fall of Trebizond (*David Komnenos)

Partial Genealogical Tables
of
Byzantine Imperial Families

An asterisk by names appearing in the tables indicates a biographical entry.

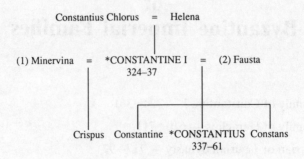

Table I. The family of CONSTANTINE I: 324–61

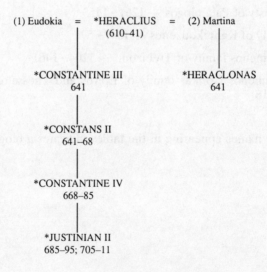

Table II. The family of HERACLIUS: 610–711

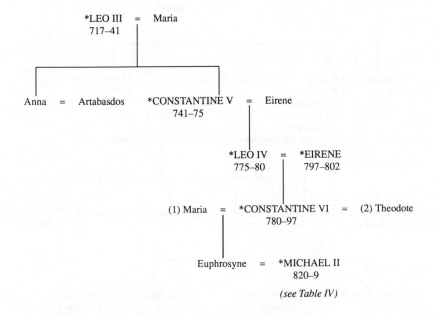

Table III. The Syrian or Isaurian dynasty: 717–97

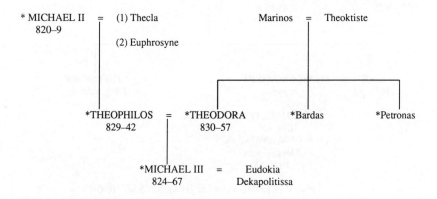

Table IV: The Amorian dynasty: 820–67

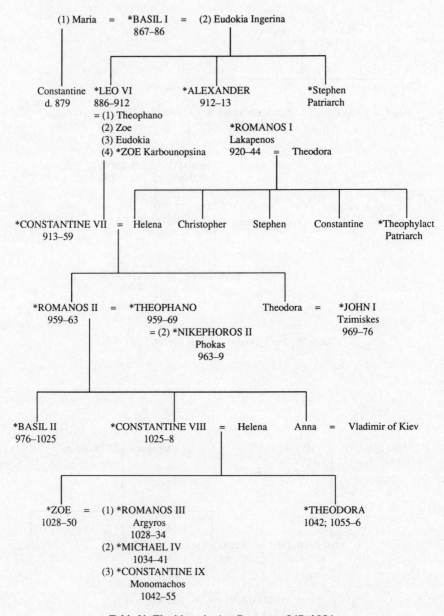

(1) Maria = *BASIL I = (2) Eudokia Ingerina
867–86

Constantine *LEO VI *ALEXANDER *Stephen
d. 879 886–912 912–13 Patriarch
= (1) Theophano
(2) Zoe *ROMANOS I
(3) Eudokia Lakapenos
(4) *ZOE Karbounopsina 920–44 = Theodora

*CONSTANTINE VII = Helena Christopher Stephen Constantine *Theophylact
913–59 Patriarch

*ROMANOS II = *THEOPHANO Theodora = *JOHN I
959–63 959–69 Tzimiskes
= (2) *NIKEPHOROS II 969–76
Phokas
963–9

*BASIL II *CONSTANTINE VIII = Helena Anna = Vladimir of Kiev
976–1025 1025–8

*ZOE = (1) *ROMANOS III *THEODORA
1028–50 Argyros 1042; 1055–6
1028–34
(2) *MICHAEL IV
1034–41
(3) *CONSTANTINE IX
Monomachos
1042–55

Table V. The Macedonian Dynasty: 867–1056

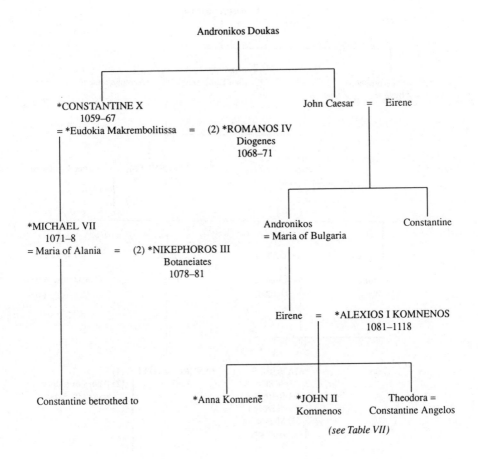

Andronikos Doukas

*CONSTANTINE X
1059–67
= *Eudokia Makrembolitissa   =   (2) *ROMANOS IV
Diogenes
1068–71

John Caesar   =   Eirene

*MICHAEL VII
1071–8
= Maria of Alania   =   (2) *NIKEPHOROS III
Botaneiates
1078–81

Andronikos
= Maria of Bulgaria

Constantine

Eirene   =   *ALEXIOS I KOMNENOS
1081–1118

Constantine betrothed to

*Anna Komnenē

*JOHN II
Komnenos

Theodora =
Constantine Angelos

(see Table VII)

Table VI. The family of Doukas 1059–78

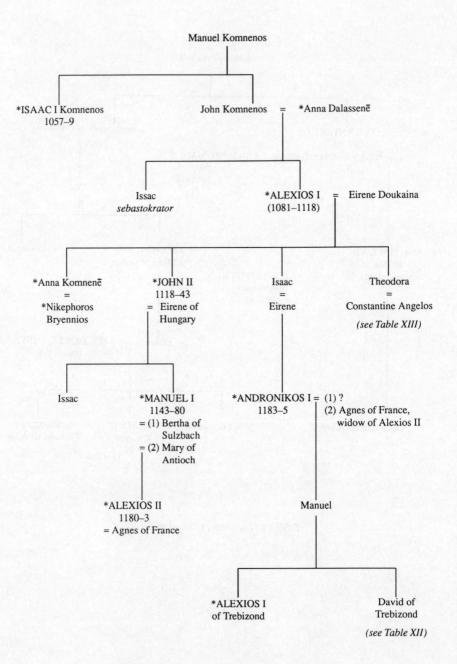

Manuel Komnenos

*ISAAC I Komnenos
1057–9

John Komnenos = *Anna Dalassenē

Issac
sebastokrator

*ALEXIOS I = Eirene Doukaina
(1081–1118)

*Anna Komnenē
=
*Nikephoros
Bryennios

*JOHN II
1118–43
= Eirene of
Hungary

Isaac
=
Eirene

Theodora
=
Constantine Angelos
(see Table XIII)

Issac

*MANUEL I
1143–80
= (1) Bertha of
Sulzbach
= (2) Mary of
Antioch

*ANDRONIKOS I = (1) ?
1183–5   (2) Agnes of France,
widow of Alexios II

*ALEXIOS II
1180–3
= Agnes of France

Manuel

*ALEXIOS I
of Trebizond

David of
Trebizond
(see Table XII)

Table VII. The family of Komnenos 1081–1185

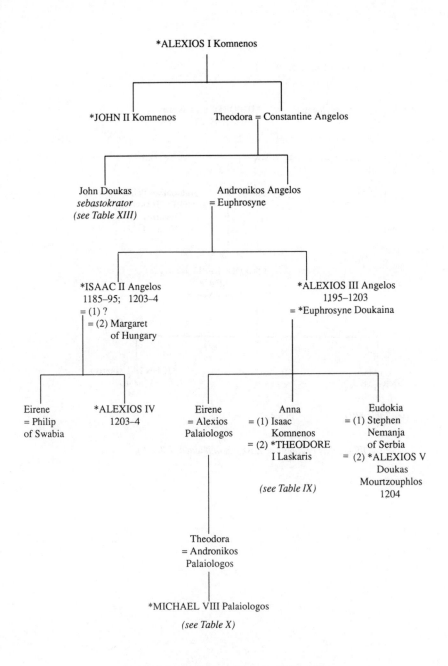

Table VIII. The family of Angelos 1185–1204

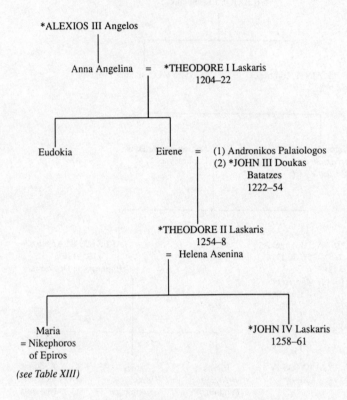

*ALEXIOS III Angelos

Anna Angelina = *THEODORE I Laskaris
1204–22

Eudokia   Eirene = (1) Andronikos Palaiologos
                           (2) *JOHN III Doukas
                               Batatzes
                               1222–54

*THEODORE II Laskaris
1254–8
= Helena Asenina

Maria   *JOHN IV Laskaris
= Nikephoros   1258–61
of Epiros

(see Table XIII)

Table IX. The family of Laskaris at Nicaea 1204–61

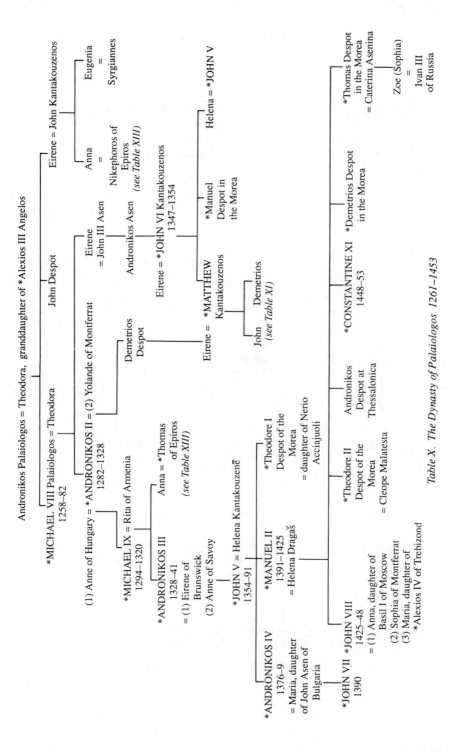

Table X. The Dynasty of Palaiologos 1261–1453

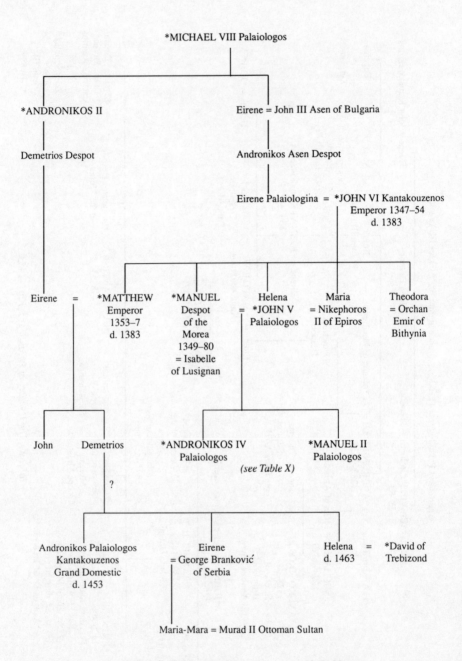

*MICHAEL VIII Palaiologos

*ANDRONIKOS II

Demetrios Despot

Eirene = John III Asen of Bulgaria

Andronikos Asen Despot

Eirene Palaiologina = *JOHN VI Kantakouzenos
Emperor 1347–54
d. 1383

Eirene = *MATTHEW
Emperor
1353–7
d. 1383

*MANUEL
Despot
of the
Morea
1349–80
= Isabelle
of Lusignan

Helena
= *JOHN V
Palaiologos

Maria
= Nikephoros
II of Epiros

Theodora
= Orchan
Emir of
Bithynia

John   Demetrios

?

*ANDRONIKOS IV
Palaiologos
(see Table X)

*MANUEL II
Palaiologos

Andronikos Palaiologos
Kantakouzenos
Grand Domestic
d. 1453

Eirene
= George Branković
of Serbia

Helena   =   *David of
d. 1463   Trebizond

Maria-Mara = Murad II Ottoman Sultan

Table XI. The family of Kantakouzenos 1347–83

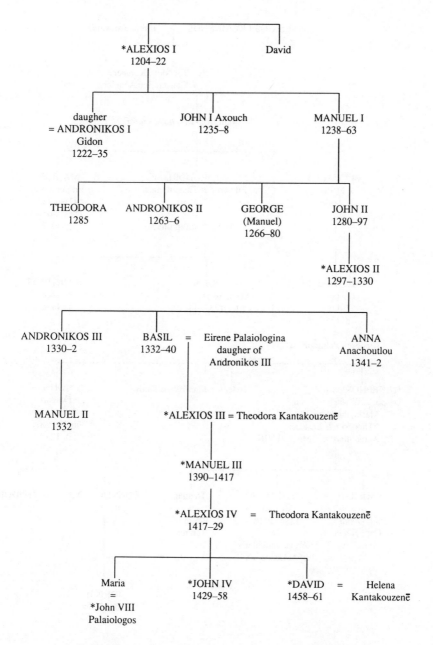

Table XII. The Komnenos family of Trebizond 1204–1461

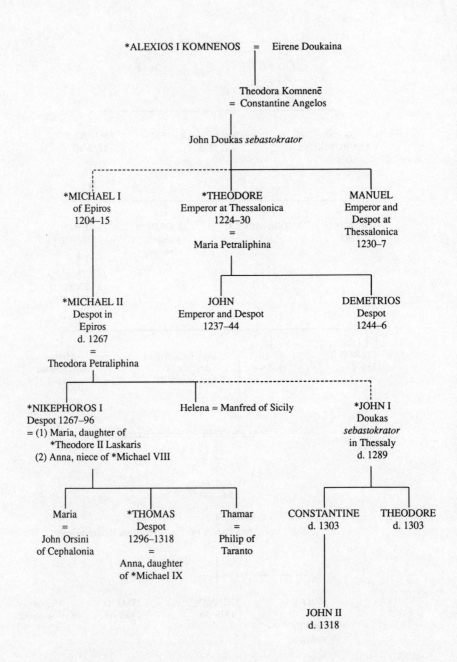

*ALEXIOS I KOMNENOS = Eirene Doukaina

Theodora Komnenē
= Constantine Angelos

John Doukas *sebastokrator*

*MICHAEL I
of Epiros
1204–15

*THEODORE
Emperor at Thessalonica
1224–30
=
Maria Petraliphina

MANUEL
Emperor and
Despot at
Thessalonica
1230–7

*MICHAEL II
Despot in
Epiros
d. 1267
=
Theodora Petraliphina

JOHN
Emperor and Despot
1237–44

DEMETRIOS
Despot
1244–6

*NIKEPHOROS I
Despot 1267–96
= (1) Maria, daughter of
*Theodore II Laskaris
(2) Anna, niece of *Michael VIII

Helena = Manfred of Sicily

*JOHN I
Doukas
sebastokrator
in Thessaly
d. 1289

Maria
=
John Orsini
of Cephalonia

*THOMAS
Despot
1296–1318
=
Anna, daughter
of *Michael IX

Thamar
=
Philip of
Taranto

CONSTANTINE
d. 1303

THEODORE
d. 1303

JOHN II
d. 1318

Table XIII. The Komnenos Doukas family of Epiros & Thessalonica 1204–1318

A

Acacius Patriarch of Constantinople 472—89

Acacius (Akakios) was Patriarch at a time when the eastern church was deeply divided over the question of the relationship between the divine and human natures of Christ. The Monophysites, who believed that they were one, had been condemned as heretics at the Council of Chalcedon in 451, but they remained a powerful religious and political force in Egypt and Syria. In 475—6 Acacius fell foul of the usurper *Basiliscus who was a Monophysite. In 482, however, he helped the Emperor *Zeno to devise a compromise formula called the *Henotikon* or Edict of Union. It was accepted by the Patriarchs of Alexandria, Jerusalem and, after some trouble, Antioch. But the Pope, Felix III, denounced it and excommunicated Acacius, who retaliated in like manner. The resulting rift in the church universal came to be known as the Acacian schism. It was not healed until *Justin I came to the throne in 518. Both Pope and Patriarch then condemned to oblivion the name of Acacius. He died in November 489. His successors were Fravitas, who was Patriarch for one year only, and then *Euphemius.

BIBL. Grumel 1972: 111—26; *DHGE* I; cols. 244—8

Agathias (*c.* 532—82) historian and poet

Agathias was born in Myrina in Asia Minor and educated first in Alexandria and then, after 551, in Constantinople, where he studied law and practised as an advocate (*scholasticus*). He lived through the great earthquake of 557 and died about 582. He wrote a *History* in five books beginning at the year 552, where the *Wars* of *Procopius leave off, and continuing to 558. It was never finished. Its main theme is the campaigns of *Narses against the Goths, Vandals and Persians, mainly from eyewitness accounts. Agathias was also a poet and a leading light in a literary circle at the court of *Justinian, with his friend *Paul the Silentiary. Most of his poems are in the form of occasional verses, epigrams, love-poems and elegies, somewhat long-winded and convoluted in style. More than a hundred of them by himself and his friends were included in later anthologies.

BIBL. Keydell 1967; Frendo 1975; Cameron 1970; Hunger 1978, I: 303—9

Akindynos, Gregory (*d.* 1348) monk and theologian

He was the chief theological adversary of Gregory *Palamas and the doctrine of Hesychasm. His friends Nikephoros *Gregoras and the Patriarch *John XIV Kalekas sided with him. All three were condemned at a council in Constantinople in 1347. He died in exile in 1348; and his memory was again anathematised when Hesychasm was declared to be Orthodox in 1351.

BIBL. *PLP* no. 495; Hero 1983

Akropolites, George (*d*. 1282) statesman and historian

He served as Grand Logothete or Chancellor of the Empire first at Nicaea and then in Constantinople after 1261. He had studied under Nikephoros *Blemmydes and was himself the teacher of the Patriarch *Gregory II (George of Cyprus) and the Emperor *Theodore II Laskaris. In Constantinople he taught philosophy and mathematics. He also travelled as an imperial ambassador; and in 1274 he represented his Emperor *Michael VIII at the second Council of Lyons, where he professed union with the Roman church which he later repudiated. He wrote rhetorical and theological treatises; but his major work is his *History* of the Empire in exile at Nicaea from 1203 to 1261. His son Constantine Akropolites became Logothete about 1282 and wrote numerous *Lives* of saints and other works.

BIBL. *PLP* no. 518; for the *History, see* Heisenberg 1903; Wirth 1978

Alexander Emperor 912–13

Alexander was the brother and co-Emperor of *Leo VI and took over the government when Leo died in May 912. Dissolute and feckless, he was indifferent to affairs of state. His main achievement was to provoke the Bulgarian ruler Symeon to war by withholding the tribute that Leo had agreed to pay him. He died of over-indulgence in June 913, leaving Leo's son *Constantine VII as heir.

BIBL. Vasiliev 1968: 216–19; Jenkins 1966: 227–30

Alexios I Komnenos Emperor 1081–1118

Alexios was the third son of John Komnenos and his ambitious wife Anna *Dalassenē and a nephew of the Emperor *Isaac Komnenos. The family were rich landowners who favoured stronger action against the Empire's enemies, especially the Seljuq Turks in the east and the Normans in the west. Since the downfall of *Romanos IV in 1071 there had been no shortage of candidates for the throne. Alexios skilfully worked his way to the head of the queue and displaced the elderly *Nikephoros III in 1081. He was crowned Emperor in April. His first concern was to drive back the Normans led by Robert Guiscard who had invaded northern Greece from across the water in Italy. It was a bitter and costly war and victory was achieved only with the help of the Venetians, whom Alexios rewarded with extensive privileges of free trade. Guiscard died in 1085, though his son Bohemond was to return to the attack in 1107. In 1091 Alexios defeated the Pechenegs who had for long been a menace on the Danube frontier. The Turks were less tractable, though he came to terms with their Sultans in 1081 and again in 1093.

It was for reinforcements against the Turks that Alexios appealed to Pope Urban II in 1095. His appeal helped to inspire the First Crusade a year later. He had asked for a small force of mercenaries. What he provoked was, as his daughter *Anna Komnenē observed, a mass movement of peoples from west to east bent on the liberation of faraway Jerusalem. The crusaders, for all their oaths of loyalty to the Emperor, set up their own principalities on Byzantine territory, thereby contributing to the disintegration of the Empire. Alexios had hoped to halt that process by centralizing all authority in Constantinople. But he could not prevent his own class of landed gentry from expanding their estates and even rewarded them by granting them more property in return for military service. He was more successful in enforcing uniformity of thought on his people, suppressing the religious heresy of the dualist Bogomils and the intellectual heresies of such as John *Italos. His Orthodox piety was sincere. His church censured him only when he deployed some of its treasure for military purposes.

Alexios saved his Empire from the rocks on which it had seemed likely to founder before 1081. He was a successful statesman as well as a soldier. He gave stability to the ruling class by making the establishment a family concern, partly through judicious marriages, partly by the gift of honorific titles to loyal supporters. He himself married *Eirene of the rival family of Doukas and, through his son *John II who succeeded him when he died in August 1118, he was the father of a dynasty which lasted for over a hundred years.

BIBL. Chalandon 1900; Angold 1984: 114—49

Alexios II Komnenos Emperor 1180—3

Alexios was only eleven years old when his father, *Manuel I, died in September 1180, although he was already married to Agnes of France, the eight-year old daughter of Louis VII. His mother, Mary of Antioch, acted as regent. The evident concentration of authority in the hands of westerners provoked a wave of anti-Latin feeling in Byzantium which brought the late Manuel's cousin *Andronikos Komnenos to the throne. Alexios and his mother were murdered in 1183.

BIBL. Ostrogorsky 1968: 394—6

Alexios III Angelos Emperor 1195—1203

Alexios III dethroned and imprisoned his brother *Isaac II in April 1195. He was a weak, corrupt and selfish ruler, dominated by his dynamic wife *Euphrosyne Doukaina. His short reign witnessed the further dissolution of the Empire, leaving it vulnerable to the machinations of its western enemies. Serbia and Bulgaria finally broke away as autonomous kingdoms whose rulers looked to Rome for recognition of their sovereignty. The intervention of the Fourth Crusade in the dynastic affairs of Constantinople brought Isaac II back to his throne in July 1203. Alexios fled and after many adventures sought refuge with his cousin, *Michael I Komnenos Doukas, the independent ruler of Epiros. He made his last bid for power in Asia Minor, where he incited the Seljuq Sultan to help him snatch the imperial crown from the Emperor in exile at Nicaea, *Theodore I Laskaris. He was captured in 1210 and ended his days in a monastery at Nicaea.

BIBL. Brand 1968: 117—57

Alexios IV Angelos Emperor 1203—4

He was the son of the Emperor *Isaac II, with whom he was imprisoned in Constantinople following the coup d'état of his uncle *Alexios III in 1195.

3

He escaped to the west in 1201 and persuaded the leaders of the Fourth Crusade, then being planned, to make their pilgrimage by way of Constantinople. He promised rich rewards if they would reinstate his father and himself as Emperors. That he had no means of fulfilling his promises quickly became clear after the crusaders had done what he asked in 1203. Their presence and their conduct in Constantinople prompted revolt led by *Alexios (V) Doukas, who was proclaimed Emperor in January 1204. In February Alexios IV was strangled. His father Isaac died a few days later.

BIBL. Brand 1968: 215–16, 229–30, 236, 241–50; Queller 1977

Alexios V Doukas Mourtzouphlos Emperor 1204

When the young *Alexios IV failed to reward the leaders of the Fourth Crusade who had put him on his throne, a conspiracy was formed in Constantinople to be rid of him and of his patrons. Its leader was Alexios Doukas Mourtzouphlos, a son-in-law of the former Emperor *Alexios III. He caused Alexios IV to be imprisoned and murdered and had himself crowned Emperor in February 1204. He represented the anti-Latin faction in Byzantium. He refused to meet any of the crusaders' demands and thus gave them the excuse to take the city by force, as they did in April 1204. Mourtzouphlos, so called because of his bushy eyebrows, fled. But he was caught, brought back and executed. He had reigned for four months; and he was the last Byzantine Emperor to wear the crown in Constantinople for fifty-seven years, until the descendants of the crusaders were evicted by *Michael VIII Palaiologos in 1261.

BIBL. Polemis 1968: no. 126; Queller 1977: 123–4, 127, 129–38, 140–7

Alexios I Komnenos Emperor of Trebizond 1204–22

Alexios and his brother David were grandsons of the Emperor *Andronikos I Komnenos, who was murdered in 1185. Just before the Fourth Crusade in 1204 they set up an autonomous principality at Trebizond on the southern coast of the Black Sea. Alexios claimed the title of Emperor and the name of Grand Komnenos, both of which passed to his heirs. His Byzantine Empire in miniature, protected by its patron St Eugenios, endured until the Ottoman Turks conquered Trebizond in 1461. Alexios had to fight for its survival against *Theodore I Laskaris at Nicaea, who also claimed the imperial title, and against the Seljuq Turks, to whom he was obliged to pay tribute. He died in February 1222, leaving his Empire to his son-in-law Andronikos I Gidon (1222–35), who was succeeded first by John I Axouch (1235–8) and then by Alexios's son Manuel I (1238–63).

BIBL. Miller 1926; Janssens 1969

Alexios II Komnenos Emperor of Trebizond 1297–1330

He was the ninth of the independent rulers of Trebizond, the Empire founded by *Alexios I Komnenos in 1204. His father was the Emperor John II Komnenos (1280–97). He married a Georgian princess and had six children. His sons Andronikos III and *Basil succeeded him.

Alexios III Komnenos Emperor of Trebizond 1349—90

He was the second son of *Basil Komnenos of Trebizond. He came to his throne with the support of the Byzantine Emperor *John VI, whose relative, Theodora Kantakouzenē, he married. Their portraits are to be seen on the charter with which Alexios endowed the monastery of Dionysiou on Mount Athos in 1374. He was succeeded by his son *Manuel III.

BIBL. Nicol 1968: no. 35

Alexios IV Komnenos Emperor of Trebizond 1417—29

Alexios was a son of *Manuel III of Trebizond. He maintained the independence of his Empire by paying tribute to most of his neighbours and potential enemies, the Turkoman chieftains, the Mongols and the Genoese. He married Theodora of the family of Kantakouzenos, by whom he had six children, among them *John IV and *David Komnenos, the last two Emperors of Trebizond. His daughter Maria was the third wife of the Byzantine Emperor *John VIII.

BIBL. Nicol 1968: no. 62

Alexios Stoudites Patriarch of Constantinople 1025—43

Abbot of the monastery of Stoudios in Constantinople, Alexios was made Patriarch by the Emperor *Basil II in 1025. Basil died soon afterwards and Alexios loyally supported the Macedonian dynasty as represented by the Empresses *Theodora and *Zoe, though he disapproved of Zoe's third marriage to *Constantine IX. He was a stickler for clerical and monastic discipline, for canon law and for the suppression of heresy, especially in the eastern provinces. He died in February 1043 and was succeeded as Patriarch by *Michael I Keroullarios.

BIBL. Grumel 1936: 245—65; Hussey 1986: 127—9

Anagnostes, John (15th century) chronicler

He was the otherwise unknown author of an eye-witness account of the final capture of Thessalonica by the Ottoman Turks in March 1430 and of a Monody or Lament on the fall of the city.

BIBL. Tsaras 1958; *PLP* no. 839

Anastasios II Emperor 713—15

Anastasios changed his name from Artemios when he was proclaimed Emperor after the army had dethroned *Philippikos-Bardanes in June 713. He was a civil servant and not a soldier but he was aware of the threat from the Arabs and he took measures for the defence of Constantinople. He chose the island of Rhodes as a strategic base for a counter-offensive and appointed the future Emperor *Leo III to defend Syria against the Arabs. He also disclaimed the heretical pronouncements of Philippikos on the will of Christ (Monotheletism), thus mending his fences with the Pope. The Opsikian troops of Asia Minor, however, rebelled when posted to Rhodes and, after six months of civil war, put up *Theodosios III as their own candidate for the throne in 715. Anastasios fled to

Thessalonica and became a monk. He was executed by Leo III in 720 after an attempt to regain his throne.

BIBL. Ostrogorsky 1968: 154–5

Anastasios Patriarch of Constantinople 730–54

He had been *synkellos* or associate of the Patriarch *Germanos I who resigned in 730 in protest against the iconoclastic policy of the Emperor *Leo III. Anastasios was prepared to do his Emperor's bidding and therefore stayed in office as Patriarch from 730 until his death in January 754, though he was excommunicated by the Pope. His successor was *Constantine II.

BIBL. Grumel 1936: 8–9; *DHGE* II: cols. 1465–6.

Anastasius I Emperor 491–518

When the Emperor *Zeno died childless in April 491, the people of Constantinople demanded an Emperor of Roman stock instead of another foreigner. Through the influence of Zeno's widow Ariadne, Anastasius, an elderly civil servant and economist, was elected. He legitimized his position by marrying her. The Isaurians of Zeno's race, whom *Leo I had brought into Constantinople, resented their loss of power and Anastasius had to suppress them by force and transplant thousands of them to Thrace, thus breaking their ascendancy for ever. In the face of growing barbarian pressure from the Danube frontier he built a Long Wall on the landward side of Constantinople, running forty-one miles from the Sea of Marmora to the Black Sea. Of great importance for the future was his reorganization of the Empire's economic structure by reforming and improving the system of taxation and by stabilizing the copper coinage (*follis*) in relation to the gold *solidus* introduced by *Constantine I. His economic measures were successful and lasting though unpopular, especially among the farmers on whom he imposed a new land tax. His religious policy was even less to the taste of his people. At his accession he had sworn before the Patriarch *Euphemius that he would protect the Orthodox Christian faith; yet he adhered to the Monophysite belief in the single divine and human nature of Christ which had been declared heterodox in 451. This endeared him to the Egyptians and Syrians who believed the same. But it cost him the support of the Byzantines. His reign was punctuated by a series of revolts, the most dangerous being led by Vitalian, his general in Thrace. It was put down in 515 and Anastasius died three years later, in July 518, at the age of eighty. He had probably intended that his nephew should succeed him. But his throne passed to *Justin I.

BIBL. Charanis 1974; Bury 1923, I: 429–52; Jones 1964, I: 230–7

Anatolius Patriarch of Constantinople 449–58

Anatolius was appointed after the death of *Flavian. He seems to have been the first Patriarch to officiate at the coronation of an Emperor in Constantinople, *Leo I, in 457, thereby imparting a religious aura to a ceremony which had hitherto been purely civil and military.

BIBL. Grumel 1972: 85–101; *DHGE* II: cols. 1497–1500; Ostrogorsky 1968: 61

Andronikos I Komnenos Emperor 1183–5

A cousin of the Emperor *Manuel I, Andronikos had led a colourful career of treason, imprisonment and exile. He was about sixty when Manuel died in 1180 leaving his young son *Alexios II under the regency of his mother Mary of Antioch. In 1182 Andronikos marched on Constantinople at the head of his Paphlagonian troops, who incited the mob to massacre all westerners in the city, and set himself up first as regent and then as Emperor. He was crowned as such in September 1183. Alexios and his mother were murdered; and to legitimize his position Andronikos married the child bride of Alexios, Agnes of France. He had come to power on the crest of a wave of anti-Latin feeling. The people at first hailed him as their saviour, for he pledged to protect them from the rapacity of the ruling aristocracy. The aristocracy fought back. The Empire began to disintegrate. In 1185 one Isaac Komnenos set up his own realm on Cyprus. The ruler of Serbia, Stephen Nemanja, declared his kingdom to be independent. The westerners, mindful of the massacre in Constantinople in 1182, took their revenge. The King of Hungary invaded the Empire. The Normans, in alliance with the German Emperor Frederick Barbarossa, marched into northern Greece and sacked Thessalonica in 1185. The fear that Constantinople would be their next stop caused panic in the capital. The mob which had brought Andronikos to power turned against him and proclaimed *Isaac (II) Angelos as Emperor. Andronikos was caught trying to escape, brought to the Hippodrome and there brutally murdered in September 1185. He was the last of the emperors of the family of Komnenos which had ruled since 1081.

BIBL. Jurewicz 1962; Brand 1968: 30–75

Andronikos II Palaiologos Emperor 1282–1328

He was the eldest son of *Michael VIII who nominated him as co-Emperor in 1272. Ten years later he came to the throne and at once won the favour of his church and people by renouncing his late father's policy of union with the Roman church. But it was too late to repair the eastern frontiers which his father had neglected; and his reign was marked by the steady advance of the Turks into Asia Minor. In 1303, in despair, Andronikos accepted the help of the Catalan Company of mercenaries, who had been fighting in Sicily. The Catalans were expensive and unruly and contributed more to the ruin of the economy and the devastation of the land than to the discomfiture of the Turks, whom they encouraged to cross over into Europe.

Andronikos was a pious intellectual. He was mesmerized by his puritanical Patriarch *Athanasios I; and he transferred to the Patriarchs the authority over the monasteries of Mount Athos which had traditionally belonged to the Emperor. His remedies for the military and economic deficiencies of his Empire were to reduce its armed forces and disband its navy; to devalue its gold coinage; and to impose heavier taxes. To keep the Serbians at bay he gave his infant granddaughter in marriage to their king. For trade and defence by sea he had hoped to rely on the Italians trading in Constantinople. The Venetians suspected him of siding with their rivals from Genoa and went to war, first with the Genoese and then with Andronikos. Peace was restored in 1302. In the east, however, his failure was more consequential. The incursion of the Turks into Asia Minor drove thousands of destitute refugees over to Constantinople. There was unrest in the towns and revolt in the provinces. Some of the younger generation felt that a new ruler was needed. Their hero was the Emperor's grandson, *Andronikos III, whom he disinherited in 1320. The old Emperor's long reign went out in civil war. He was forced to abdicate in May 1328, became a monk and died in February 1332.

Perhaps his greatest service was his patronage of learning, literature and the arts. His Grand Logothete (Chancellor) was the polymath Theodore *Metochites; and scholars, poets, historians and theologians frequented his court. He married twice, first to Anne of Hungary by whom he had two sons, *Michael IX and Constantine; second to Yolande (Eirene) of Montferrat, who gave him four sons. Yolande quarrelled with him over the inheritance of her sons and went to live as Empress in Thessalonica, where she died in 1317.

BIBL. Laiou 1972; Nicol 1972: 99–149

Andronikos III Palaiologos Emperor 1328–41

Andronikos was the elder son of *Michael IX who died in 1320, and a grandson of *Andronikos II, who disinherited him. His cause was championed by a group of the younger aristocracy, among them the later *John VI Kantakouzenos, fighting for what they believed to be his rights. In 1325 he was reinstated as co-Emperor; three years later he forced his grandfather to abdicate and took sole possession of the throne. In 1329 he was defeated in battle by Orchan, Emir of the Ottoman Turks, at Pelekanon in Bithynia; and in 1333 he formally acknowledged that most of Asia Minor belonged to Orchan by right of conquest. His policy of rapprochement with the Turks was upset by the Italians who had commercial interests in the eastern Mediterranean, and by the Pope's formation of a league of Christian powers against the Muslims. His greatest achievements were his reform of the legal administration and the judiciary and his recovery of the provinces of Epiros and Thessaly in northern Greece, which had been defiantly separatist since the time of the Fourth Crusade. In all his enterprises Andronikos was guided by his friend John Kantakouzenos, his Grand Domestic or commander-in-chief. He married twice, first to Adelaide (Eirene) of Brunswick and second to Anne of Savoy, who outlived him for many years and claimed to be regent for her son *John V when Andronikos died in June 1341.

BIBL. Bosch 1965; Nicol 1972: 159–90

Andronikos IV Palaiologos Emperor 1376–9

Andronikos was the eldest son of the Emperor *John V, against whom he rebelled. In 1373 he was imprisoned and half blinded for his part in a plot organized by a son of the Ottoman Sultan Murad I. The Genoese as well as the Turks saw him as a useful pawn in their own games of power politics; and in August 1376, with the help of both, he escaped and made himself Emperor in Constantinople, arresting his father and his two brothers. He rewarded the Genoese by granting them the island of Tenedos, a deed which provoked a long war between Genoa and Venice. He rewarded the Turks by surrendering Gallipoli. He was Emperor for barely three years. In July 1379 his father, subsidized by the Venetians, fought his way back into Constantinople. In 1381 Andronikos was allowed to rule over an appanage in Thrace. There he died in June 1385. His son *John VII inherited his restless and selfish ambition.

BIBL. Nicol 1972: 285−93

Anna Komnenē (Comnena) (1083−c. 1153) historian

The eldest daughter of the Emperor *Alexios I Komnenos and *Eirene Doukaina, Anna was born in December 1083. As a child she was betrothed to *Constantine Doukas, son of her father's late rival *Michael VII. After his premature death she married *Nikephoros Bryennios. When her father died in 1118 she aspired unsuccessfully to thwart the succession to the throne of her younger brother *John II. She spent her remaining years in enforced retirement, devoting herself to scholarship and to the composition of her celebrated *Alexiad*, the history of her father's reign. It remains one of the gems of Byzantine literature. It is written in an archaizing form of Greek calculated to display the erudition of an author who, for a medieval woman, was astonishingly well read and highly cultured. Completed after 1148, it is unashamedly a panegyric of her father Alexios, who is the central heroic figure of the piece. It is therefore less than impartial. Yet it is the major source of our knowledge of the revival of the Empire in the eleventh and twelfth centuries and of the Byzantine confrontation with the Normans, the crusaders, the Seljuq Turks and the Pechenegs. It is at the same time a very personal document, revealing the often passionate likes and dislikes of the princess Anna, the only female historian that Byzantium produced. She had two sons and one daughter and outlived her husband by some fifteen years, dying about 1153. Her Epitaph was composed by George *Tornikes.

BIBL. Leib 1937−45; Sewter 1969; Buckler 1929; Hunger 1978, I: 400−9

Anthemius of Tralles (*d.* 534) mathematician and architect

Anthemius was the son of a doctor in Tralles in western Asia Minor. He studied mathematics and engineering, probably at Alexandria, and was called to Constantinople by the Emperor *Justinian I. The church of St Sophia, the Holy Wisdom, had been burnt down in the Nika riot in 532. Justinian commissioned Anthemius to build a new church which would be a fitting symbol of the new age of the Christian Roman Empire. Anthemius had studied the mathematical principles of vaulting; his colleague, Isidore of Miletos, had written a commentary on Heron of Alexandria's treatise on vault construction. It was their architectural expertise and skill that designed and created the new church of the Holy

Wisdom, the largest domed building in the world — a church, as *Procopius said, 'the like of which has never been seen since Adam nor ever will be'. The work was done at phenomenal speed and Anthemius lived to see its completion. He died about 534.

BIBL. Hunger 1978, II: 230

Anthimus Patriarch of Constantinople 535—6

Anthimus was a secret believer in the Monophysite heresy. His election as Patriarch was secured by *Justinian's wife *Theodora, who was of the same religious persuasion. Pope Agapetus, who visited Constantinople in 536, refused to communicate with him and forced him to resign in favour of *Menas in March 536. He was anathematized along with other heretics.

BIBL. Grumel 1972: 165—8; *DHGE* III: col. 531

Antonios I Kassimatas Patriarch of Constantinople 821—37

Antonios had been Bishop of Syllaion in Pamphylia and a leading figure at the council held in Constantinople in 815 at which iconoclasm was reaffirmed. The Emperor *Michael II chose him as Patriarch when *Theodotos died in 821. He outlived the Emperor by eight years and died in January 837, to be succeeded by *John VII Grammatikos.

BIBL. Grumel 1936: 41—2

Antonios II Kauleas Patriarch of Constantinople 893—901

He was appointed Patriarch by the Emperor *Leo VI when *Stephen I died in 893. A virtuous ascetic, he succeeded in restoring good relations between Constantinople and Rome and peace within his own church after the storms of the Photian schism. He was canonized and his *Life* was written by a contemporary, Nikephoros Philosophos.

BIBL. Grumel 1936: 131—3; Beck 1959: 563

Antonios IV Patriarch of Constantinople 1389—90; 1391—7

He performed the coronation of the Emperor *Manuel II Palaiologos in Constantinople in February 1392. He was active in seeking help against the Turks from the rulers of Poland, Hungary and Russia; and he is especially celebrated for his rebuke to Basil I, Grand Duke of Moscow, who had ceased commemorating the Byzantine Emperor's name in the liturgy.

BIBL. *PLP* no. 1113

Apokaukos, Alexios (*d.* 1345) Grand Duke

He gave the impression of being an unscrupulous social climber with an eye to the main chance, though he is said to have been a scholar who studied medicine under Theodore *Hyrtakenos. He took the side of *Andronikos III in the war against his grandfather in 1320 and of *John VI Kantakouzenos against his opponents in 1341. As a result, although an upstart, he gained great power, wealth and influence and the title of

Grand Duke or High Admiral. But later he turned against John VI and sided with his adversary, the Empress Anne of Savoy, who made him Prefect of the City. He was murdered by some of his political prisoners in Constantinople in June 1345. His son John Apokaukos, whom he had made governor of Thessalonica, declared for John VI as soon as he heard of his father's death. He too was murdered.

BIBL. *PLP* no. 1179

Apokaukos, John Bishop of Naupaktos *c.* 1200–33
After a spell in the service of the Patriarchate in Constantinople John was appointed as Metropolitan of Naupaktos about 1200. It has been said, without much evidence, that he was a nephew of the historian Constantine *Manasses. Naupaktos, on the northern shore of the Gulf of Corinth, lay in the state of Epiros, which declared its independence after the Fourth Crusade in 1204. As its senior bishop, John was a loyal supporter of the political ambitions of its rulers *Michael I and *Theodore Komnenos Doukas. He presided over the synod at Arta which upheld Theodore's right to the title of Emperor in 1224. But he was uneasy about the resulting break with the Patriarchs at Nicaea, who claimed jurisdiction over the church in Epiros. He was upstaged by Demetrios *Chomatianos, Archbishop of Ochrida, who had no such scruples; and in his declining years John retired to a monastery in Epiros. His many surviving letters and other documents form one of the main sources for the early history of what came to be called the Despotate of Epiros.

BIBL. Nicol 1957; Karpozilos 1973

Arcadius Emperor 395–408
Arcadius was seventeen years old when his father *Theodosius I died in January 395, having nominated him as Emperor in the east. He was managed by a series of regents, first Rufinus and then, when he was murdered, by Eutropius and Anthemius. His younger brother Honorius, nominated as Emperor in the west, was likewise controlled by his adviser, the Romanized German Stilicho. Arcadius was weak in mind and in character. The Visigoths, whom his father had placated, rose in arms again under Alaric, devastating the Balkans and Greece and menacing Constantinople. Arcadius bought them off and diverted them to Italy and the west. He married Eudoxia, daughter of a Romanized Frank, whose hedonistic style of life was publicly condemned by the Patriarch *John I Chrysostom. He died in January 408, leaving his title to his young son *Theodosius II.

BIBL. Bury 1923, I; Jones 1964, I

Arethas (*c.* 850–944) Bishop of Caesarea, theologian and scholar
Born in Patras, Arethas studied at Constantinople, perhaps under *Photios. He became a deacon and then, about 902, Metropolitan of Caesarea, though living mainly in Constantinople. He is best known for his work on classical Greek texts, for he commissioned and commented

11

upon manuscripts of Aristotle, Euclid, Lucian and Plato. A great number of these survive, some from his own library and with his own marginalia, written in the minuscule Greek script which revolutionized scholarship in the ninth century. His manuscript of the *Iliad*, now in Venice, is the oldest witness to the text. His works of Christian literature include commentaries on the Psalms, on the Pauline Epistles, on the Apocalypse and on several church fathers. There are also homilies, speeches and letters. As a churchman he was more interested in canon law than in theology; though he had a reputation for spite and obstinacy and for tergiversation in the controversies that divided his church, amply proved by his conduct over the scandalous fourth marriage of the Emperor *Leo VI.

BIBL. Jenkins 1966: 219–26; Beck 1959: 591–2; Wilson 1983: 120–6

Arsacius Patriarch of Constantinople 404–5
He was a brother of the Patriarch *Nectarius and when *John I Chrysostom was dismissed in 404 he was elected to succeed him, although aged eighty. He died in November 405 and was replaced by *Atticus.

BIBL. *DHGE*, IV: col. 742

Arsenios Autoreianos Patriarch of Constantinople 1254–60; 1261–4
Appointed Patriarch by *Theodore II Laskaris in 1254, Arsenios performed the joint coronation of *Michael VIII Palaiologos and *John IV Laskaris at Nicaea and then of Michael VIII alone at Constantinople in 1261. Later he excommunicated Michael for his treatment of John IV. In 1264 he was deposed. His action and his memory inspired a faction in the Byzantine church calling themselves the Arsenites who refused to recognize any subsequent Patriarchs and remained in schism until 1310.

BIBL. *PLP* no. 1694

Athanasios I Patriarch of Constantinople 1289–93; 1303–9
Athanasios was a fanatically rigorist and ascetic monk appointed as Patriarch by the Emperor *Andronikos II Palaiologos. His reformist zeal proved so unpalatable that he had to resign in October 1293. In January 1303, after an ominous earthquake, the Emperor implored him to return. The people admired him for his charitable labours on behalf of the poor in Constantinople, especially for the refugees from the Turks. The Emperor was often under his spell. But the bishops and clergy were discouraged by his fanaticism and his calls to repentance. He resigned again in September 1309 and retired to a monastery. Many of his letters to the Emperor and other officials have survived, providing unique insights into the social and political life of the time.

BIBL. Talbot 1975; *PLP* no. 415

Athanasios the Athonite (*c*. 920–*c*. 1004) monk
The founder of the monastery of the Great Lavra on Mount Athos, Athanasios was the son of well-to-do parents in Trebizond. He began his career as a scholar and teacher in Constantinople; but he soon renounced

the world and entered a monastery on Mount Kyminas in Bithynia. Its abbot was an uncle of the future Emperor *Nikephoros II Phokas with whom Athanasios became friends. In 958 he joined what was then the loosely organized colony of hermits on Mount Athos, though he was persuaded to accompany Nikephoros on his expedition to reconquer Crete from the Arabs in 960−1. He then returned to Athos; and Nikephoros rewarded him by endowing a new monastic settlement there, to which he vowed that he would himself retire one day. Work on the buildings began in 963 and Nikephoros, who became Emperor in that year, granted the new monastery an imperial charter. The introduction of more ordered monasticism on Athos did not go unchallenged by the hermits but their differences were partly resolved by the Emperor *John I Tzimiskes who issued another charter in 972. About 970 Athanasios composed the *typikon* or rules for the monks of his Great Lavra. They incorporated the ideals of coenobitic or communal monastic life as they had been formulated by *Theodore of Stoudios. The Great Lavra was the first such foundation on Mount Athos; and Athanasios, as its abbot, set the pattern for other Athonite monasteries. He was killed about 1004 when the dome of his church collapsed.

BIBL. Petit 1906; Noret 1982; Lemerle *et al.* 1970−82

Attaleiates, Michael (*c.* 1028−*c.* 1085) historian

Born in Constantinople, he became a lawyer and senior civil servant in the reigns of *Romanos IV and *Michael VII, whose achievements he narrates in his *History*, which he dedicated to the Emperor *Nikephoros III. It covers the period from 1034 to 1079. Much of it is based on personal observation and experience. It is reliable for its facts and of interest for its sociological content.

BIBL. Presle and Bekker 1853; Kazhdan 1984a; Hunger 1978, I: 382−9

Atticus Patriarch of Constantinople 406−25

Atticus came from Armenia and was a monk from an early age. He was made Patriarch on the death of *Arsacius, with whom he seems to have plotted the downfall of *John I Chrysostom. His election, after months of intrigue, deepened the division in the church, until he was forced to rehabilitate the name of Chrysostom. He died in October 425 and his successor as Patriarch was *Sisinnius I.

BIBL. Grumel 1972: 27−36; *DHGE* V: cols. 161−6

Axouch, John (*d. c.* 1150) Grand Domestic

The Axouch (or Axouchos) family were of Seljuq Turkish origin. John was captured as a boy. The Emperor *Alexios I Komnenos adopted him as a companion for his own son *John (II), who later made him Grand Domestic or commander-in-chief of the Byzantine army. He gave invaluable service to John when he became Emperor in 1118 and to *Manuel I in 1143. He died about 1150. He was also interested in philosophy and theology and wrote an Encomium of the Emperor John II. He had a son,

Alexios Axouch, who also served Manuel I as a military commander; but he was suspected of treason and forced to enter a monastery.

BIBL. Angold 1984: 152–3, 190–1; Hunger 1978, I: 124–5; Beck 1959: 625

Axouch, John Komnenos (*d*. 1201) pretender

He was a grandson of John *Axouch, whose son Alexios had married Maria, granddaughter of the Emperor *John II, through whom he acquired the name of Komnenos. John was, evidently with justification, nicknamed 'the Fat.' He led a conspiracy against the Emperor *Alexios III Angelos and was briefly acclaimed Emperor and crowned by a monk in St Sophia in July 1201. He was rounded up and executed.

BIBL. Brand 1968: 122–4

B

Balsamon, Theodore (second half 12th century) canon lawyer

Born and educated in Constantinople, he rose to become *chartophylax* or archivist of the Great Church, in effect the Patriarch's deputy. About 1190 he was appointed Patriarch of Antioch, but he continued to reside in Constantinople. He was the most learned of all Byzantine canonists and is best known for his Commentary on the seventh-century canonical collection known as the *Nomokanon* in Fourteen Titles, which he composed in the reign of *Manuel I Komnenos. His opinions and rulings on the authority of the Emperor in ecclesiastical affairs and of the Patriarch in secular matters came as near as any Byzantine lawyer ever came to drawing the line between things temporal and things spiritual.

BIBL. Beck 1959: 657−8

Bardanes, George Bishop of Corfu 1219−*c.* 1235

Bardanes was a student of Michael *Choniates at Athens before the Latin conquest of the Empire in 1204. He was elected as Metropolitan of Kerkyra (Corfu) in 1219 by a synod convened by John *Apokaukos on the recommendation of the then ruler of Epiros, *Theodore Komnenos Doukas. He fully supported Theodore's claim to imperial authority over church and state in defiance of the emperors and patriarchs in exile at Nicaea. He went on a diplomatic mission to Italy in 1231 and there engaged in a discussion with a Franciscan on the subject of Purgatory, probably the first of its kind. His correspondence, especially with the patriarchs at Nicaea, is a prime source for the history of the separatist state of Epiros.

BIBL. Nicol 1957; Hoeck and Loenertz 1965

Bardanes Turcus (8th to 9th century) military commander

He was an Armenian soldier, created commander (*monostrategos*) of five of the Themes or military districts in Asia Minor by the Emperor *Nikephoros I. In 803 his rebellious troops proclaimed him Emperor. He was at first supported by three of his officers, Michael the Amorian, Leo the Armenian and Thomas the Slav. Bardanes never ascended the throne and his revolt, never more than half-hearted, collapsed. The first two of his colleagues, however, were each in due course to become Emperor, *Michael III and *Leo V; while the third, *Thomas the Slav, came very near it. Bardanes surrendered and became a monk, though in 804 he was blinded, apparently against his Emperor's wishes.

BIBL. Treadgold 1988: 129−35, 196−7; Jenkins 1966: 119−123

Bardas Caesar (*d.* 865) statesman and soldier

Bardas was a brother of the Empress *Theodora and one of her chief

15

advisers when her husband *Theophilos died in 842. He was early ousted by her favourite and his rival *Theoktistos; but he came into his own when her son the Emperor *Michael III asserted his personal authority in 856. Theoktistos was murdered and Bardas was honoured with the rank of Caesar as the Emperor's friend, policy maker and administrator. His private life was not without blemish; and the Patriarch *Ignatios excommunicated him for adultery. But he was a distinguished statesman, soldier and patron of learning. Though it may be exaggerating to credit him with the foundation of an imperial 'university' at Constantinople, his name is associated with the furtherance of higher education and scholarship in the city. He also co-operated with the Patriarch *Photios in the conversion of the Slavs to Christianity and fully supported him in his disagreement with the Roman church. He quickly became a target of the upstart and ambitious *Basil (I) who worked his way into the favour of Michael III; and in April 865 Basil murdered him.

BIBL. Ostrogorsky 1968: 219—22, 227—9, 231—5

Barlaam of Calabria (d. 1348) scholar and monk

Barlaam was an Orthodox monk from Calabria in south Italy and abbot of a monastery in Constantinople from 1330—41. As a scholar his erudition was much admired by the Emperors *Andronikos III and *John VI. Andronikos sent him on a confidential mission to the Pope at Avignon in 1339 to put the Byzantine point of view on the union of the churches. There he met Petrarch to whom he later tried to teach Greek. As a philosopher he quarrelled with Nikephoros *Gregoras; as a theologian he crossed swords with Gregory *Palamas. He turned to denouncing and ridiculing the Hesychast monks whom Palamas had inspired; and in June 1341 he was condemned at a council of bishops in Constantinople. He went back to Italy, where the Pope made him Bishop of Gerace, where he died in 1348.

BIBL. *PLP* no. 2284

Basil I Emperor 867—86

Born in 826, Basil came of an Armenian family who had settled in Macedonia. The imperial dynasty which he founded was thus known as the Macedonian. He had no breeding, no education and no money when he came to seek his fortune in Constantinople. By native wit and cunning he rose to become a courtier and close friend of the Emperor *Michael III, who made him his co-Emperor in 866. He reached the summit of his ambition by murdering first the Emperor's uncle, the Caesar *Bardas, and then the Emperor himself, in September 867. The Macedonian dynasty, like that of the Palaiologos family in later times, was thus founded on crime. But it lasted for 189 years and brought to the Byzantine Empire its greatest glory and prestige.

Basil's immediate predecessors left an Empire fit not merely to survive but also to expand. In 867 Bulgars, Slavs and Russians were all at peace. The Arabs in the east had been forced to accept a frontier well-defended on the Byzantine side. Its weakest point lay in Cilicia, where an added nuisance was a rebellious Manichean Christian sect, the Paulicians, who were in league with the Arabs. Basil led his army against them, captured their headquarters in 872, and by so doing was able to push his frontier further east into Arab territory. Inexperienced though he was, Basil saw the Arab problem as one affecting the west as well as the east. He might emulate *Justinian by reconquering some of the western provinces. With this in mind he restored the imperial navy and sought the co-operation of the Frankish Emperor Louis II in the defence of southern Italy, proposing the marriage of his eldest son Constantine to Louis's daughter. The Arabs, however, already held Crete and in 878 almost completed their conquest of Sicily by capturing Syracuse. Basil also made his peace with the Papacy by dismissing the Patriarch *Photios, whose appointment had led to schism, and reinstating *Ignatios; though Photios was recalled in 877 with the approval of Rome. Part of Basil's plan for a new era after the dark age of iconoclasm was a revision or 'purification' of the law. He did not live to see its completion, though a provisional code of law (*Procheiros Nomos*) for everyday use in the courts and an Introduction (*Epanagogē*) were produced in his time. His eldest son Constantine died in 879, a tragedy that affected Basil's reason. Constantine had been the child of his first marriage. His second wife was Eudokia Ingerina, former mistress of *Michael III, who gave him three sons, *Leo, *Stephen and *Alexander. It was Leo (VI) who succeeded him when he died in a hunting accident in August 886.

BIBL. Vasiliev 1968: 1–114; Ostrogorsky 1968: 233–41; Jenkins 1966: 183–97.

Basil II Emperor 976–1025

When *John I Tzimiskes died in January 976, Basil and his brother *Constantine VIII were aged eighteen and sixteen. They had been over-shadowed by usurpers posing as their guardians, first *Nikephoros (II) Phokas and then John Tzimiskes. Yet they were the sons of *Romanos II, the great-grandson of *Basil I, and so the legitimate heirs of the Macedonian dynasty. In 976 Basil determined to make this fact clear. John I had no male heir to challenge him. But his brother-in-law, Bardas *Skleros, was proclaimed Emperor by his troops; Bardas *Phokas, a nephew of *Nikephoros II, also rebelled; and the pot was stirred by the chamberlain Basil, who saw himself as a kingmaker. The first years of Basil II's reign were thus taken up by civil wars. Not until 989 did he feel secure, having beaten his rivals and banished the scheming Basil. The experience hardened and embittered him.

The domestic problems of Byzantium gave its enemies their chance. The Bulgars rebelled and, under the leadership of their ruler Samuel, built up an empire that stretched from the Adriatic across the Balkans to the Black Sea. Basil's solution to the perennial problem of Bulgarian insubordination was military conquest and annexation; and for fifteen years, with methodical ruthlessness, he directed annual campaigns to break the resistance and the will of the rebels. Samuel's army was finally annihilated at a battle in July 1014. He died three months later, his ambitions and his empire in ruins. Basil's barbarous treatment of his prisoners of war earned him the nickname of Boulgaroktonos, the Bulgar-slayer. By 1019 the conquest was complete and Bulgaria was divided into three provinces as an integral part of the Byzantine Empire. His pre-occupation with the north did not lead Basil to neglect his eastern frontiers, where he frightened the Arabs on two occasions and personally supervised the annexation of Georgia to his Empire. Within that Empire he penalized the landowning aristocracy and protected the small farmers and peasants who were so vital to the upkeep of the army. In foreign affairs he maintained diplomatic relations with Russia, with Venice and with the western Empire. He gave his sister Anna in marriage to Vladimir of Kiev and so prompted the conversion of Russia to Orthodox Christianity in 988−9. He gave a relative, Maria Argyropoulaina, in marriage to the son of the Doge of Venice in 1004; and his niece *Zoe was betrothed to the young Otto III of Germany, though he died before the wedding took place. At the end of his life Basil was preparing for the reconquest of Sicily from the Arabs. But he died in December 1025 at the age of sixty-eight. He had never married and he was succeeded by his brother *Constantine VIII. His death marked the end of the golden age of the Macedonian dynasty.

BIBL. Schlumberger 1900; Ostrogorsky 1968: 298−315; Jenkins 1966: 301−31

Basil II Kamateros Patriarch of Constantinople 1183−6

Basil was appointed Patriarch by the Emperor *Andronikos I on the resignation of the Patriarch *Theodosios I in August 1183. He performed the coronation of Andronikos in St Sophia and became his chief supporter among the hierarchy. In the rioting that attended the downfall of Andro-nikos in 1185, Basil was dragged out of his palace and forced to set the crown on the head of the Emperor *Isaac II Angelos. He was deposed in February 1186 and brought to trial by his successor *Niketas (II) Mountanes.

BIBL. Grumel 1947: 174−7; *DHGE* VI: cols. 1129−30

Basil Komnenos Emperor of Trebizond 1332−40

The second son of *Alexios II Komnenos of Trebizond, Basil married Eirene Palaiologina, a natural daughter of the Byzantine Emperor *Andronikos III. He repudiated her in favour of his mistress who gave him four children, one of whom became Emperor of Trebizond as *Alexios III. He gave his two daughters as brides to local Turkoman chieftains. By such marriages the Empire of Trebizond survived.

BIBL. Miller 1926: 44−6

Basil the Great (c. 329−79) Bishop of Caesarea and saint

Basil was born into a wealthy Christian family at Caesarea in Asia Minor. He studied there and at Constantinople and Athens, where he made friends with *Gregory of Nazianzus. Then, prompted by his pious sister Macrina, he set up a monastic community at Annesi in Pontos. He travelled among the monks of Egypt. In 370, on the death of *Eusebius, he was made Bishop of Caesarea. His ecclesiastical career was largely devoted to the defence of the Christian creed as formulated at the Council of Nicaea in 325 against the persistent influence of the Arian heresy which that council had condemned. His numerous writings had a lasting effect, not least on the development of organized monasticism. They include his *Longer* and *Shorter Rules* for the conduct of monastic life; the *Hexaemeron* or nine sermons on the six days of Creation; his *Treatise on the Holy Spirit*; his *Address to the Young* on the proper use of pagan literature by Christians; and numerous letters. He was the brother of *Gregory of Nyssa; and he is revered as a saint by the eastern and western churches.

BIBL. Quasten 1960: 204–36; von Campenhausen 1963: 84–100

Basiliscus Emperor 475–6

He was the brother of the Empress Verina, wife of *Leo I, for whom he commanded a disastrous expedition to recover North Africa from the Vandals in 468. When the Emperor *Zeno came to power in 474, Verina conspired with Basiliscus to seize the throne. Things did not go quite as she had wanted; for it was Basiliscus and not her own favourite who was proclaimed Emperor when Zeno fled. He reigned in Constantinople for twenty months and achieved little but discord; for he was a Monophysite heretic, anathema to the Patriarch *Acacius and disliked by his Orthodox subjects. When Zeno came back from exile in August 476, Basiliscus with his wife and family were rounded up and executed.

BIBL. Bury 1923, I: 390–3

Belisarius (c. 505–65) general

Belisarius was the leading military commander of the Emperor *Justinian I and the strategist of most of the fighting that led to the reconquest of the Empire's western provinces. His early career is obscure but his most active period is well documented by the historian *Procopius, who was with him on many of his campaigns. He married Antonina, a friend of the Empress *Theodora. He first came to notice as a commander against the Persians in Mesopotamia; and he impressed Justinian by his prompt and brutal suppression of the Nika riot in Constantinople in 532. He was chosen to lead the expedition for the recovery of North Africa from the Vandals in 533, which he achieved in a matter of months. He was then given command of the force sent to liberate Sicily and Italy from the Ostrogoths. Sicily fell in 535 and in a brilliant series of campaigns Belisarius went on to capture Naples, Rome and Ravenna in 541. The Goths offered to surrender if he would become their Emperor. He wisely refused. But he was recalled to Constantinople and posted again to Mesopotamia, where the Persians had violated their truce. There he was charged with disloyalty and saved from disgrace only by the intervention of his wife's friend Theodora. After Belisarius left Italy the Goths returned to the attack, led by Totila. Justinian sent him back to restore order in 544 but with insufficient resources. Four years later, when his protectress Theodora died, he was summoned to Constantinople. The command in Italy passed to *Narses. Thereafter he lived in retirement, though in 559 he was ordered to beat back a raid by the Huns. He never complained of his Emperor's ingratitude even when falsely accused of conspiracy in 562. He died in March 565 . In later centuries he became the hero of many legends and stories.

BIBL. *see under* *Justinian I

Bessarion (1403–72) Bishop of Nicaea and Cardinal

Born at Trebizond, Bessarion studied at Constantinople and at Mistra under George *Gemistos Plethon. He became a monk in 1423 and was appointed Bishop of Nicaea in 1437. His scholarship inclined him to Platonism although he understood and admired western scholasticism; and at the Council of Ferrara-Florence which he attended in 1438–9 he became convinced that Greek and Latin theology were not incompatible. He was such an enthusiastic supporter of the reunion of Christendom that he went over to the Roman church and settled in Italy, where the Pope made him a Cardinal and ultimately titular Latin Patriarch of Constantinople. He died at Ravenna in November 1472. He was an assiduous collector of Greek manuscripts and in 1468 he presented his collection to the Library of St Mark in Venice. His numerous rhetorical and philosophical works include a defence of Plato against his detractors, letters, poems and funeral orations. He was equally at home in Latin and in Greek.

BIBL. Mohler 1923–7, 1942; *PLP* no. 2707

Blastares, Matthew (*d*. 1350) lawyer

A monk in Thessalonica from 1335, Blastares is best known for his collection (*Syntagma*) of rulings in canon and civil law, which was translated at an early date into Serbian and widely known in the Slav world.

BIBL. *PLP* no. 2808

Blemmydes, Nikephoros (1197–1272) monk and scholar.

He was a monk and then abbot of a monastery near Ephesos. Having left Constantinople with his parents after the Latin conquest in 1204, he eventually found his way to Nicaea. There he studied medicine for seven years and was a successful teacher. His pupils included the Emperor *Theodore II Laskaris and George *Akropolites, whom he instructed in philosophy, mathematics and astronomy. He was nominated as Patriarch in 1254 but declined the honour. His many and varied writings comprise philosophical, rhetorical and medical treatises; poems; an address to Theodore II on the duties of an Emperor; and his own Autobiography.

BIBL. Works *in MPG*, vol. 142; Autobiography, ed. and trs. *in* Munitiz 1988.

Boilas, Eustathios (*d*. 1059) landowner

He is most famous for his Will which is preserved in an eleventh-century manuscript. He was a well-to-do landowner from a Cappadocian family and attained the rank of *protospatharios*. For reasons not clear, he was forced to migrate to the wilder country on the borders of Armenia and Georgia, which had been annexed to the Empire by *Basil II about 1000. There he cleared and cultivated the land and turned the desolate area into a productive estate, with his own mansion containing a library and two chapels. His Will, with its inventory of his possessions, is a uniquely informative document of the eleventh century.

BIBL. Vryonis 1957

Branas, Alexios (*d*. 1187) soldier

The Branas family were among the great landowners of the eleventh century, their estates being concentrated around Adrianople (Edirne) in Thrace. Alexios served the Emperor *Andronikos I Komnenos in war against the Hungarians and against the Emperor's political enemies in Bithynia. He took command of the army that drove the Normans out of Thessalonica in 1185 after the overthrow of Andronikos. He then rebelled against the new Emperor *Isaac II Angelos and was killed trying to force his way into Constantinople. His son, Theodore Branas, was one of those who put *Alexios III Angelos on to the throne in 1195 and served him as a military commander.

BIBL. Brand 1968: 80−2, 170−4, 273−4

Bryennios, Nikephoros (1062−1136) historian

He was the son of Nikephoros Bryennios, pretender to the throne in 1077. He married *Anna Komnenē, daughter of the Emperor *Alexios I, in 1097 and served Alexios and his son *John II as a soldier and a civil servant, being honoured with the title of Caesar. He began a *History* of the rise to power of his wife's family but died before finishing it. It covers the years from 1070 to 1079.

BIBL. Gautier 1975; Hunger 1978, I: 394−400

C

Chalkokondyles, Laonikos (*c*. 1423—90) historian
Chalkokondyles was the last Byzantine historian. He was born at Athens, studied with George *Gemistos Plethon, and lived in Constantinople until the Turkish Conquest in 1453. His *History* covers the years from 1298 to 1463. Its theme is not so much the decline and fall of Byzantium as the origins and rise to power of the Ottoman Turks. His narrative is larded with historical and geographical digressions in the manner of Herodotus.

BIBL. Darkó 1922—7; Miller 1922; Hunger 1978, I: 485—90

Chomatianos, Demetrios Archbishop of Ochrida 1217—35
Scholar, canonist and theologian, Chomatianos was appointed to the Archbishopric of Ochrida (Ohrid) in 1217 on the recommendation of the separatist ruler of Epiros *Theodore Komnenos Doukas, without reference to the Patriarch at Nicaea who claimed jurisdiction over Epiros. He had no reservations about the autonomy of his church nor about Theodore's political ambitions; and it was he who crowned Theodore as Emperor after he had conquered Thessalonica from the Latins in 1224. He claimed that the coronation of emperors was one of the many traditional prerogatives of his autocephalous see. He is best known for his many surviving works, extensive correspondence and written judgments in ecclesiastical and civil cases brought before his tribunal.

BIBL. Works *in* Pitra 1891; Nicol 1957

Choniates, Michael (Akominatos) (*c*. 1138—*c*. 1222) Bishop of Athens
Michael was the elder brother of Niketas *Choniates, from Chonai in Asia Minor. He was a pupil of *Eustathios of Thessalonica, studied in Constantinople and served on the Patriarch's staff before being appointed Metropolitan of Athens in 1182. He was evicted from his see by the crusaders after 1204 and took refuge on the island of Keos within sight of his beloved Attica. He declined invitations from the rulers in exile in Epiros and in Nicaea to settle at their courts. His literary works include homilies, poems and funeral orations; and his numerous letters are a mine of information about the social, political and intellectual life of his time.

BIBL. Lambros 1879—80; Stadtmüller 1934

Choniates, Niketas (*c*. 1150—1215) statesman and historian
The younger brother of Michael *Choniates, he studied at Constantinople and entered the civil service, becoming secretary to the Emperors *Alexios II and *Isaac II. In 1189 he was governor of the province of Philippopolis (Plovdiv) in Thrace and then Grand Logothete or Chancellor in Constantinople. During the Latin conquest of the city in 1204 he lost everything. He found refuge in Nicaea with the Emperor *Theodore I Laskaris. His

major literary work is his *History*, briefly covering the period from the reign of *John II Komnenos (1118−43) and in greater detail from that of *Manuel I to the capture of Constantinople in 1204, of which he gives a vivid and moving account. It is one of the most valuable and informative of all Byzantine histories. He also compiled a huge theological compendium, the *Treasury of Orthodoxy*.

BIBL. Dieten 1975; Magoulias 1984; Beck 1959: 663−4; Hunger 1978, I: 429−41

Chortasmenos, John (*c*. 1370−*c*. 1436/7) Bishop of Selymbria
He was a notary in the Patriarchate in Constantinople, where he lived during the Turkish blockade of the city from 1394 to 1402. Though constantly complaining of poverty, he had a good library and supplemented his income by teaching. Among his pupils were Mark *Eugenikos, *Bessarion and *Gennadios (George) Scholarios. In later life he became a monk and was then appointed Bishop of Selymbria in Thrace. His surviving works include letters, many to the Emperor *Manuel II, poems, and an interesting collection of moral precepts for the successful conduct of upper class life in his time.

BIBL. Hunger 1969; Nicol 1979; 117−20

Choumnos, Nikephoros (*d*. 1327) statesman and scholar
A pupil of the later Patriarch *Gregory II (George of Cyprus), Choumnos began his diplomatic career under the Emperor *Michael VIII and became prime minister for *Andronikos II, giving his daughter in marriage to the Emperor's son John. He was governor of Thessalonica from 1309−10. He was adept at trimming his sails to the prevailing political and religious winds. As a scholar he had a celebrated academic quarrel with his social and political rival Theodore *Metochites. His literary, philosophical and scientific works are heavily and consciously indebted to ancient Greek models.

BIBL. Verpeaux 1959

Christodoulos (1020−93) monk of Patmos
He was born in Nicaea and became a monk on Mount Olympos in Bithynia about 1040. In 1088, through the intercession of *Anna Dalassenē, mother of the Emperor *Alexios I Komnenos, he was granted the island of Patmos to found there the still flourishing monastery of St John the Theologian. By imperial decree it was declared to be an autonomous institution. Christodoulos died in Euboia in 1093 but his body was brought back to his monastery on Patmos. He wrote the *typikon* or charter of rules for his monks and also his last will and testament, both of which documents survive.

BIBL. Beck 1959: 646−7

Christopher of Mitylene (*c*. 1000−50) poet
Christopher Mitylenaios was a civil servant and supreme judge in Paph-

lagonia. He composed epigrams which display an acerbic wit and reveal much about the social life and customs of his time. He also wrote a metrical calendar for the liturgical year of the church.

BIBL. Kurtz 1903; Follieri 1980—1; Beck 1959: 607

Chrysoloras, Manuel (*d*. 1415) scholar and diplomat

He was a pupil of Demetrios *Kydones, whose example he followed by joining the Roman church. Having served his friend the Emperor *Manuel II as ambassador to Italy, he was appointed to teach Greek in Florence in 1396. In 1408 he went as ambassador to Paris, and then to London and Venice. In 1414 he attended the Council of Constance, where he died in April 1415. Among his students was the Italian humanist Francesco Filelfo. Chrysoloras played a significant part in the renaissance of Greek studies in Italy. Among his literary works, the Greek grammar which he composed (*Erotemata*) was especially influential.

BIBL. Cammelli 1941

Constans II Emperor 641—68

The grandson of *Heraclius and son of *Constantine III, Constans II was eleven years old when, after the banishment of his uncle *Heraclonas, he was raised to the throne, at first under the regency of the Senate in Constantinople. By 650 the Arabs had occupied Alexandria, completed the conquest of Egypt and built ships to terrorize the Greek islands. In 655 Constans took command of a fleet against them, but he was defeated off the south coast of Asia Minor. Four years later, thanks to political upheavals in the Arab world, he was able to make a treaty with them. This gave him time to campaign against the Slavs in the north and to deport large numbers of them to Asia Minor.

In an attempt to settle the religious dissension in his Empire, Constans issued a document called the *Typē* which forbade any further discussion about the nature of Christ. It satisfied none of the warring factions in the church and was condemned by the Pope, whom he summoned to Constantinople. Latterly he led an army by way of Greece to Italy, where he fought the Lombards with some success. Having visited Naples and Rome, he settled in Sicily, probably intending to use it as a base for warfare against the Arabs in the west. His tyrannical behaviour, however, and his unorthodox religious views made him unpopular. He was murdered at Syracuse in September 668; and one of his courtiers, Mezesios, was hailed as Emperor. The revolt was put down by the governor of Ravenna who was loyal to the son and heir of Constans, *Constantine IV. He was nicknamed Pogonatus because of his long and bushy beard.

BIBL. Ostrogorsky 1968: 114—23; Jenkins 1966: 36—42

Constantine I the Great Emperor 324—37

Flavius Valerius Constantinus was the son of Constantius Chlorus and Helena and was born in the 280s at Naissus (Nis). He was brought up at Nikomedia by the Emperor Diocletian, after whose abdication in 305 he joined his father in the west. His father died in 306 and his troops proclaimed Constantine as their Emperor at York. A long series of wars between the claimants to imperial power brought him to the throne after he had defeated his brother-in-law Maxentius at the Milvian Bridge near Rome in 312 and then the eastern Emperor Licinius in Thrace in 324.

Constantine's reforms of the army, the administration and the economy would hardly have been possible without the work of his great predecessor Diocletian. But the two most consequential of his achievements owed nothing to those who had ruled before him. One was his adoption of Christianity. The other was the foundation of his own city of Constantinople as the Second or the New Rome in May 330. These were essential elements in the formation of what has come to be called the Byzantine Empire, centred round a capital city built on the site of the ancient Greek colony of Byzantium and imbued with the spirit of the Christian religion which previous emperors had tried to stifle by persecution. The sincerity of Constantine's conversion has often been questioned; but his own writings and those of his friend *Eusebius of Caesarea attest his personal conviction that he was the servant of God on earth, committed to the protection and triumph of what was then a minority religion. He involved himself deeply in the furtherance of the Christian faith and to unanimity among its adherents, as in the Donatist schism in North Africa or in the theological controversy stirred up by the followers of Arius in Alexandria, who effectively denied the divinity of Christ. It was in the fond hope of resolving that controversy that Constantine summoned and presided over the First Council of the church at Nicaea in 325, thus setting another precedent for Christian Roman or Byzantine emperors to follow.

As a commander and strategist he was uncommonly successful. He transformed the economy of the Empire by introducing the new gold coin (*solidus*) which was to remain the standard unit of currency for centuries. He was extravagant in the building of public monuments, not least churches. As a person, however, and for all his publicly professed Christianity, he was brutal and capricious; and, though the circumstances are obscure, he must be held guilty of the murder of his son Crispus and his second wife Fausta. He was baptized on his deathbed and died near Nikomedia on 22 May 337. To the pagans he became a god. The Christians venerated him as the Thirteenth Apostle and a saint. He divided his Empire between his three surviving sons, Constantine (II), who took the western portion, *Constantius, who took the east, and Constans, who took the central area.

BIBL. Baynes 1972; Jones 1964, I; Barnes 1981; Barnes 1982; Dagron 1974

Constantine III Emperor 641.

He was the son of *Heraclius by his first wife Eudokia. His father had willed that he should share the succession and the government with his half-brother *Heraclonas; but he died after three months of becoming co-Emperor, in May 641. He left a son, *Constans, who became Emperor in September 641.

BIBL. Ostrogorsky 1968: 112–13

Constantine IV Emperor 668–85

Constantine was the eldest son and successor of *Constans II, who was murdered in 668. His reign saw the first decisive phase in the struggle between Byzantium and the Arabs. For four years, from 674–8. Constantinople was under siege by Arab ships and armies. It was saved by the strength of its walls but also by the energy and initiative of Constantine IV. In 678 the Arab fleet was repulsed, largely thanks to the newly-invented Greek fire, the Byzantine secret weapon. At the same time the Arab army was defeated in Asia Minor. Their Caliph was forced to sign a thirty-year treaty with the Emperor and to pay him an annual tribute. Constantine was less successful on his northern frontier. A tribe of Bulgars who appeared at the Black Sea mouth of the Danube about 670 defeated the troops that he sent to dislodge them. He was obliged to treat with their ruler and to pay him tribute, thus formally recognizing the existence of a Bulgar and Slav Kingdom on Byzantine territory. To resolve the disputes in the church, he convened the Sixth Oecumenical Council at Constantinople in 680–1. There the compromise formulae defining the nature of Christ, which had been proposed by previous emperors and patriarchs, were condemned and the doctrines of the Council of Chalcedon (451) were accepted as the truth, or as near the truth as any human mind could get in such matters. Constantine died in September 685 aged only thirty-three, leaving the throne to his son *Justinian II.

BIBL. Ostrogorsky 1968: 123–9; Jenkins 1966: 42–50

Constantine V Emperor 741–75

Constantine's father *Leo III made him his co-Emperor in 720 when he was only two years old, and he duly succeeded to the throne in June 741. His succession was challenged by his brother-in-law, the general Artabasdos. But by 743 Constantine was in control of his capital and his Empire. He was an even more fervent iconoclast than his father and he propagated his beliefs by theological arguments as well as by brute force. In 754 he summoned a council of bishops which sanctioned and formulated iconoclasm, or the destruction of all religious images, as the policy of church and state. Constantine was later remembered for his savage perscution of those who opposed that policy, especially the monks; though his most eloquent opponent, *John of Damascus, could not be silenced. He was also remembered, however, for his victorious military leadership in campaigns against the Arabs and the Bulgars. On the other hand, by concentrating his resources on the east and the north, he left Italy open to the Lombards, who captured Ravenna in 751 and so put an end to the Byzantine province established there by *Justinian I. Constantine's later detractors nicknamed him Kopronymos since he was alleged to have fouled the font at his baptism. He married as his first wife a Khazar princess, by whom he had a son, *Leo IV, who succeeded him when he died fighting the Bulgars in September 775.

BIBL. Ostrogorsky 1968: 165–75; Jenkins 1966: 68–73, 84–9

Constantine VI Emperor 780—97

Constantine was ten years old when his father *Leo IV died in 780. He remained under the tutelage of his mother the Empress *Eirene until 790 when he asserted his independence and reigned alone. In 792, however, he unwisely recalled and reinstated her as his imperial partner. On the field of battle he was defeated by the Arabs and by the Bulgars, though he suppressed a revolt by some of his troops in Asia Minor in 793. On the domestic front he scandalized the church by divorcing the wife whom his mother had selected for him in order to marry his mistress Theodote and make her his Empress. His mother made the most of his disgrace if she did not engineer it; and in August 797 she had him imprisoned and blinded. He died soon afterwards, leaving her as sole ruler. He was the last of the Isaurian or Syrian dynasty inaugurated by the Emperor *Leo III.

BIBL. Speck 1978; Treadgold 1988: 89—110

Constantine VII Porphyrogenitus Emperor 913—59

Constantine Porphyrogenitus ('born in the purple') was the only son of *Leo VI by his fourth wife *Zoe Karbounopsina. The Patriarch *Nicholas (I) Mystikos had disallowed Leo's marriage and questioned Constantine's legitimacy. When Leo's brother *Alexander died in June 913, the Patriarch none the less had to act as regent for Constantine, then aged seven. Alexander had provoked Symeon of Bulgaria to war; and it was the Patriarch who had to face the consequences. He averted the crisis for a while by flattering Symeon with a crown and a title. But in 914 Constantine's mother Zoe took over the regency herself and brought Symeon to war again. The day was saved by the admiral of the fleet *Romanos (I) Lakapenos, who deliberately undermined Zoe's power, made himself regent and gave his daughter Helena in marriage to the young Constantine.

For the next twenty-four years Constantine reigned under the shadow of his brilliant father-in-law. Not until 944, when Romanos was removed, did he come into full possession of his inheritance. He had not chafed at being overshadowed for so long, for he was by nature a scholar and an antiquarian rather than a man of action. He is best remembered for his three great works: on the administration of the Empire; on the ceremonies of the court; and on the Themes or military districts of the provinces. The first was compiled for the edification of his son and heir *Romanos II. All are of unique historical and geographical value. Constantine also stimulated and patronized intellectual and creative activity among others, not least in the writing of history by the continuators of the chronicler *Theophanes. He himself wrote the history of the reign of his grandfather *Basil I. As a ruler he held firmly to the policies of his father-in-law, Romanos I. The Bulgarian crisis had passed; the eastern frontier was held against the Arabs; and among the diplomatic successes of his reign was the conversion to Christianity of the Russian princess, Olga of Kiev, who paid a state visit to Constantinople in 957. Constantine died in November 959, leaving his throne to his son *Romanos II.

BIBL. Jenkins and Moravcsik 1967; Jenkins 1962; Reiske 1829—30; Vogt 1935—40; Pertusi 1952; Toynbee 1973

Constantine VIII Emperor 1025−8

He was the brother and successor of *Basil II with whom he had been co-Emperor for almost fifty years, though he had been content to play a very subordinate role. Basil's death in 1025 unleashed numerous revolts of the landed aristocracy who had suffered from his legislation. Constantine suppressed them with cruel savagery. Almost his only act of statesmanship was to sanction the marriage of his sister Anna to Vladimir of Kiev. He had three daughters but no sons. On his deathbed he arranged that his second daughter *Zoe should marry an elderly senator, *Romanos (III) Argyros; and it was he who succeeded Constantine when he died in November 1028.

BIBL. Ostrogorsky 1968: 320−2

Constantine IX Monomachos Emperor 1042−55

Constantine became Emperor through his marriage to the Empress *Zoe in 1042. Each had been married twice before. He was a pleasantly decadent aristocrat with a taste for pleasure and extravagance that Zoe shared, to the detriment of the treasury and the economy. Nominally he ruled in concert with the two Empresses of the Macedonian family, Zoe and her sister *Theodora. But he also brought his mistress, a coquette called Skleraina, to live in the palace and invented an imperial title for her so that she could appear at all state functions with the Empresses. This scandalized the Patriarch and the church but left Zoe unmoved. Constantine's ineffectiveness was twice challenged by pretenders to his throne and twice he was saved, mainly by chance. He lived on the legacy of stability created by his greater predecessors. He sensed no danger from the Seljuq Turks who appeared on the Armenian frontier. Instead of strengthening the defences of his Empire he reduced the numbers of his troops. His attempt to enlist the help of the Pope against the growing threat from the Normans in southern Italy resulted in the schism between the churches of Rome and Constantinople in 1054, which his troublesome Patriarch *Michael (I) Keroullarios constrained him to approve. In his favour it must be said that Constantine promoted a revival of learning and scholarship by founding, in 1045, the schools of higher education in philosophy and in law, the one headed by Michael *Psellos, the other by *John Xiphilinos, the future Patriarch John VIII. He died in January 1055 leaving his throne to his elderly sister-in-law *Theodora.

BIBL. Ostrogorsky 1968: 333−7; Jenkins 1966: 345−7, 357−8; Angold 1984: 24−30, 36−48, 56−62

Constantine X Doukas Emperor 1059−67

Constantine came to the throne on the recommendation of Michael *Psellos as the nominee of the Emperor *Isaac I, who abdicated in December 1059. His wife, *Eudokia Makrembolitissa, was a niece of the Patriarch *Michael (I) Keroullarios. The Doukas family represented the civilian aristocracy of Constantinople who despised the military families of the provinces. Constantine almost made it his business to neglect the army and the defences of the Empire, with disastrous consequences. In the west the Normans overran the south of Italy; in the north the Hungarians occupied Belgrade and the Pechenegs and Cumans broke across the Danube deep into the Balkans; while in the east the Seljuq Turks, who had captured Baghdad in 1058 and set up their Sultanate in place of the Arab Caliphate, advanced westwards into Byzantine Asia Minor. Even Michael Psellos, who had made him Emperor, had to admit that Constantine's foreign policy was a failure. He died in May 1067. His widow Eudokia, after a short spell as regent for her three sons, was persuaded to marry *Romanos IV Diogenes.

BIBL. Polemis 1968: no. 12; Ostrogorsky 1968: 341−4

Constantine XI Palaiologos Emperor 1449−53

Constantine XI was the last Byzantine Emperor. The fourth son of *Manuel II, he was nominated to the succession by his brother *John VIII who died childless in October 1448. Two of his brothers disputed his appointment but the matter was resolved by their mother, the dowager Empress Helena. Constantine, who was serving in the province of the Morea (Peloponnese), was invested as Emperor at Mistra in January 1449. In February the Ottoman Sultan Murad II died and was succeeded by his young but formidable son Mehmed II, who soon made it clear that the conquest of Constantinople was his prime objective. In 1451 he began his encirclement and blockade of the city. Constantine made tireless and heroic efforts to defend it and to stir the conscience of his western allies by upholding the union of the churches proclaimed at the Council of Florence. But he laboured in vain. A few courageous Venetians fought in the final defence of Constantinople. But the relief promised by their government and by the Pope arrived too late. Before his decisive assault on the walls, the Sultan Mehmed invited the Emperor to surrender and vacate his city. Constantine replied that he would sooner die. It was the last communication between a Christian Emperor and an Ottoman Sultan. Constantinople was captured on Tuesday, 29 May 1453 and Constantine was last seen fighting as a common soldier at its walls. He had no issue from his two marriages.

BIBL. Runciman 1965

Constantine II Patriarch of Constantinople 754−66

He was appointed by the iconoclast Emperor *Constantine V after an interregnum of some six months following the death of the Patriarch *Anastasios. He attended the last session of Constantine's iconoclast council in August 754 and gave his approval to its decrees. He held office as a time-serving iconoclast Patriarch until August 766, when the Emperor removed him for alleged implication in a conspiracy. A year later he was executed. His successor was *Niketas I.

BIBL. Grumel 1936: 9−11

Constantine III Leichoudes Patriarch of Constantinople 1059−63

He was chief minister of the Emperor *Constantine IX and a close

29

friend of Michael *Psellos, of the future Patriarch *John VIII Xiphilinos, and of John *Mavropous. He was dismissed from the imperial service in 1055; but the Emperor *Isaac I appointed him Patriarch in succession to *Michael I Keroullarios in February 1059. Psellos wrote a Eulogy of him when he died in 1063.

BIBL. Grumel 1947: 17−19; Hussey 1986: 138

Constantine-Cyril (*c*. 827−69) missionary and saint

Constantine was born at Thessalonica and changed his name to Cyril when he became a monk. He succeeded his friend *Photios as professor of philosophy at Constantinople, and was a diplomat as well as a scholar. He went on embassies to the Arabs in 855−6 and to the Khazars in 860−1. In 862 Rostislav, ruler of the newly-born Slav kingdom of Moravia, asked the Emperor *Michael III to send him missionaries capable of preaching Christianity in the Slav language. Constantine and his brother *Methodios were appointed for the task. Both were natives of Thessalonica, a Greek-speaking city surrounded by Slavs. They were well-equipped linguistically and culturally to spread the Gospel in the Slavonic tongues. Constantine's unique contribution to the enterprise was the invention of a Slav alphabet so that the Scriptures and the liturgy could be translated from Greek. The earlier form of this new script was the Glagolitic; but this was superseded by the Cyrillic, which was adapted from the Greek uncial alphabet with some additional signs to represent sounds which do not occur in the Greek language. Constantine and his brother led their mission to Moravia in 863. Their arrival was resented by Frankish missionaries from the west who were committed to the use of Latin, a language foreign to the Slavs. The Pope, Hadrian II, invited Constantine and Methodios to Rome to discuss the matter; and there Constantine died in February 869. He was canonized by both eastern and western churches.

BIBL. Dvornik 1970; Vlasto 1970; Obolensky 1971

Constantius Emperor 337−61

*Constantine I left his Empire to be divided between his three surviving sons, Constantine II, Constantius and Constans (I), Constantius received Constantinople and the eastern portion. The conflict that ensued was religious as well as political, for Constantius subscribed to the Arian form of the Christian creed while his brothers held to that defined at the Council of Nicaea in 325. This led to long and bitter disruption in the church, the Nicene creed being championed most vigorously by Athanasius of Alexandria. Much of Constantius's reign was spent in warfare against the Persians in the east and the barbarian tribes on the Danube frontier. He was intolerant of paganism and offended the adherents of the old Roman religion. He died childless in November 361 and was succeeded by his cousin *Julian who represented the pagan reaction to Christian bigotry.

BIBL. Jones 1964, I: 112−20

Cosmas Indicopleustes (6th century) geographer

A much-travelled spice merchant from Alexandria, Cosmas wrote an account of his impressions to substantiate his cosmological theory. His work, known as the *Christian Topography*, attempts to describe the *cosmos* in terms of Christian principles and revelations as against the theories of pagan geographers. His name implies that he had sailed to India but he probably got no further than the Black Sea, the Red Sea and the Persian Gulf.

BIBL. Wolska-Conus 1968, 1970, 1973; Wolska 1962

Cyril Patriarch of Alexandria 412−44

Cyril was a native of Alexandria and a nephew of its Patriarch, Theophilus, whom he succeeded in 412. He came to prominence in the defence of Orthodox belief against the doctrines of *Nestorius who was made Patriarch of Constantinople in 428. Their dispute over theology had deep political undertones, for Cyril was convinced of the superiority of his apostolic see of Alexandria over the upstart church of Constantinople. Both appealed to Rome and Pope Celestine condemned what he considered to be the new heresy of Nestorius. The Emperor *Theodosius II then called a Council at Ephesos in 431 at which Nestorius was denounced in twelve anathemas drawn up by Cyril. The Bishop of Antioch and other Nestorians held a separate synod at which they condemned Cyril. The Emperor had both of them put in prison. But Cyril was allowed to escape back to Alexandria. For all the purity of his theology, he was an ambitious, unscrupulous and intolerant prelate, feared as a persecutor of pagans, Jews and heretics. His immense literary output includes commentaries on the Scriptures, dogmatic and polemical works against the Arians and Nestorians, a diatribe against the pagan Emperor *Julian, letters and sermons. He was canonized at an early date as the last of the Greek Fathers and Doctors of the church universal.

BIBL. Quasten 1960: 116−42; von Campenhausen 1963: 158−70

Cyril of Skythopolis (*c.* 524−*c.* 558) monk and hagiographer

Cyril, who came from Skythopolis in Palestine, was a monk in the monastery of St Sabas near Jerusalem. His devotion to the eremitic, ascetic life led him to compile a hagiographical corpus of monks and hermits, many of whom he had known. Among the most interesting from the historical point of view are his *Lives* of St Sabas, St Euthymius and St Theodosius.

BIBL. Schwartz 1939; Beck 1959: 408−10

D

Dalassenē, Anna (*c.* 1030–1101/2) princess

Anna was the mother of the Emperor *Alexios I Komnenos. She worked hard to get him to the throne and was a tireless promoter of the interests of the great family of Komnenos into which she had married. Her husband was John Komnenos, brother of the Emperor *Isaac I who abdicated in 1059, a dereliction of family duty for which Anna never forgave him. She was for a time exiled in 1071 as a result of her dynastic machinations. Her son Alexios had such confidence in her many talents that he made her regent in Constantinople with supreme authority in justice and finance when he was called away to fight the Normans just after his accession in 1081. Her granddaughter *Anna Komnenē gives a vivid and sympathetic account of her, though she is reticent about her later life.

BIBL. Diehl 1906a: 317–42; Cheynet 1986: 95–9

David Komnenos Emperor of Trebizond 1458–61

The last of the Emperors of Trebizond, David was a brother of *John IV Komnenos, whom he succeeded in 1458. Constantinople had fallen to the Sultan Mehmed II five years before; and in anticipation of the expected Turkish attack on Trebizond, David looked far afield for allies. He was in touch with the Pope and with Philip, Duke of Burgundy. He was none the less forced to surrender to the Sultan's army and navy in August 1461. The city of Trebizond was spared; but the Empire which had lasted since 1204 was extinguished. David was deported to Adrianople (Edirne) where, after some time in prison, he and most of his family were executed in 1463. His wife, Helena Kantakouzenē, had nine children. She is said to have buried the corpses of her murdered husband and sons and to have died of grief. Her two surviving children were forced to become Muslims.

BIBL. Nicol 1968: no. 72

Demetrios Palaiologos Despot of the Morea 1449–60

Demetrios was the fifth son of the Emperor *Manuel II. In 1438–9 he attended the Council of Ferrara-Florence with his brother, the Emperor *John VIII. When his elder brother *Constantine (XI) was proclaimed Emperor in 1449, Demetrios joined his youngest brother *Thomas as Despot at Mistra in the Morea (Peloponnese). Their constant quarrelling led to unrest and rebellion and provoked the intervention of the Turks, who caused Demetrios to surrender Mistra on 29 May 1460. The Sultan spared his life and granted him a pension and a small estate. He died as a monk in 1470.

BIBL. Runciman 1980: 86–92

Dositheos of Jerusalem Patriarch of Constantinople 1189—91 *See* Niketas II Mountanes Patriarch

Doukas (*c*. 1400—62) historian

Doukas (Ducas), whose first name was probably Michael, was the author of a *History* of the fall of the Byzantine Empire and the rise of the Ottoman Turks, from 1341 to 1462, in greater detail from 1389. His description of the Turkish siege and capture of Constantinople in 1453 is particularly vivid, although he was not there at the time. Little is known about his ancestry or his life, most of which he spent in the service of the Gattilusi, the Genoese lords of Lesbos. He may have died during the Turkish siege of the island in 1462. He evidently knew Turkish as well as Italian and he was a fervent supporter of union between the eastern and western churches.

BIBL. Grecu 1958; Magoulias 1975; *PLP* no. 5685

Doukas, Constantine porphyrogenitus (1074-c. 1095)

He was the only son of the Emperor *Michael VII Doukas and his Caucasian wife, Maria of Alania. As a boy he was betrothed, for diplomatic purposes, to a daughter of the Norman leader Robert Guiscard. When this engagement was broken, Guiscard made it his pretext for invading Byzantium. Constantine was accorded special privileges by the Emperor *Alexios I, who was infatuated with his beautiful mother Maria; and he styled himself co-Emperor. He was then betrothed to Alexios's daughter *Anna Komnenē. But he died about 1095 before they were married, having already been upstaged as heir apparent to the throne by Alexios's son *John (II), who was born in 1087. Constantine's portrait appears on the holy crown of Hungary.

BIBL. Polemis 1968: no. 23

Doukas, John Caesar (*d. c.* 1088)

John was the brother of the Emperor *Constantine X Doukas, who gave him the title of Caesar and relied upon him as a trusted adviser. He was a friend and correspondent of Michael *Psellos and the owner of large estates in Thrace and in Bithynia, to which he retired when *Romanos IV came to the throne. After the defeat of Romanos at Manzikert in 1071, John, with the help of Psellos, caused his nephew *Michael VII Doukas to be made Emperor and ordered the blinding of Romanos. He was taken prisoner by the Norman rebel, Roussel de Bailleul, with whom he then joined forces and by whom he was proclaimed Emperor. His bid for power was thwarted and he became a monk; though later he helped and advised the Emperor *Alexios I Komnenos. He had two sons by his wife Eirene, Andronikos and Constantine. Andronikos was the father of *Eirene Doukaina, who married Alexios I.

BIBL. Polemis 1968: no. 13

Doukas, John (*c*. 1064—*c*. 1135) soldier

John was a son of Andronikos Doukas (*d*. 1077) and a grandson of the

Caesar John *Doukas, who reared him as an orphan. He was posted as governor of Dyrrachion (Durazzo) in Albania after the Normans had been expelled in 1085. He was there until 1092, when he was transferred to Asia Minor to recapture Lesbos and other islands from the Turks. He also put down rebellions in Crete and Cyprus and fought many victorious campaigns against the Turks on the mainland of Asia Minor. He was a correspondent of *Theophylact of Ochrida.

BIBL. Polemis 1968: no. 26

E

Eirene Empress 797–802

Eirene came from Athens and married the Emperor *Leo IV. When he died in 780 she became regent for her infant son *Constantine VI. She survived two attempted coups d'état. She had some political flair but no military talent. Her overriding obsession was the restoration of holy pictures to their traditional place in Orthodox worship after half a century of iconoclasm. To this end she summoned a Council of the church to undo the work of that called by *Constantine V in 754. She proceeded with caution, for much of the army was iconoclast by persuasion. The Council was finally held at Nicaea in 787, presided over by the Patriarch *Tarasios, whom Eirene had appointed; and its bishops gratified her by declaring iconoclasm to be a heresy. In 790 she was temporarily ousted by her son Constantine whom she had bullied into an unwanted marriage. But in 797, having engineered his disgrace, she had him arrested and blinded. She then reigned as sole Emperor (*basileus* in the masculine gender) for five years, from 797 to 802, until her minister of finance, *Nikephoros (I), seized the throne and banished her to Lesbos, where she died in August 803. In the last year of her reign Charlemagne is reported to have made her an offer of marriage which, if accepted, might have changed the course of European history. In the eyes of the church Eirene's devotion to the icons outweighed her crime against her son. She was canonized after her death.

BIBL. Ostrogorsky 1968: 175–82; Jenkins 1966: 90–104; Runciman 1978; Treadgold 1988: 60–126

Eirene Doukaina Empress 1081–1123

Eirene was the eldest daughter of Andronikos Doukas and a granddaughter of the Caesar John *Doukas. She married the Emperor *Alexios I Komnenos, against the wishes of his mother Anna *Dalassenē, and was crowned Empress by the Patriarch *Kosmas I in 1081. Eirene is a central figure in the *Alexiad* written by her daughter Anna Komnenē, who describes her marriage as a happy one after some initial problems. She had seven children. When her husband died in 1118 she became a nun in the convent of the Theotokos Kecharitomenē in Constantinople, which she had restored. Like her more famous daughter, Eirene was a cultured woman and a patron of learning, with a special interest in theology. Her portrait is to be seen in the Pala d'Oro in St Mark's in Venice.

BIBL. Polemis 1968: no. 26

Eirenikos, Nicholas (first half 13th century) poet

A near relation of the Patriarch *Theodore II Eirenikos, Nicholas was archivist (*chartophylax*) of the Empire in exile at Nicaea after 1204. He

composed some verses in celebration of the wedding of the Emperor
*John III Batatzes to Constance (Anna), daughter of the German Emperor
Frederick II in 1244. They are of interest for the study of Byzantine court
ceremonial.

BIBL. Heisenberg 1973: 97—112

Epiphanius Patriarch of Constantinople 520—35
He had the difficult task of being the first Patriarch under the Emperor
*Justinian, who had a firm belief in his own position as head of the
church. In 520 Epiphanius sent his profession of faith to the Pope emphasiz-
ing his adherence to the Orthodox creed of the Council of Chalcedon and
his condemnation of the Monophysite heresy. He died in June 535 and
was succeeded as Patriarch by *Anthimus.

BIBL. Grumel 1972: 159—63; Beck 1959: 375—6

Esaias Patriarch of Constantinople 1323—32
He was a monk appointed to succeed *Gerasimos I as Patriarch. When
in 1327 the Emperor *Andronikos II ordered him to excommunicate his
grandson, *Andronikos III, Esaias boldly refused. He was confined in a
monastery until the civil war was over in May 1328, when he was brought
out in triumph and reinstated.

BIBL. Darrouzès 1977: 78—126; Nicol 1972: 167—9

Eudokia Makrembolitissa Empress 1067; 1071
A member of the families of Doukas and of Makrembolites, Eudokia
was a niece of the Patriarch *Michael I Keroullarios and a relative of
Michael *Psellos. She became the second wife of the Emperor *Constantine X Doukas and mother of several children. When he died in 1067 she
acted as Empress-regent for her three sons, *Michael VII, Andronikos
and Constantine. She had vowed never to take another husband; but in
December 1067 she was persuaded to marry *Romanos IV Diogenes and
reigned with him until he was deposed in August 1071. For two months
she was sole Empress once again, until her son Michael VII took over as
Emperor. She withdrew to a convent and died as a nun some time after
1081; though there was a moment when she considered taking as her third
husband *Nikephoros III Botaneiates.

BIBL. Polemis 1968: no. 12

Eugenikos, Mark (*d*. 1445) Bishop of Ephesos
He was a pupil of George *Gemistos Plethon and later a tutor of
*Gennadios (II) Scholarios. He was appointed Metropolitan of Ephesos
in 1437 and in the following year went with the Byzantine delegation to
the Council of Ferrara-Florence, where he played a very active part. He
was later accused of bigotry because he had refused to sign the decree of
union at Florence in 1439. But he soon became the hero of the anti-
unionist faction in Constantinople; and he was the only Byzantine delegate
to the Council to be canonized as a Confessor by the Orthodox church for

his consistent and vociferous opposition to the union of the eastern and western churches. In his quieter moments he was a Hesychast monk of deep spirituality. Many of his anti-Latin polemics survive as well as ascetical works and letters.

BIBL. *PLP* no. 6193

Euphemius Patriarch of Constantinople 490−6
When *Anastasius I was elected Emperor in 491, Euphemius as Patriarch extracted from him a written profession of his Orthodox belief. This he produced in evidence against the Emperor when it became clear that Anastasius was in fact a heretical Monophysite. Euphemius was deposed and exiled in 496. His successor was the Patriarch *Macedonius II.

BIBL. Grumel 1972: 131−6; Charanis 1974

Euphrosyne Doukaina Empress 1195−1203
She was the wife of the Emperor *Alexios III Angelos, whose nefarious ascent to the throne she contrived in 1195. She was a headstrong woman who had the courage and the drive that her husband lacked. She came of the same family as the Patriarch *John X Kamateros. In 1196 it was rumoured that she had a secret lover. She was driven from the palace. But she had influential friends, among them the powerful Constantine *Mesopotamites. After six months she was recalled and took over almost all the reins of government. When, in July 1203, the Emperor *Isaac II was liberated and reinstated by the knights of the Fourth Crusade, Euphrosyne fled from Constantinople with her husband. She followed him on his wanderings and took refuge with his cousin *Michael I Komnenos Doukas, the independent ruler of Epiros. She died at his capital at Arta about 1211. She had three daughters. One of them, Eudokia, married *Alexios V Doukas; another, Anna, married the Emperor in exile at Nicaea, *Theodore I Laskaris.

BIBL. Polemis 1968: no. 101

Eusebius of Caesarea (*c*. 260−*c*. 339) Bishop and historian
Eusebius Pamphili, so-called after his mentor the learned theologian Pamphilus in his native Caesarea, was a priest who lived through and subsequently described the persecution of the Christians by the Emperor Diocletian (284−305). He was made Bishop of Caesarea about 313. The most famous of his many written works is his *Ecclesiastical History* covering events in the church from its foundation to the year 324. He played a major part at the first Council of the church held at Nicaea in 325. His place in the later development of the Byzantine church and state, however, was assured through his relationship with the first Christian Roman Emperor, *Constantine I, whom he knew and admired, and whose *Life* (*Vita Constantini*) he wrote soon after the Emperor's death in 337. In the speeches which he delivered to celebrate the thirtieth year of Constantine's reign (the *Tricennalia*) in 335−6 Eusebius first adapted to Christian thought the ancient Hellenistic theory of the monarch as the image of God and the

Roman Empire as the earthly reflection of the kingdom of Heaven.

BIBL. Drake 1967; Winkelmann 1975; Williamson 1965; Barnes 1981

Eustathios Bishop of Thessalonica *c.* 1179—*c.* 1195

Born about 1115 and educated at Constantinople, Eustathios rose through the ranks of the patriarchal chancery and judiciary. As a deacon he was appointed master of the rhetors (orators) under the Patriarch *Michael III about 1170 and about 1179 became Metropolitan of Thessalonica. He continued to teach rhetoric there; and among his pupils was Michael *Choniates, later Bishop of Athens. For various reasons, not all of them clear, he was not popular in Thessalonica and had to leave it for a while. But he was back by 1185 and wrote an eye-witness account of the siege and sack of the city by the Normans in that year. He himself was taken prisoner. He died about 1195 and was succeeded by Constantine *Mesopotamites. As a scholar Eustathios is famous for his extensive commentaries on the *Iliad* and the *Odyssey* and his works on Pindar and Aristophanes. As a cleric and theologian he is noted for his series of Lenten homilies, his treatise on monastic reform, his commentary on St John of Damascus and some hagiographical works. As an orator he composed a funeral oration on the Emperor *Manuel I and addresses to various dignitaries. His letters are also preserved.

BIBL. Hunger 1978, I: 426—9; Wilson 1983: 196—204; Kazhdan 1984b

Eustathios Patriarch of Constantinople 1019—25

A western source reports that in 1024 the Patriarch Eustathios, with the approval of the Emperor *Basil II, wrote to Pope John XIX asking him to recognize the autonomy of the church of Constantinople.

BIBL. Grumel 1936: 244—5; Runciman 1955: 35—6

Eustathios Romaios (first half 11th century) judge

Eustathios 'the Byzantine' was an eminent jurist in Constantinople who held the ranks of *protospatharios* and Magister and served as a judge of the Hippodrome court in the time of the Emperors *Basil II and *Romanos III. Many of his rulings were transcribed and collected by an anonymous subordinate under the title of the *Peira*. They provide uniquely rich material on the social, economic and agrarian conditions of the early eleventh century.

BIBL. Weiss 1973; Oikonomides 1986

Eustratios Garidas Patriarch of Constantinople 1081—4

As successor to *Kosmas I, it fell to Eustratios to do his Emperor's bidding by presiding over the trial and condemnation for heresy of John *Italos in 1082. His heart was not in it and it was even said that he was sympathetic to the accused. He resigned in July 1084.

BIBL. Grumel 1947: 32—9; *DHGE* XVI: cols. 48—9

Euthymios I Patriarch of Constantinople 907–12

He was a monk and the spiritual adviser of the Emperor *Leo VI. When the Patriarch *Nicholas I Mystikos refused to absolve the Emperor of his sins, Euthymios was made Patriarch in his place. He was stripped of his rank and title, however, when Nicholas was recalled in 912 and withdrew to a monastery, where he died in August 917. His sanctity was recognized in 921; and his *Life*, written by an anonymous author in the tenth century, is a valuable historical source.

BIBL. Karlin-Hayter 1970; Grumel 1936: 146–7; Beck 1959: 549–50

Euthymios II Patriarch of Constantinople 1410–16

Archimandrite of the monastery of Stoudios in Constantinople, Euthymios was a friend and correspondent of the Emperor *Manuel II, who sent him on a mission to the Pope in 1384. In October 1410 he was appointed to succeed *Matthew I as Patriarch.

BIBL. *PLP* no. 6268

Eutychius Patriarch of Constantinople 552–65; 577–82

A monk from Amaseia in Asia Minor, Eutychius was appointed Patriarch in August 552 after the death of *Menas. He loyally supported the theological opinions of *Justinian I until, in his last years, the Emperor thought himself into the heresy of aphthartodocetism, which Eutychius and his colleagues could only condemn. The Emperor had him arrested and banished in January 565. He was succeeded by *John III Scholasticus; though he was reinstated in October 577 and died as Patriarch in April 582.

BIBL. Grumel 1972: 177–81, 189–92; *DHGE* XVI: cols. 94–5

Evagrius (*c.* 536–*c.* 600) church historian

Born in Syria, he studied philosophy and rhetoric. About 588 he went with Gregory, Patriarch of Antioch, to Constantinople, where he held various public offices and was known as Evagrius Scholasticus. His major work was an *Ecclesiastical History* in six books, a sequel to the histories of the church by *Socrates, *Sozomen and *Theodoret, covering the years from 431 to 593.

BIBL. Bidez and Parmentier 1898

F

Flavian Patriarch of Constantinople 446–9

He succeeded *Proclus. He was made a saint because of his steadfastness in the face of the new challenge to Orthodoxy posed by the Monophysites, who believed that Christ had but one, single and divine nature. He died in August 449 and was replaced by *Anatolius.

BIBL. Grumel 1972: 75–84; *DHGE* XVIII: cols. 390–5

G

Gabalas, Matthew Bishop of Ephesos 1329—51

Matthew (Matthaios) became a monk in 1322 and was appointed as Metropolitan of Ephesos in 1329. He was a pupil of *Theoleptos of Philadelphia and a correspondent of Nikephoros *Gregoras, with whom he shared an antipathy towards Gregory *Palamas, for expressing which he was condemned and relieved of his office in 1351. He wrote many letters and orations and died between 1355 and 1360.

BIBL. *PLP* no. 3309

Gazes, Theodore (*c*. 1400—75) scholar

Theodore Gazes (Gaza in Latin) was a native of Thessalonica who settled in Italy. He learnt Latin at Mantua and about 1447 he became the first Professor of Greek at Ferrara. He was later in Rome, Naples and Calabria. A friend of Cardinal *Bessarion, of Francesco Filelfo and other Italian humanists, he wrote many literary and philosophical works and translations from Latin into Greek. He was a formative figure in the revival of Greek studies in the west.

BIBL. *PLP* no. 3450

Gemistos, George Plethon (*c*. 1360—1452) philosopher

Born as George Gemistos in Constantinople, he adopted the name Plethon out of his admiration for Plato. He is said to have learnt the teachings of Zoroaster from a Jewish scholar. His own pupils included Cardinal *Bessarion and Mark *Eugenikos; and he corresponded with *Gennadios (II) Scholarios and the Italian humanist Francesco Filelfo. About 1405 he left Constantinople to live at Mistra in the Morea (Peloponnese) and there he studied and taught for most of his long life. He was present at the Council of Ferrara-Florence in 1438—9 as a lay observer; and the experience confirmed his belief that Christianity had been tried and found wanting. Twenty years earlier he had laid before the Emperor *Manuel II and his son, the Despot *Theodore II Palaiologos, detailed plans for reforming the administration, the economy, the social structure and the defence of the Despotate of the Morea along the lines of Plato's *Republic*. Later in life his classical studies and his disenchantment with Christianity led him to propose the salvation of society through a return to the ideals of ancient Greece supported by a revived 'Hellenic' religion, its ethical system based not on the Christian faith but on platonic and neoplatonic philosophy. He committed his ideas to writing in a treatise called *The Book of the Laws*. His former friend, the future Patriarch Gennadios II, found it so blasphemous that he ordered it to be burnt; only fragments survive. His other major work was on the differences between Aristotle and Plato, which originated as lectures which he gave in Florence. As an original thinker and philosopher Plethon had no equal in his own milieu. He was more acclaimed in Renaissance Italy, where his influence prompted Cosimo de' Medici to found the Platonic Academy in Florence. He died at Mistra in June 1452. Twelve years later his remains were exhumed and carried to Rimini by Sigismondo Malatesta, over whose relative Cleope, wife of the Despot Theodore, he had pronounced a funeral oration in 1433. His tomb in Rimini bears the inscription: 'Prince of Philosophers in his time'.

BIBL. Woodhouse 1986; *PLP* no. 3630

Genesios, Joseph (mid 10th century) historian
A member of a well-known Constantinopolitan family of the ninth and tenth centuries, Genesios wrote a *History of the Emperors* (*Basileiai*) in four books. It covers the years 813 to 886 and the reigns of *Leo V, *Michael II, *Theophilos, *Michael III and, more briefly, *Basil I. It was composed between 944 and 959 at the invitation of the Emperor *Constantine VII in whose service Genesios was employed. This explains his bias in favour of Basil I as against his predecessors; for Basil was Constantine's grandfather. None the less Genesios is uniquely informative about many events.

BIBL. Lesmüller-Werner and Thurn 1978; Hunger 1978, I: 351−4

Gennadios I Patriarch of Constantinople 458−71
The eastern church venerates him as a saint for his staunch support of the Emperor *Leo I in defence of the Orthodox creed as defined at the Council of Chalcedon in 451. He was celebrated for his writings, commentaries on the Scriptures and dogmatic works, few of which have survived. He died in November 471 and was succeeded as Patriarch by *Acacius.

BIBL. Grumel 1972: 103−9; Quasten 1960: 525−6

Gennadios II Scholarios Patriarch of Constantinople 1454−6
George Kourtesis Scholarios was born about 1405 and studied at Mistra in the Morea (Peloponnese). As secretary of the Emperor *John VIII he attended the Council of Ferrara-Florence, being an expert in western philosophy and theology. He signed the document of the union of the churches there proclaimed in 1439. But he changed his mind when back in Constantinople and became, after Mark *Eugenikos, the hero and spokesman of the anti-union faction. In 1450 he was tonsured as a monk with the name of Gennadios. After the Turkish conquest of Constantinople in 1453, the Sultan Mehmed II selected and invested him as the first Patriarch of Constantinople under the Ottoman dispensation. He died after 1472. His many writings have survived.

BIBL. Petit, Siderides and Jugie 1928−36; Gill, 1964: 79−94; Beck 1959: 760−2

Geometres, John Kyriotes (10th century) poet
A court official in Constantinople, Geometres became a monk in the monastery of Kyrou and, late in life, Bishop of Melitene. He wrote

epigrams and poems about contemporary events, such as the campaigns of the Emperor *Basil II against the Bulgars, as well as religious works in verse and prose.

BIBL. Works *in MPG*, vol. 106; Beck 1959: 553–4

George II Xiphilinos Patriarch of Constantinople 1191–8
The Emperor *Isaac II Angelos claimed the right to appoint his own Patriarchs. In 1191 he selected George Xiphilinos as a compromise candidate after the trouble that had arisen over the appointment of *Niketas (II) Mountanes and his rival Dositheos. George II is noted for his efforts to tighten episcopal control over the monasteries. He resisted the change of rulers in 1195 when *Alexios III seized the palace and imprisoned Isaac II. But he gave in and recognized Alexios as Emperor. He died in July 1198 and was succeeded by *John X Kamateros.

BIBL. Grumel 1947: 181–9

George of Cyprus *see* **Gregory II** Patriarch of Constantinople

George the Monk (mid 9th century) chronicler
George Monachos or Hamartolos (the Sinner), a regular attribute of Byzantine monks, wrote a *World Chronicle* stretching from Adam to the year 842. He completed it in 866–7. It is written in a simple style, a work of monkish piety for popular consumption and edification, and very popular it proved to be. It was translated into Old Slavonic and into Georgian in the eleventh to twelfth centuries. A sequel, under the name of Georgius Continuatus, was written in the reign of *Nikephoros II Phokas taking the tale on to the death of *Romanos I in 948.

BIBL. de Boor 1904; Georgius Continuatus *in* Bekker 1838; Hunger 1978, I: 347–51

George of Pisidia (first half 7th century) poet
A deacon and archivist of St Sophia in Constantinople, he was the author of religious and historical poems all but one written in the Byzantine dodecasyllabic verse, which he may have invented. His poems on the Persian campaigns and victories of the Emperor *Heraclius and on the Avar and Persian attack on Constantinople in 628 are of great historical value. His *Hexaemeron* is a poem about the creation of the world.

BIBL. Pertusi 1959; Hunger 1978, II: 112–13

George Synkellos (*d*. 810–11) chronicler
George was a monk who became *synkellos* or private secretary to the Patriarch *Tarasios (784–806) in Constantinople and wrote a *World Chronicle* from Adam up to the accession of the Emperor Diocletian in 284. Much of it is no more than chronological tables. It was continued by his friend *Theophanes.

BIBL. Mosshammer 1984; Hunger 1978, I: 331–2

Gerasimos I Patriarch of Constantinople 1320—1

He succeeded the Patriarch *John XIII Glykys, having formerly been abbot of the Mangana monastery in Constantinople.

BIBL. *PLP* no. 3783

Germanos I Patriarch of Constantinople 715—30

He was the first Patriarch under the iconoclast regime of the Emperor *Leo III. He had formerly been Bishop of Kyzikos and not noted for his strength of mind. When, however, in 730 the Emperor issued a formal decree ordering the destruction of all religious images, Germanos refused to sign it and was forced to abdicate. He was succeeded by *Anastasios and died in 733. Many of his letters survive.

BIBL. Grumel 1936: 1—8; Lamza 1975; Beck 1959: 473—5

Germanos II Patriarch of Constantinople 1223—40

He was appointed by the Emperor *John III Batatzes, in succession to the Patriarch *Manuel II, as the third of the Patriarchs in exile at Nicaea. He was enthroned in January 1223. He challenged the unauthorized appointment of bishops in Epiros being sanctioned by its secular rulers; and he disputed the claim of *Theodore Komnenos Doukas to the title of Emperor. In 1232 he sent a deputy to Epiros to reassert his jurisdiction; and thereafter the clergy in Epiros recognized the Patriarch at Nicaea as their spiritual head. He also corresponded with the Latin Patriarch of Constantinople about the treatment of Greek priests in Latin-occupied territories.

BIBL. Laurent 1971a: 41—109

Glabas *see* **Isidore Glabas**

Glykas, Michael (*d.* after 1200) chronicler

Michael Glykas, also known as Sikidites, was on the secretarial staff of the Emperor *Manuel I until 1159, when he was partially blinded on a charge of heresy. He wrote a *Chronicle* of events from the Creation to 1118 which is a popular confabulation of theology and curiosities. His more scholarly work is an exegesis of certain problems (*Aporiai*) in the Holy Scriptures. Under the name of Myron Sikidites he also stirred up a theological controversy over the question of transubstantiation in the Eucharist which divided the church during the patriarchate of *John X Kamateros.

BIBL. Bekker 1836a; Eustratiades 1906, 1912; Hunger 1978, I: 422—6; Beck 1959: 343—4

Gregoras, Nikephoros (*d.* 1361) scholar and historian

Reared by his uncle John, Bishop of Herakleia Pontica, whose *Life* he later wrote, Gregoras was a pupil of Theodore *Metochites. Although a layman, he was a leading opponent of the theology of Hesychasm as expounded by Gregory *Palamas. As a result he fell out with his friend

*John (VI) Kantakouzenos. He had earlier fallen out with *Barlaam of Calabria, whose denunciation he welcomed; for he disapproved of Latin theology and scholasticism. He served the Emperor *Andronikos II as an ambassador and frequented his court as a scholar. In 1349 he declined an invitation to be Patriarch. His opposition to Palamas led to his being condemned in 1351 along with Gregory *Akindynos and other anti-Palamites. He was confined to the Chora monastery (Kariye Djami) in Constantinople, where he applied himself to his writing. He was liberated when *John V came to the throne. Many attempts were made to win him over. But he was determined to be a martyr; and he died, still protesting, in 1361.

Gregoras was one of the greatest polymaths of the fourteenth century. Though latterly obsessed with theology, he was a mathematician and astronomer. He foretold eclipses; he proposed a reform of the Julian Calendar; he devised a new method of reckoning the date of Easter; and he wrote a treatise on the construction of the astrolabe. His *History* in thirty-seven books covers the period from 1320 to 1359 and is a major source for the age in which he lived. Many of his letters survive as well as rhetorical, hagiographical, philosophical, philological and scientific works. He also wrote funeral orations on the Emperors *Andronikos II and *Andronikos III.

BIBL. Schopen 1829, 1830, 1855; Guilland 1926; *PLP* no. 4443

Gregory II Patriarch of Constantinople 1283−9
Gregory is otherwise known as George of Cyprus, where he was born and educated at a Latin school. Later he studied philosophy and mathematics under George *Akropolites in Constantinople. He was at first in favour of the union of the eastern and western churches proclaimed in 1274, but he changed his mind after 1282. He was made Patriarch by the Emperor *Andronikos II in March 1283 and presided over the synod in 1285 at which the former Patriarch *John XI Bekkos and other unionists were denounced. In a document (*Tomos*) which he presented to that synod he tried to define more clearly the Orthodox position on Trinitarian theology. Some thought it to be heretical and Gregory was forced to resign in March 1289. Many of his letters and other writings survive as well as his Autobiography.

BIBL. Papadakis 1983; *PLP* no. 4590

Gregory III Mammē Patriarch of Constantinople 1445−51
He attended the Council of Ferrara-Florence in 1438−9 and was a devoted adherent of the union of the eastern and western churches. As such he was elected to succeed the Patriarch *Metrophanes II after a vacancy of some months. Unable to win over the opponents of the union in Constantinople, he left in August 1451 and settled in Rome, where he died in 1459. He had no successor until the appointment as Patriarch of *Gennadios II in 1454. He was thus the last Patriarch of Byzantine Constantinople.

BIBL. *PLP* no. 4591

45

Gregory of Nazianzus (*c*. 330–*c*. 389) theologian and saint

Born near Nazianzus in Cappadocia in Asia Minor, Gregory was the son of a convert to Christianity who became Bishop of Nazianzus. He was educated at Caesarea, Alexandria and Athens, where he made friends with *Basil, later Bishop of Caesarea, whose monastery at Annesi he joined. He was ordained as a priest in 362 and although nominated to a bishopric he never took it up, preferring the seclusion of a monastery in Isauria. After the death of the Emperor *Valens, who had favoured the Arian heresy, Gregory became champion of the Orthodox creed of Nicaea in Asia Minor and in Constantinople. The council convened there in 381 by the Emperor *Theodosius I proposed him as bishop of the capital; but the appointment was challenged and Gregory withdrew. He lived the rest of his life in rural retirement, writing and corresponding with his many friends. He was and is generally recognized as one of the foremost interpreters of the theology of the Trinity as it had first been formulated by the Fathers at the Council of Nicaea in 325. His sermons elaborate the doctrine, especially his *Five Theological Orations*. Some of his other speeches provide valuable historical material. His many other works include a long autobiographical poem.

BIBL. Quasten 1960: 236–54; von Campenhausen 1963: 101–14; Ruether 1969

Gregory of Nyssa (*c*. 335–*c*. 394) theologian and saint

He was the brother of *Basil the Great and friend of *Gregory of Nazianzus, and became Bishop of Nyssa in Cappadocia about 372. He attended the Council at Constantinople called by the Emperor *Theodosius I in 381 and thereafter was an eloquent preacher on state occasions in the capital. Like his brother Basil, Gregory was much concerned with the synthesis between Platonic and Christian philosophy. He was less concerned with the misguided beliefs of the Arian heretics who denied the divine nature of Christ. That he was more of a scholar than a man of action is shown by the number and the range of his written works. They include: *The Creation of Man*, a continuation of Basil's *Hexaemeron*; the *Great Catechesis* or Religious Instruction; *On Not Three Gods*, about the nature of the Trinity; *On Virginity*; and his *Life of Macrina*. He is revered as a saint by the eastern and western churches.

BIBL. Quasten 1960: 254–96; von Campenhausen, 1963: 115–25

Gregory of Sinai (*d*. *c*. 1340) monk

Gregory Sinaites was one of the first preachers and practitioners of the mystical doctrine and contemplative technique of Hesychasm. He came by way of Mount Sinai, Cyprus, Jerusalem and Crete to Mount Athos; and there he instructed the later Patriarch *Kallistos I and many other hesychast monks. Turkish raids on Mount Athos obliged him and his disciples to flee and Gregory made his way to the mountains of Paroria in northern Bulgaria, where he founded a Greco-Slav monastic community under the patronage of the Tsar John Alexander. There he died some time after 1337. His influence on the development of the spiritual and ascetic life in

Byzantium and eastern Europe was great. His *Life* was written by his disciple Kallistos and he left some ascetic writings of his own.

BIBL. *PLP* no. 4601

H

Harmenopoulos, Constantine (*d. c.* 1359) lawyer

A civil servant and supreme judge (*nomophylax*) in Thessalonica from 1347, he is best known for his compendium of civil and criminal law in six books (*Hexabiblos*), which had a profound effect on legal development in the countries of eastern Europe.

BIBL. *PLP* no. 1347

Heraclius Emperor 610–41

Probably of Armenian descent, Heraclius (Herakleios) was the son of the governor of Carthage, to whom the people of Constantinople appealed for rescue from the tyranny of the Emperor *Phokas. In October 610 he successfully dethroned the tyrant and took his place as Emperor. He was faced with the internal collapse of the Empire and with the aggression of its foreign enemies, the Avars and Slavs in the north and the Persians in the east. He had at first some success. But in 613 the Persians struck back, stormed Antioch and Damascus and captured Jerusalem, massacring the Christians and stealing the relic of the True Cross. Other Persian forces invaded Armenia and Egypt, capturing Alexandria in 619. Simultaneously the Slavs and their masters, the Avars, laid siege to Thessalonica and advanced almost to the walls of Constantinople.

In 622 Heraclius led his own army to fight the Persians and drove them out of Asia Minor. In 626, however, the Avars, in league with the Persians, marched on Constantinople; the Slavs brought ships to blockade the city; while a Persian army moved up to the Bosporos. The combined assault was miraculously repulsed; and in the autumn of 627 Heraclius again invaded Persia. At the end of that year he overwhelmed the Persian army in a great battle at Nineveh. The Persian king was deposed and his son made peace with the Emperor, restoring Armenia, Syria, Palestine and Egypt to Byzantine rule. In 630 Heraclius personally replaced the Cross in the church of the Holy Sepulchre in Jerusalem. The Slavs seized their chance to break away from domination by the Avars, a move which Heraclius skilfully encouraged.

Heraclius was probably responsible for initiating the division of the provinces into militarized zones or Themes, which began in Asia Minor. Each Theme was commanded by a *strategos* or military governor; and soldiers and their families were settled in them as freehold farmers on condition of hereditary service in the armed forces. The system, developed by succeeding Emperors, benefited the army, the economy and agriculture. Heraclius also decreed that Greek was to replace Latin as the official language of the Roman Empire. He himself adopted the Greek title of *basileus* instead of the Latin *imperator*. To bring peace to the church he approved the doctrine proposed by his Patriarch *Sergios I, that Christ had a single will (Monotheletism) and enshrined it in an edict called the *Ekthesis* in 638.

In his last years it became clear that the defeat of the Persians had left the way open for the Arabs, who poured into Syria and Palestine. Jerusalem was again in infidel hands by 638. Heraclius died a sick and disappointed man in February 641. He had married twice, first to Eudokia who died in 612, and then to Martina, who was his niece, a fact that caused scandal. He left the succession to be shared between *Constantine III, son of Eudokia, and *Heraclonas, eldest of his nine children by Martina.

BIBL. Ostrogorsky 1968: 91–112; Jenkins 1966: 15–35

Heraclonas Emperor 641

Heraclonas (or Heracleonas) was the son of the Emperor *Heraclius by his second wife, Martina. In his will Heraclius stated that Heraclonas, then aged fifteen, should reign jointly with his half-brother *Constantine III. But Constantine died in May 641; and rumour had it that Martina and her son had poisoned him. In September 641 political and military pressure caused the deposition, mutilation and exile of both in favour of the son of Constantine, *Constans II.

BIBL. Ostrogorsky 1968: 112–14

Holobolos, Manuel (13th century) monk and scholar

As secretary to the Emperor *Michael VIII, Holobolos was disgraced and mutilated for expressing sympathy for the infant *John IV Laskaris whom Michael had dispossessed. He became a monk with the name of Maximos. But in 1267 he was appointed orator of St Sophia and head of the revived patriarchal school in Constantinople. He suffered again under Michael VIII because of his change of heart on the matter of union with the church of Rome. After 1282 the new Emperor, *Andronikos II, restored him to favour. He was one of the very few of his contemporaries who knew Latin; and he translated some of the works of Boethius into Greek. He wrote hymns, poems and scholia on Aristotle and Theocritus.

BIBL. Constantinides 1982: 50–9

Hyrtakenos, Theodore (*d. c.* 1328) schoolmaster.

A pedagogue rather than a scholar, Hyrtakenos ran a fee-paying school in Constantinople, partly patronized by the Emperor *Andronikos II. Theodore *Metochites and the later Patriarch *John (XIII) Glykys sent their sons there; and Alexios *Apokaukos was his student. His surviving letters reveal the financial and other hardships of a struggling schoolmaster in fourteenth-century Constantinople.

BIBL. Constantinides 1982: 93–5

I

Ignatios Patriarch of Constantinople 847−58; 867−77

He was a son of the Emperor *Michael I and he was appointed as Patriarch, somewhat uncanonically, by the Empress *Theodora when *Methodios I died in 847. He had been a monk from his youth and noted for his piety, though not for his tact or tolerance. When Theodora was evicted by her son *Michael III in 857, Ignatios fell foul of the new regent, the Caesar *Bardas, and excommunicated him in 858. For this he was demoted and banished to an island. His successor was the Patriarch *Photios. When *Basil I came to power over the dead body of Michael III in 867, he at once dismissed Photios and recalled Ignatios to the Patriarchate. The church was split between Photians and Ignatians. But Ignatios held his office and even made his peace with Photios before he died in October 877.

BIBL. Grumel 1936: 64−71, 95−100; Hussey 1986: 69−82

Ignatios the Deacon (8th to 9th century) poet and hagiographer

Born about 770, he was a pupil of the learned Patriarch *Tarasios, rising to become professor of rhetoric and poetry in the patriarchal school and later Bishop of Nicaea. He was then a professed iconoclast, an aberration of which he repented after 842. He wrote poetry, including a poetic version of Aesop's *Fables*, and hagiographies, among them *Lives* of the Patriarchs Tarasios and *Nikephoros I.

BIBL. Works *in MPG*, vol. 117; Beck 1959: 511−12

Isaac I Komnenos Emperor 1057−9

As a child Isaac was a ward of the Emperor *Basil II. He pursued a military career and became one of a group of generals who resented the power of the civilian bureaucracy in Constantinople. He was proclaimed Emperor by his troops in Paphlagonia in June 1057. *Michael VI was made to abdicate. In September Isaac was crowned by the Patriarch *Michael (I) Keroullarios who had supported him, but with whom he soon quarrelled and whom he felt bound to dismiss. Isaac did much to strengthen the defences of the Empire. In 1059 he led campaigns against the Hungarians and the Pechenegs on the Danube frontier. He robbed the civil aristocracy and even the church of their property to finance his army. It was the combination of these powerful interests, together with ill health, that caused him to abdicate in December 1059. He became a monk and died in 1061. On the advice of Michael *Psellos, he had named as his successor *Constantine X Doukas.

BIBL. Angold 1984: 48−55; Ostrogorsky 1968: 338−41

Isaac II Angelos Emperor 1185−95

One of a provincial family which had come to prominence under

50

the Emperor *Manuel I, Isaac found himself hailed as Emperor in Constantinople by the mob who had murdered the tyrant *Andronikos I Komnenos in September 1185. The immediate crisis was resolved when his army, commanded by Alexios *Branas, drove the Normans out of Thessalonica and back to Italy. But Isaac was unable to prevent the further disintegration of the Empire. Revolt broke out in Bulgaria. Branas, sent to suppress it, was proclaimed Emperor by his troops. He was defeated; but in 1187 Isaac had to recognize the existence of a new and autonomous Bulgarian kingdom. In the same year he renewed and extended the trade concessions for Venetian merchants in Constantinople and elsewhere. In 1189, fearful of the approach of the Third Crusade, he signed a treaty with Saladin, Sultan of Egypt, an act which western Christendom regarded as the darkest treachery. Frederick Barbarossa, leader of the Crusade, bullied Isaac into ferrying his men across to Asia Minor. He had some success over the rebellious Serbians in 1190; but he failed to break the spirit of the Bulgarians. He was about to lead a second campaign against them, supported by his father-in-law Bela of Hungary, when he was dethroned by his brother *Alexios III Angelos in April 1195. He was blinded and incarcerated together with his own son *Alexios (IV). Eight years later, in the circumstances of the Fourth Crusade, he was briefly reinstated as co-Emperor with his son, who had accompanied the Crusade to Constantinople. But in January 1204 both were overthrown by revolution; and Isaac died of old age or of fright a few days after the murder of his son in February of that year.

BIBL. Brand 1968: 76−116

Isidore I Boucheiras Patriarch of Constantinople 1347−50
Isidore was a hesychast monk on Mount Athos, a disciple of *Gregory of Sinai and a friend of Gregory *Palamas. In May 1347 he was appointed to succeed the Patriarch *John XIV Kalekas, who had earlier excommunicated him for adhering to the doctrine of Hesychasm. In 1350 he crowned *John VI Kantakouzenos as Emperor in Constantinople and appointed Palamas as Metropolitan of Thessalonica.

BIBL. *PLP* no. 3140

Isidore Glabas Bishop of Thessalonica 1380−4; 1386−96
He became a monk in 1375 and in 1380 was consecrated as Metropolitan of Thessalonica, where he had been born. The city was then under siege by the Turks; and in 1384 Isidore was reprimanded by the Patriarch *Neilos for having abandoned his flock. He was reinstated in 1386. The Turks conquered the city in the following year; and Isidore travelled to Asia Minor to try to negotiate with the Sultan. He died in Thessalonica in 1396. He wrote homilies, canonical works, and treatises on the date of Easter and the phases of the moon. He was the first to record the Turkish practice of *devshirme* or forcible recruitment of Christian children into the Ottoman army.

BIBL. *PLP* no. 4223

Isidore of Kiev Cardinal 1439−63

In 1433 he was abbot of a monastery in Constantinople and was appointed Metropolitan of Kiev in 1436. At the Council of Ferrara-Florence in 1438−9 he played a leading part as one of the Byzantine spokesmen for the union of the eastern and western churches. Pope Eugenius IV made him a Cardinal in August 1439 and designated him as papal legate to Russia. But when he took the decree of union to Moscow he was arrested by the Grand Duke Basil II. He escaped to Italy. In 1452 he went to Constantinople as the Pope's representative to declare and celebrate the union in the cathedral of St Sophia. In the sack of the city after the Turkish conquest in 1453 he was captured but ransomed and got back to Italy, where he died in April 1463. Among his Italian humanist friends were Guarino of Verona and Francesco Filelfo. He left letters, orations, philosophical and theological works.

BIBL. *PLP* no. 8300

Italikos, Michael (mid 12th century) scholar

He was a scholar and orator who taught philosophy and rhetoric in Constantinople in the reigns of *John II and *Manuel I Komnenos. In 1147 he was appointed Bishop of Philippopolis (Plovdiv). His patroness was the Empress *Eirene Doukaina, for whom he wrote a Eulogy. Some of his letters and rhetorical compositions also survive.

BIBL. Gautier 1972; Moravcsik 1983: 432

Italos, John (second half 11th century) philosopher

John Italos was a Greek from the south of Italy who came to Constantinople. He studied with Michael *Psellos whom, about 1075, he succeeded as Professor of Philosophy during the reign of *Michael VII Doukas, with whose family he had influence. His lectures drew large audiences but their content worried the authorities. Psellos claimed to have revived the study of Plato. Italos challenged the cardinal principle of Byzantine thought, that philosophy was the handmaid of religion. His platonic and neoplatonic researches seemed to be at odds with the revealed truths of Christian theology. He was charged with corrupting the young and with heresy. The Patriarch *Kosmas declined to intervene. His successor *Eustratios Garidas and his synod, urged to action by monastic pressure, met to consider the condemnation of Italos. Their meeting was broken up by a mob thirsting for his blood. The Patriarch handed the matter over to the Emperor. In March 1082 *Alexios I convened a tribunal at which Italos was obliged to recant and abjure his heretical ideas and was forbidden to continue teaching. There may have been political understones in his trial and condemnation. But it was stage-managed by the Emperor; and it was no accident that its culmination came on the Feast of Orthodoxy, when the impious teachings of all the deviationists, beginning with the iconoclasts, were annually anathematized. The charges against Italos were henceforth added to the list as a warning to future Christians against the snares of 'Hellenism' or pagan philosophy.

Italos was a vexatious character not given to compromise and disliked as a rude and arrogant foreigner by such as the Emperor's daughter, *Anna Komnenē. But his public denunciation silenced original thought and scholarship in Byzantium for many years. Among his surviving works is a collection of replies to ninety-three philosophical questions put to him by Michael VII and others. He also wrote commentaries on Aristotle and a treatise on dialectic addressed to Michael's brother.

BIBL. Joannou 1956; Gouillard 1967; Hussey 1937; Clucas 1981

J

Joel (12th to 13th century) chronicler

Joel was the author of a *World Chronicle* summarizing events from Adam up to the Latin conquest of Constantinople in 1204. It has no literary and little historical value.

BIBL. Bekker 1837b; Hunger 1978, I: 476

John I Tzimiskes Emperor 969–76

John Tzimiskes (from Tshemeshgadzak, near Melitene-Malatiya, in Mesopotamia) came of a military family. His mother was a Phokas; and it was the Emperor *Nikephoros II Phokas who, seeing his prowess as a soldier, made him commander of the eastern armies in 963. John became the willing paramour of the Emperor's wife, *Theophano, and her accomplice in his murder in 969. Once she had paved his way to the throne he no less willingly accepted the conditions imposed by the Patriarch *Polyeuktos, that the murderers of Nikephoros be punished and that the wicked Theophano be banished. The Patriarch then crowned him as the Emperor John I in December 969. Having disposed of his mistress, he took to wife a daughter of the late *Constantine VII, Theodora. She was an aunt of the two legitimate heirs of the Macedonian house, *Basil II and *Constantine VIII, of whom John, like his predecessor, claimed to be guardian. The Phokas family struck back. Bardas *Phokas, a nephew of Nikephoros, was proclaimed Emperor in Caesarea; and Leo, Nikephoros's brother, staged a coup in Constantinople. Both were silenced.

Nikephoros had rashly invited the Russians to invade Bulgaria. Once there they declined to go home. John's first task was to chase them out, which he did with great success, defeating the Russian prince Svjatoslav and capturing the Bulgarian king Boris. Against the Arabs in the east he led brilliant campaigns, humiliating the Emir of Mosul on the Tigris river and the Fatimid Caliphs of Egypt. By 975 all the coastline from Caesarea to Antioch and most of the inland cities were once again Byzantine. John seemed to be within striking distance of Baghdad and of Jerusalem. In the west he poured oil on the rough diplomatic waters stirred up by Nikephoros Phokas by agreeing to give the German Emperor Otto a Byzantine princess as wife for his son. In April 972 the wedding of Otto II to Theophano, probably John's niece, was celebrated in Rome. The promise of further military and diplomatic victories was, however, cut short by John's death in January 976 at the age of fifty-one. He may have died of typhoid; but almost all the sources allege that he was poisoned by his chamberlain Basil, who saw his power slipping from him. The throne was at once occupied by the rightful heir of the Macedonian house, *Basil II.

BIBL. Ostrogorsky 1968: 293–8; Jenkins 1966: 291–9

John II Komnenos Emperor 1118–43

John was the eldest son of *Alexios I who had named him heir to the throne in 1092. The succession was disputed by his sister, the historian *Anna Komnenē, who hoped to secure the crown for her husband Nikephoros *Bryennios. But John was crowned in August 1118. His father had left the Empire in good shape, surrounded though it was by enemies and potential trouble-makers: the Turks in Asia Minor the crusaders in Syria and Palestine, the Normans in south Italy, the Venetians, the Serbians and the Hungarians in Europe. John was able to keep them all at bay and impressed them with the strength and confidence of his government. He had married a Hungarian princess and so could exert some influence in that quarter. He dealt forcibly with the Serbians and with the last remnants of the Pechenegs on the Danube frontier. He withdrew the trading privileges which his father had granted to Venice, on the ground that the conduct of Venetian merchants in Constantinople posed a threat to law and order in his Empire; though he relented in 1126 on certain strict conditions. Against the Norman kingdom in Italy, created when Roger II was crowned in Sicily in 1139, he made an alliance with the German Emperor Lothair II. In the east his victorious campaigns against the Seljuq Sultans and their rivals the Danishmend emirs as well as the Armenians brought his armies to the borders of Syria. In 1137 the city of Antioch, which the crusaders had illegally held since 1098, surrendered to him. He was on his way to make the surrender complete when he died after a hunting accident in April 1143, having named his fourth son, *Manuel I Komnenos, as his heir.

BIBL. Chalandon 1912; Angold 1984: 150–9

John III Doukas Batatzes Emperor at Nicaea 1222–54

John was the second of the Emperors in exile at Nicaea after the Fourth Crusade. He married Eirene, daughter of *Theodore I Laskaris, whom he succeeded in 1222. His succession was disputed by Theodore's brothers. His most dangerous rival, however, was the independent ruler of Epiros, *Theodore Komnenos Doukas, who captured Thessalonica from the Latins in 1224 and claimed the title of Emperor. His pride was humbled by the Bulgarians in 1230, but his Empire of Thessalonica lived on. John III regarded the Bulgarian Tsar John Asen as his ally. His son married Asen's daughter; and in 1235 and 1236 they joined forces to attack Constantinople. Their alliance then broke up and Asen died in 1241. In 1242 John III marched on Thessalonica and clipped the wings of its self-styled Emperor. Four years later he annexed Thessalonica and much of northern Greece to his Empire of Nicaea. The extension of that Empire into Europe isolated the feeble Latin regime in Constantinople.

John had his own contacts among the Latins. He almost convinced the Pope that a deal might be done over the possession of Constantinople if the Byzantine church accepted obedience to Rome. Long and fruitless negotiations took place. He was also in touch with Frederick II of Hohenstaufen and married Frederick's illegitimate daughter Constance. He might well have transferred his capital to Constantinople by diplomacy had he lived longer. It was his wise statesmanship and strategy that raised the Empire of Nicaea to the status of an international power and made that transfer possible a few years after his death at Nymphaion in November 1254. He had made Nicaea a microcosm of the Byzantine Empire, its frontiers secure and well guarded, with a sound if frugal economy and near self-sufficiency in its food production. He also patronized the founding of charitable institutions, churches and monasteries and encouraged Greek literature and scholarship. His popularity was such that he was canonized as a local saint after his death.

BIBL. Angold 1975; Polemis 1968: no. 72

John IV Laskaris Emperor at Nicaea 1258.

John was the only son and heir presumptive of the Emperor *Theodore II Laskaris who died in August 1258. He was then only eight years old. As his guardian and regent his father had appointed the Patriarch *Arsenios, together with one George Mouzalon, a man despised by the aristocracy of Nicaea. Some of them contrived Mouzalon's assassination in favour of *Michael (VIII) Palaiologos, who assumed the regency in September 1258 and soon proclaimed himself Emperor. He was crowned as such along with John IV. But after the recovery of Constantinople from the Latins in 1261 Michael was crowned alone. The young John was left behind in Nicaea. Before long he was blinded and imprisoned in a castle on the Sea of Marmora. The Patriarch Arsenios, who condemned the crime, was dismissed. The political and ecclesiastical consequences were felt for many years to come. In 1290 the Emperor *Andronikos II, the son and successor of Michael Palaiologos, privately visited John IV in his prison, either to beg forgiveness for his father's crime or to seek recognition of his own title to the imperial crown.

BIBL. Polemis 1968: no. 76

John V Palaiologos Emperor 1354–91

John, the first son of *Andronikos III, was nine years old when his father died. His mother, Anne of Savoy, backed by the Patriarch *John XIV Kalekas, overruled the reasonable claim of her late husband's closest adviser, *John (VI) Kantakouzenos, to act as regent, Civil war broke out between the supporters of the rival candidates. After six years of fighting Kantakouzenos entered Constantinople in February 1347 and was crowned as Emperor, giving his daughter Helena in marriage to John V. In December 1354 he abdicated and John V came into his full inheritance.

In the same year the Ottoman Turks made their first permanent settlement in Europe at Gallipoli. John pinned his hopes on help from the western Christian world. In 1355 he appealed to the Pope, offering to bring the church of Constantinople under obedience to Rome in return for papal protection of his Empire. Ten years later, when that hope had dimmed, he went to seek comfort from King Louis the Great of Hungary, again to no avail. The Bulgarians detained him on his way home and he had to be rescued by his cousin Amadeo of Savoy, who had brought a small armada to Constantinople and regained Gallipoli from the Turks.

Amadeo persuaded John to visit the Pope in person; and in 1369, in Rome, he made his personal submission of obedience to Pope Urban V. On his return journey he was held in Venice as an insolvent debtor. His son *Manuel (II) hurried to bail him out. He got back to Constantinople in 1371 only to learn that the Turks had won their first great victory on European soil by defeating the Serbians in a battle on the Marica river.

Despairing of any material reward for his spiritual sacrifices in the west John then declared himself to be a vassal of the Ottoman Sultan Murad I. His son *Andronikos IV rebelled, imprisoned his father and reigned in his place from 1376 to 1379. John recovered his throne with help from the Turks and the Venetians; and for a few years the fragments of his Empire were held together by a fragile consensus between the members of his family. John reigned as Emperor in Constantinople; his first son Andronikos IV in Thrace; his second son Manuel II in Thessalonica; and his fourth son *Theodore as Despot at Mistra in the Peloponnese. Each, however, was at the mercy of the Turkish Sultan, who captured Thessalonica in 1387 and won his second decisive victory in Europe at the battle of Kossovo in 1389. In 1390 John's throne was seized by his grandson, *John VII. His loyal son Manuel again came to his rescue. But the Sultan was displeased and summoned Manuel to his court. John then shut himself up in his palace and died in February 1391, disenchanted by his Christian friends in the west and in thrall to his Muslim enemies in the east. His widow Helena survived him for a few years and died as a nun. He was succeeded by his second son *Manuel II Palaiologos.

BIBL. Halecki 1930; Nicol 1972: 265–309

John VI Kantakouzenos Emperor 1347–54

The family of Kantakouzenos (Cantacuzenus) were aristocratic and wealthy landowners. John came to prominence during the civil war that brought *Andronikos III to the throne (1321–8). He was a loyal friend of Andronikos who made him Grand Domestic or commander-in-chief. When Andronikos died in 1341 John expected to act as regent for his infant son *John V Palaiologos. He was thwarted by the dowager Empress, Anne of Savoy, and the Patriarch, *John XIV Kalekas. For nearly six years he waged war against them, basing himself in Thrace. There his partisans proclaimed him Emperor in October 1341. He had support from the Serbian ruler Stephen Dušan and from some of the Turkish emirs who saw profit to be made from civil war in Byzantium. John gave his daughter Theodora as wife to Orchan, the Emir of Bithynia. After bitter setbacks the tide of war turned in his favour. In May 1346 he was crowned Emperor at Adrianople; and in February 1347 he entered Constantinople, where a second coronation in May set the seal on his title. He posed, however, simply as co-Emperor with the young John V, to whom he gave his daughter Helena in marriage.

John VI had many ideas for the revival of his Empire. But the people distrusted him as a representative of the aristocracy. The citizens of Thessalonica rebelled and turned their city into a commune governed or terrorized by a faction called the Zealots. Not until 1350 did John restore order there, and then only with the help of Turkish troops. In the first year of his reign the Black Death decimated the population of Byzantium and enabled the Serbians to invade and occupy northern Greece. John proposed to end the dependence of his Empire on the Venetians and the Genoese by rebuilding a fleet. The Italians were resentful and he was forced to take sides in the perennial war between Venice and Genoa. The Turks too were unpredictable allies. His problems mounted when John V began to assert his own right to the throne by force. John's eldest son *Matthew took up the challenge and was crowned as co-Emperor in 1353. Matters came to a head after John's Turkish friends occupied Gallipoli in March 1354. In November John V was hailed as the lawful Emperor in Constantinople. In December John VI abdicated. He spent the rest of his long life as a monk, though his advice as an elder statesman was often sought. One of his successful achievements had been to appoint his second son *Manuel Kantakouzenos as governor of the Byzantine province of the Morea (Peloponnese); and it was there, at Mistra, that John died in June 1383.

During his retirement he wrote theological works, many in defence of the mystical doctrine of the Hesychasts as formulated by his friend Gregory *Palamas. As Emperor he had presided over the council in 1351 which had declared Hesychasm to be Orthodox. He is more celebrated for the *History* which he composed in the form of Memoirs; a polished apologia for his career between 1320 and 1357.

BIBL. Schopen 1828–32; Nicol 1968: no. 22; Weiss 1969; Hunger 1978, I: 465–75

John VII Palaiologos Emperor 1390

John was the only son of *Andronikos IV. The Genoese and the Ottoman Turks favoured him and encouraged the coup d'état by which he ousted his grandfather *John V and became Emperor in Constantinople in April 1390. In September, however, his reign was cut short by the intervention of his uncle *Manuel (II) who, with Venetian help, reinstated John V as Emperor. He took charge of Constantinople during Manuel's absence in the west from 1399 to 1402; and it fell to him to make terms with Suleiman, son of the late Sultan Bajezid, after the dismemberment of the Ottoman dominions by the Mongols at the battle of Ankara in 1402. In 1403 he was sent to govern Thessalonica; and there he died in September 1408. He may have had a son who predeceased him, having been nominated as the Emperor Andronikos V.

BIBL. Dölger 1931; Nicol 1972: 320–8, 334–9

John VIII Palaiologos Emperor 1425–48

John was the first of the six sons of *Manuel II, who made him co-Emperor in 1421. In June 1422 the Ottoman Sultan Murad II laid siege to Constantinople. There was little else left of the Byzantine Empire, except for the Morea (Peloponnese) where John had served his apprenticeship as a provincial governor. Thessalonica, also under blockade by the Turks, was governed by John's brother Andronikos; but in 1423 he ceded it to the Venetians, who held it until the Turks broke in and destroyed the city in 1430. Before he died in 1425 Manuel had counselled his son John against making compromises with the Christians of the west to stimulate a crusade for the salvation of Constantinople. John could see no alternative. In 1430 he opened discussions with the papacy. Pope Eugenius IV (1431–47) invited him to lead a delegation to a Council to be convened at Ferrara, at which the union of the eastern and western churches might be proclaimed. The Byzantines, as reformed Christians, would then qualify for a crusade for their rescue from the Turks. John took with him his Patriarch *Joseph II and a host of bishops, priests and laymen. They reached Italy in March 1438. He worked hard to control his prelates at the Council, first at Ferrara and then at Florence, whither it moved in 1439; and in July of that year the union of the churches under Rome was declared to have occurred.

The announcement caused deep bitterness and open unrest in Constantinople and those who had subscribed to the union were denounced as traitors. The reward that John VIII had expected, the promised crusade, finally set out in 1443, led by the King of Hungary. It was annihilated by the Turks at Varna on the Black Sea in November 1444. The Sultan Murad took his revenge on those who had assisted it by devastating Greece and routing its surviving leaders at Kossovo in 1448. John VIII died in October of that year, disillusioned by his western friends and mistrusted by most of his subjects. He had married three times: first to Anna, daughter of Basil I of Moscow; then to Sophia of Montferrat; and then to Maria, daughter of *Alexios IV Komnenos, Emperor of Trebizond. But he had no issue. It was his wish that the eldest of his five brothers, *Constantine XI, should succeed him.

BIBL. Gill 1958; Gill 1964; Nicol 1972: 346–86

John I Chrysostom Patriarch of Constantinople 398–404

John, called Chrysostomos or golden-mouthed because of his eloquence, was born in Antioch about 347, the son of a military officer and a Christian mother. He studied law under the pagan Libanius and also theology. After a short retreat as a hermit, he went back to Antioch where he was ordained and acquired renown as a preacher. In 398, in the reign of the Emperor *Theodosius I, he was appointed Patriarch of Constantinople, an office which he accepted with reluctance. He was more of a reforming moralist than a theologian. His homilies attracted wrapt audiences among the common people since he often inveighed against the unchristian profligacy of the rich. He made enemies in high places and particularly provoked the Empress Eudoxia, wife of *Arcadius, by denouncing her in public as a Jezebel. The Emperor felt bound to dismiss and banish him. By popular request he was soon recalled; and once back in the capital he again denounced the luxury-loving Empress. In June 404 he was finally deposed and exiled to faraway Cucusus in Armenia. He continued, however, to keep in touch with his friends by letter. Three years later he was banished to an even remoter spot; but he died on the journey, in September 407. Some thirty years after his death his remains were solemnly laid to rest in Constantinople by the son of Arcadius and Eudoxia, *Theodosius II. He is revered as a saint in the eastern and western churches.

BIBL. Grumel 1972: 13−26; Quasten 1960: 424−82; Attwater 1959

John III Scholasticus Patriarch of Constantinople 565−77

Appointed Patriarch in the last year of the reign of the Emperor *Justinian I, John was a lawyer from Antioch and representative in Constantinople of the Patriarch of Antioch. He was famous for his codification of canon law, the first of its kind in the Byzantine church. He compiled it in Antioch but revised it as Patriarch in Constantinople.

BIBL. Grumel 1972: 183−8; Beck 1959: 422−3

John IV Patriarch of Constantinople 582−95

John IV, known as the Faster, succeeded *Eutychius as Patriarch in April 582. He had a celebrated quarrel with Pope Gregory the Great over his use of title of Oecumenical Patriarch. The Pope took this to imply a claim to universal jurisdiction over the church and commanded the Emperor *Phokas to forbid its use. John also wrote a number of works on monastic discipline. He died in September 595 and was followed by Cyriacus (595−606).

BIBL. Grumel 1972: 193−201; Beck 1959: 423−4

John VII Grammatikos Patriarch of Constantinople 838−43

John Morochazanios, known as the Grammarian, was abbot of the monastery of Saints Sergius and Bacchus in Constantinople. He was a leading scholar of his day and tutor to the Emperor *Theophilos, who secured his appointment to the patriarchate in April 838 in succession to *Antonios I. He had earlier led a famously extravagant diplomatic mission to the Arab Caliph in Baghdad. He was an iconoclast by intellectual conviction and took part in the council in 815 at which the decrees of the iconoclast council of 754 were reaffirmed. When Theophilos died in 842 and his widow, the Empress *Theodora, restored the veneration of icons as official policy, John refused to collaborate and was deposed in 843 in favour of *Methodios I.

BIBL. Grumel 1936: 42

John VIII Xiphilinos Patriarch of Constantinople 1064−75

His family came from Trebizond and he was educated in Constantinople by John *Mavropous with whom, and with Michael *Psellos, he remained on friendly terms. He was appointed head of the law school (*nomophylax*) in Constantinople by the Emperor *Constantine IX in 1045. But after criticism of his teaching methods he chose to resign and to become a monk about 1050. He was made Patriarch, against his will, in 1064 in succession to *Constantine III Leichoudes. For all their long friendship, Xiphilinos and Psellos differed in their approach to philosophy, and he felt bound to excommunicate Psellos for a while on a charge of heresy.

Psellos none the less wrote his Epitaph when he died in 1075.

BIBL. Grumel 1947: 20−7; Bonis 1938; Hussey 1986: 138−40; Beck 1959: 556−7

John X Kamateros Patriarch of Constantinople 1198−1206
    John was appointed in August 1198 following the death of *George II Xiphilinos. He had formerly been archivist of St Sophia and was related to the Empress *Euphrosyne, wife of *Alexios III Angelos. He became involved in a theological controversy over transubstantiation, initiated by Myron Sikidites, the chronicler Michael *Glykas. He corresponded with Pope Innocent III. After the conquest of Constantinople by the crusaders in 1204, he was evicted from his patriarchate. Having led the refugees out of the city, he settled in Bulgaria. *Theodore I Laskaris invited him to his court in exile at Nicaea; but he declined and died in May 1206.

BIBL. Grumel 1947: 189−95

John XI Bekkos Patriarch of Constantinople 1275−82
    John Bekkos (or Beccus) was archivist of St Sophia in Constantinople. The Emperor *Michael VIII made him Patriarch in place of *Joseph I who refused to accept the policy of union with the Roman church. John had earlier been an anti-unionist himself, but a spell in prison helped him change his mind. He became the principal spokesman for the Emperor's policy and then, in 1275, Patriarch. After the union had been renounced by the Emperor *Andronikos II he was dismissed and formally condemned as a heretic in 1285 at a synod presided over by his successor *Gregory II.

BIBL. *PLP* no. 2548

John XII Kosmas Patriarch of Constantinople 1294−1303.
    He was elected after the Patriarch *Athanasios I resigned in 1293. In May 1294 he performed the coronation of *Michael IX as co-Emperor with his father *Andronikos II Palaiologos. He quarrelled with Andronikos over various matters, especially the diplomatic marriage of the Emperor's infant granddaughter to the Serbian king in 1299. In June 1303 he was obliged to stand down when Athanasios I was reinstated as Patriarch.

BIBL. *PLP* no. 90378

John XIII Glykys Patriarch of Constantinople 1315−19
    John Glykys was a lay civil servant, a scholar and a teacher and friend of Nikephoros *Gregoras. He was ordained and raised to the patriarchate in May 1315, a year after the enforced resignation of the Patriarch *Niphon.

BIBL. Kourousis 1975; *PLP* no. 4271

John XIV Kalekas Patriarch of Constantinople 1334−4/
    After the death of the Emperor *Andronikos III in 1341, John Kalekas as Patriarch claimed the regency for the young *John V Palaiologos. His claim was challenged by *John (VI) Kantakouzenos whom he

excommunicated. He crowned John V as Emperor in November 1341. In June of that year he had convened a council of bishops in Constantinople at which *Barlaam of Calabria was denounced. He took the side of Gregory *Akindynos in the dispute over Hesychasm and in November 1344 excommunicated its principal exponent, Gregory *Palamas. In 1347 he was deposed by the Empress, John V's mother; and he died as a prisoner in December of that year. He was succeeded by *Isidore I Boucheiras.

BIBL. *PLP* no. 10288

John of Cappadocia (first half 6th century) Praetorian Prefect

John came from Caesarea. He was of lowly origin but he brought himself to the notice of the Emperor *Justinian I who in 531 appointed him Praetorian Prefect, responsible for raising taxes for the supply and maintenance of the army. He was deservedly disliked, partly because he was rude, arrogant and uncultured, partly because he was ruthlessly efficient at his job of reforming the system of taxation and collecting the proceeds. Without him Justinian's expensive projects would hardly have been realizable. He was dismissed more than once as a result of his unpopularity. The Empress *Theodora detested him; but after her death in 548 he was allowed to return to Constantinople, where he was ordained as a priest and died.

BIBL. *see under* *Justinian I

John Climax (Klimakos) (*d. c.* 670) monk and theologian

John became a monk towards the end of the sixth century and spent forty years as a hermit in the desert before becoming abbot of the monastery of St Catherine at Mount Sinai. His most famous and influential work was his *Ladder of Divine Ascent* or *Klimax*, from which he took his name. It describes the thirty stages of the virtuous monk's graduation to the topmost rung of spiritual perfection. It was required reading for generations of monks and was translated into Syriac, Georgian, Latin and Arabic. He also wrote a handbook for heads of monasteries (*Liber ad pastorem*).

BIBL. Works *in MPG*, vol. 88; Beck 1959: 451−2.

John of Damascus (*c.* 675−*c.* 750) theologian and saint

John the Damascene (or Damaskenos) was the son of a rich Christian father who served the Arab Caliphs in Damascus, a position which John inherited. About 720, however, he became a monk in the monastery of St Sabas near Jerusalem and stayed there for the rest of his life. It was in the defence of Orthodoxy against the heresy of iconoclasm that he became celebrated. The fact that he lived on Arab territory put him beyond the reach of the iconoclast Emperors and allowed him a freedom of expression denied to his colleagues in Constantinople. He was dead by 754 when the iconoclast council summoned by the Emperor *Constantine V condemned his name and his memory.

In the ninth century, when the controversy was over, John was proclaimed a saint of the church universal and revered as the last great theologian of the Orthodox church. As a consequence many dogmatic and polemical works were wrongly ascribed to him. Even those that are genuinely his, however, are numerous. They include the *Fount of Knowledge* (*Pēgē Gnōseōs*), a tripartite exposition of theological truth covering the philosophical background, the heretical deviations and a manifesto of Orthodox doctrine. It had a profound influence on Christian thought in the west as well as the east. The confounding of heretics and the upholding of right belief were his obsessions; and he wrote tracts against all the major heresies of his time, particularly iconoclasm, as well as ethical and moral treatises, commentaries on the Bible, saints' lives, homilies and hymns. A curiosity among his works is his *Romance of Barlaam and Joasaph*, an Indian tale about Buddha set in Christian form, which was translated into Latin in the eleventh century and circulated widely in the west.

BIBL. Work *in MPG*, vols. 94–6; Beck 1959: 476–86

John Doukas *sebastokrator* of Thessaly 1267–89
John was the natural son of *Michael II Despot of Epiros and the half-brother of *Nikephoros of Epiros. By his father's will John inherited Thessaly with his capital at Neopatras (Hypati). The purely honorary title of *sebastokrator* was conferred on him by the Emperor *Michael VIII about 1272, in the fond hope that he would keep the peace. He remained an inveterate and troublesome enemy of the government in Constantinople until he died about 1289. His widow, daughter of a Vlach chieftain in Thessaly, outlived him and became a nun. His portrait is in the church of Porta Panagia near Trikkala which he built in 1283. His son Constantine and his grandson John carried on his struggle for independence from Constantinople. Thessaly was restored to the Byzantine Empire in 1333.

John IV Komnenos Emperor of Trebizond 1429–58
John came to the throne by assassinating his father *Alexios IV of Trebizond in 1429. He kept a precarious hold on his little Empire by judicious alliances with the neighbouring Georgian and Turkoman rulers. The Ottoman Sultan Murad II attacked Trebizond in 1442; but John was still there when Constantinople fell to the Turks in 1453. He married a Georgian princess and had three children. He died in 1458 and was succeeded by his brother *David Komnenos.

BIBL. Miller 1926: 81–97

John the Lydian (*c.* 490–*c.* 565) civil servant
John Lydus was born in Philadelphia in Lydia. About 510 he came to Constantinople where he studied philosophy, learnt Latin and entered the judiciary. He held many public offices under the Emperors *Anastasius I, *Justin and *Justinian I. His major work is an essay *On the Magistracies of the Roman State*, written about 559, in which he sets forth his researches on the history and organization of the offices and administration of Rome

from its foundation by Aeneas to the reign of Justinian I.

BIBL. Bandy 1983

John the Orphanotrophos (first half 11th century) civil servant

A man of humble birth from the eastern provinces, he applied his native wit to winning favour and influence in the administration and the court in Constantinople. One of his many offices was keeper of the imperial state orphanage (*orphanotrophos*). Being a eunuch, he could never become Emperor; but he could and did become the power behind the throne. He was ruthless, unscrupulous and widely feared and hated, especially as a collector of taxes. It was he who brought his brother *Michael IV to the attention and to the bed of the Empress *Zoe and so to the throne when her husband *Romanos III died in 1034. It was he who induced Zoe to adopt his nephew *Michael V and set him on the throne in 1041. But it was Michael V who put an end to his schemes by sending him into exile.

BIBL. Jenkins 1966: 391−4

Joseph I Patriarch of Constantinople 1266−75; 1282−3

Joseph, abbot of a monastery on Mount Galesion near Ephesos, was elected Patriarch in December 1266. In 1267 he lifted the ban of excommunication which the Patriarch *Arsenios had imposed on the Emperor *Michael VIII. But he condemned the Emperor's policy of union with the Roman church and was consequently deposed and imprisoned in favour of the unionist Patriarch *John XI Bekkos. His sympathizers, known as the Josephites, joined forces with the followers of the Patriarch Arsenios, the Arsenites, to confound the Emperor's plans; and when in 1282 the new Emperor *Andronikos II rejected the union with Rome, the then elderly Joseph was reinstated and honoured as a martyr. He died in March 1283.

BIBL. *PLP* no. 9072

Joseph II Patriarch of Constantinople 1416−39

Joseph was Bishop of Ephesos until his election as Patriarch in May 1416. He attended the Council of Ferrara-Florence with his Emperor *John VIII in 1438−9. He was a supporter of the union of the eastern and western churches but he died in Florence before the document proclaiming that union was signed.

BIBL. *PLP* no. 9073

Joseph the Philosopher (*c*. 1280−*c*. 1330) monk and scholar

Joseph, also known as Rakendytes (the monk), was born about 1200 on the island of Ithaka and studied in Thessalonica before becoming a monk. He lived as a hermit in Thessaly, Mount Athos and elsewhere and finally settled in Thessalonica. He declined election to the patriarchate and died in Thessalonica about 1330. His major work, which he never completed, was an encyclopaedia intended to reconcile the inherited wisdom of Greek antiquity with the true wisdom of Christian theology.

BIBL. Nicol 1979: 57–8

Jovian Emperor 363–4

Flavius Jovianus was proclaimed Emperor by his troops in Mesopotamia when *Julian, whom he had been serving as an officer, was killed by the Persians in June 363. He concluded a hasty peace with the enemy but he never got to Constantinople, for he died on his way there in February 364. He was a fervent Christian, devoted to the suppression of the paganism which Julian had tried to revive and to the recognition of Christianity as the state religion. He was succeeded by Valens.

BIBL. Jones 1964, I: 138–9, 150

Julian Emperor 361–3

Julian (Flavius Claudius Julianus) was a nephew of *Constantine I and a cousin of the Emperor *Constantius, whom he succeeded in 361. He was brought up as a Christian but his prolonged studies of ancient Greek philosophy at Pergamon, Ephesos and Athens led him to renounce his faith, for which the Christian church labelled him as Julian the Apostate. He represented the pagan reaction to the intolerant enforcement of Christianity by his predecessors. Inevitably he was driven to vicious acts of intolerance against the Christians in his Empire, of which he was the last pagan Roman Emperor and the last of the house of Constantine the Great. He was killed fighting against the Persians on the eastern frontier in June 363 at the age of thirty-one; and it was quickly proved that his attempt to put back the clock of history had failed.

BIBL. Browning 1975; Bowersock 1978

Justin I Emperor 518–27

Elected Emperor on the death of *Anastasius I in July 518, Justin was an Illyrian swineherd turned soldier who had risen to the rank of commander of the imperial guard (*Excubitores*) in Constantinople. He is said to have been illiterate but he knew his own mind on the abstruse theological issue of the divine and human natures of Christ; and he had no time for the Monophysites who refused to accept the ruling of the Council of Chalcedon in 451. He disavowed the compromise formula (*Henotikon*) by which the Emperor *Zeno had tried to resolve the problem and he persecuted the Monophysites. The Pope, who had condemned the *Henotikon*, consequently took the church of Constantinople back into communion. Justin was equally opposed to the Arian form of the Christian creed which prevailed in the Gothic Kingdom of Italy. He had a mind of his own in foreign affairs as well; but for most of his reign Justin's policy was suggested if not dictated by his far greater nephew *Justinian I, who succeeded him when he died aged seventy-seven in August 527.

BIBL. Vasiliev 1950

Justin II Emperor 565–78

Justin was the nephew of *Justinian I and succeeded him as Emperor in

November 565. To find the resources to pay for the defence and maintenance of the vast Empire which his uncle had acquired, he tried to economize by stopping the payment of tribute to the Persians. They went to war again in 572 and the news of their victories unhinged the Emperor's mind. His wife Sophia, acting on his behalf, bought peace by paying the Persian king even more annual tribute. On the north, the Avars and Slavs continued their infiltration into the Balkans; and in the west the Lombards carried all before them in northern Italy. The imperial government remained behind the walls of Ravenna, but it was isolated from Constantinople and from Rome. Milan fell in 569. The army that Justin sent to Italy in 575 was defeated. The Empress Sophia persuaded him to adopt the soldier *Tiberius I as his son and heir with the title of Caesar in December 574; and for the last few years of his reign Justin lived in retirement. He died in October 578.

BIBL. Barker 1966: 211–19

Justinian I Emperor 527–65

Born as Petrus Sabbatius in 483, he changed his name to Flavius Justinianus as the adopted nephew of the Emperor *Justin I, whom he succeeded in August 527. Like his uncle he was a Latin-speaking Illyrian. As Emperor he was surrounded by able administrators and soldiers; and his remarkable wife *Theodora had a great influence on him. Five years after his accession he was faced by an uprising in Constantinople, known as the Nika riot, in which much of the city was destroyed. It gave him the pretext to assert the absolute authority which he believed to be his by divine right. His main achievements thereafter were the reconquest of the lost western provinces of his Empire, the codification of the law, and the building of fortifications and churches.

The reconquest, though planned by Justinian, was the work of his great generals *Belisarius and *Narses. His reform of the law was realized by his legal adviser *Tribonian. The greatest of his churches, St Sophia or the Holy Wisdom in Constantinople, was designed and built by two eastern Greek architects, *Anthemius of Tralles and Isidore of Miletos; and the money for all his projects was raised by his brilliant but ruthless agent *John of Cappadocia. To make his western campaigns possible, Justinian made a treaty with the Persians, the age-old enemies of the Empire in the east, in 532. The work began with the recovery of North Africa from the Vandals. It was completed by the liberation of Sicily, Italy, Sardinia, Corsica and southern Spain from the Ostrogoths and Visigoths; and by 555 the Emperor could boast that the Mediterranean was once again a Roman lake. But the cost in destruction and human suffering, as well as in economic terms, had been immense; and the circumstances of war helped the spread of a virulent plague which broke out in 542. The eastern provinces had to pay the price. The Danube and Euphrates frontiers, though guarded by chains of fortresses, were undermanned; while in the east the Persians broke their treaty and destroyed Antioch in 540. Justinian was forced to pay tribute to their king to keep them at bay.

As a Christian Roman Emperor and vice-gerent of God on earth he felt duty bound to enforce uniformity of belief on his subjects and to unite church and state firmly under his control. Heresy, especially that of the Monophysites with their mistaken view of Christ's divine and human natures, must be stamped out. Nor could the teaching of pagan Greek philosophy be tolerated, except in Christian institutions. In 529 he commanded that the Platonic Academy in Athens be closed for ever. His efforts to reach some compromise with the Monophysites antagonized the church of Rome as well as many of his eastern bishops. Latterly he became obsessed with theology and was himself suspected of a recondite heresy. He died in November 565. His successors inherited his mystique of the Christian Roman *imperium*; and the brilliance of his reign was reflected in the architectural, artistic, literary, philosophical and theological creativity of sixth-century Byzantium.

BIBL. Bury 1923, II; Barker 1966; Browning 1971

Justinian II Emperor 685−95; 705−11

He succeeded his father *Constantine IV in September 685 when he was sixteen years old. The Arabs made a favourable treaty with him at the outset of his reign, which made it possible for him to attend to his other enemies. In 688 he led an army against the Slavs in Macedonia who threatened Thessalonica, forced them into submission and deported thousands of them to Asia Minor, thus strengthening the Theme system there. He also created a new Theme of Hellas in central Greece. In 691−2 he held the church council in Constantinople known as the Quinisextum or Council in Trullo (the domed chamber in the palace) which confirmed the rulings of the Fifth and Sixth Councils and was much concerned with disciplinary matters. The Pope refused to accept its rulings and Justinian tried to get him arrested. He was thwarted by the troops of Rome and Ravenna. He prided himself on his piety and had the figure of Christ stamped on his coins. But it was his pride and authoritarianism that turned people against him. The aristocracy rebelled in 695 and proclaimed *Leontios, governor of Hellas, as Emperor; Justinian's nose was cut off (which gave him the nickname of Rhinotmetos) and he was banished to the Crimea. However, after a series of adventures among the Khazars and the Bulgars, he came back as Emperor to Constantinople with the help of a Bulgarian army in 705, and Leontios was murdered. Justinian's second reign was one of terror and vengeance, although he made his peace with the papacy, and Pope Constantine visited Constantinople in 710. In December 711 he was executed with all his family and *Philippikos-Bardanes was proclaimed Emperor. Justinian II was the last of the dynasty which had begun with *Heraclius.

BIBL. Jenkins 1966: 50−60; Ostrogorsky 1968: 129−44

K

Kabasilas, Neilos Bishop of Thessalonica 1361−3

A monk and teacher, Neilos was appointed Metropolitan of Thessalonica in 1361. Although he was himself a Hesychast with a distaste for Latin theology, he numbered Demetrios *Kydones, a later convert to the Roman church, among his pupils. One of several theological tracts composed by Neilos is on the causes of the schism and the primacy of the Pope. He was an uncle of Nicholas *Kabasilas Chamaetos.

BIBL. *PLP* no. 10102

Kabasilas, Nicholas Chamaetos (*d. c.* 1365) writer and theologian

He was a native of Thessalonica and a nephew of its Bishop Neilos *Kabasilas. Chamaetos was his father's family name. He spent most of his life in Constantinople as a senior civil servant, first at the court of the Emperor *John VI Kantakouzenos about 1350. Although probably never a monk or a priest, he was proposed as a candidate for the patriarchate in 1354; and he was the author of some of the most profound and influential of all Byzantine spiritual writings, among them his *Explanation of the Divine Liturgy* and his essay *On the Life in Christ*. He also wrote discourses and speeches on the political and economic evils of his day.

BIBL. Hussey and McNulty 1960; Catanzaro 1974; Beck 1959: 780−3

Kallinikos I Patriarch of Constantinople 694−706

Kallinikos performed the coronation of the Emperor *Leontios after the rebellion against *Justinian II in 695. When Justinian came back to power in 705 he punished Kallinikos by having him blinded.

BIBL. Grumel 1972: 246

Kallistos I Patriarch of Constantinople 1350−3; 1355−63

Kallistos was a Hesychast monk on Mount Athos, a disciple of *Gregory of Sinai and a friend of Gregory *Palamas, whose theology he vindicated at the council in Constantinople convened by the Emperor *John VI Kantakouzenos. He was an admirer of John VI, who had helped make him Patriarch in June 1350; but, on constitutional grounds, he refused to crown John's son *Matthew Kantakouzenos as Emperor in 1353 and retired to a monastery. He was replaced by *Philotheos; though in 1355, when *John V became Emperor, he was reinstated as Patriarch. Kallistos was a consistent opponent of union with the Roman church. He died in 1363 while on a diplomatic mission to seek help from the Serbians. He wrote a number of homilies and hagiographies, notably a *Life* of *Gregory of Sinai.

BIBL. Gonis 1980; *PLP* no. 10478

Kaminiates, John (9th to 10th century?) chronicler

A priest in Thessalonica, Kaminiates lived through the capture of his city by the Arabs in July 904. He himself was taken prisoner. His sole surviving work is his account of this event, which contains much interesting detail about Thessalonica and its people. It has been suggested, however, that he lived not in the tenth but in the fifteenth century and that the conquerors of the city were not the Arabs but the Ottoman Turks.

BIBL. Böhlig 1973; Kazhdan 1978: 301—14

Kananos, John (1422) chronicler

Kananos (Cananus) was the author of an eye-witness account of the siege of Constantinople by the Ottoman Sultan Murad II in 1422.

BIBL. Pinto 1977; Hunger 1978, I: 482—4

Kantakouzenos see **John VI** Emperor; **Manuel** Despot; **Matthew** Emperor

Kasia (first half 9th century) poetess

Kasia (Ikasia or Casia) was the daughter of an aristocratic Byzantine family. As such she was selected to parade in the bride show for the Emperor *Theophilos in 830. The young Emperor was astounded by her beauty but taken aback by her prompt riposte to his remark that woman was the root of all evil. He picked instead on a less outspoken girl called *Theodora. Kasia became a nun. She was opposed to the Emperor's iconoclasm; and she corresponded with *Theodore of Stoudios. She wrote poems in the form of short epigrams as well as hymns, some of which are still sung in the Orthodox church.

BIBL. Hunger 1978, II: 168

Kedrenos, George (11th to 12th century) chronicler

Kedrenos (Cedrenus) compiled a *World Chronicle* from the Creation to the year 1057. It contains nothing original apart from the passages taken from sources now lost. The bulk of it (covering the years from 811 to 1057) derives almost word for word from *Skylitzes.

BIBL. Bekker 1838—9; Hunger 1978, I: 393—4

Kekaumenos (mid 11th century) soldier and writer

Kekaumenos (Cecaumenus) composed a work known as the *Strategikon* during the reign of *Michael VII. He addressed it to his son as a manual of advice gained from his long experience as a military commander and provincial governor. Despite its title, the work offers much more than strategic or military counsel. It reflects the conservative, pious and rather suspicious views of one who felt that standards were falling and that the old order was passing away. Kekaumenos might be called the Byzantine Polonius; but he also in passing imparts much historical information about Byzantium and its neighbours in the eleventh century.

BIBL. Wassiliewsky and Jernstedt 1896; Moravcsik 1983: 350—2

Kinnamos, John (*c*. 1144−*c*. 1203) historian

Kinnamos (Cinnamus) was secretary of the Emperor *Manuel I. He wrote a *History* (*Epitome*) beginning with the reign of *John II Komnenos (1118) and going into greater detail from the accession of Manuel I in 1143 up to 1176. He clearly had access to the court and to official documents and therefore constitutes a prime source for most of the twelfth century.

BIBL. Meineke 1836; Brand 1976; Hunger 1978, I: 409−15

Kodinos (Pseudo), George (mid 14th century) writer

He was the author of a work on the ecclesiastical and secular offices and dignities of Constantinople, formerly attributed to one George Kodinos (Codinus). It was compiled in the reign of the Emperor *John VI Kantakouzenos and it provides unique information on the customs and ceremonies of the Byzantine court, the ritual of coronation and the pecking order of dignitaries of church and state in the fourteenth century.

BIBL. Verpeaux 1966

Kosmas I Patriarch of Constantinople 1075−81

Kosmas followed *John VIII Xiphilinos as Patriarch in August 1075. He disapproved of the third marriage of the Emperor *Nikephoros III; and he forbade *Alexios I Komnenos to repudiate his wife *Eirene Doukaina, whom he crowned as Empress. He resigned in May 1081, leaving to his successor, *Eustratios Garidas, the problem of judging the alleged heresies of John *Italos.

BIBL. Grumel 1947: 27−32

Kosmas II Attikos Patriarch of Constantinople 1146−7

He was appointed in April 1146 to replace *Michael II Oxeites, who had charged him with heresy. He at once absolved and released one of his fellow suspects, the monk Niphon. Kosmas was a close friend of Isaac Komnenos, brother of the Emperor *Manuel I, and was suspected not only of heresy but also of plotting to put Isaac on the throne. Manuel convened a synod in Constantinople in February 1147 at which Kosmas was accused of being a fellow-traveller with heretics and was deposed. He refused to accept the verdict and excommunicated those who had pronounced it. He was succeeded by the elderly Nicholas IV Mouzalon (1147−51).

BIBL. Grumel 1947: 97−8; Angold 1984: 229; Beck 1959: 661

Kourkouas, John (first half 10th century) general

John Kourkouas (Gourgen) was an Armenian soldier who rose to become Captain of the Guard in Constantinople and then Domestic or commander of the eastern armies against the Arabs under the Emperor *Romanos I Lakapenos, whom he served faithfully for over twenty years. His brilliant strategy carried the Byzantine frontiers well beyond the Euphrates, north into Armenia and south towards Edessa and Aleppo. It was he who rescued from Edessa the sacred *mandilion*, the cloth on which Christ had imprinted His face, and sent the holy relic to Constantinople. He also distinguished himself in the defence of Constantinople against the Russians in 941. He was dismissed when Romanos I was dethroned in 944.

BIBL. Runciman 1929: 69, 135−50; Jenkins 1966: 241, 245−7, 251

Kritoboulos, Michael (15th century) historian
A member of a leading family on the island of Imbros, Kritoboulos came to terms with the Ottoman Turks after the fall of Constantinople and was allowed to govern his island from 1456. He wrote a *History* of the years from 1451 to 1467 and dedicated it to the conquering Sultan Mehmed II. Though unashamedly pro-Turkish, Kritoboulos had access to Ottoman as well as Greek sources. His history is therefore singularly informative, not least about the capture of Constantinople in 1453.

BIBL. Reinsch 1983; Riggs 1954; *PLP* no. 13817

Kydones, Demetrios (1324−97/8) statesman
Born into an aristocratic family in Thessalonica, Kydones supported *John (VI) Kantakouzenos in the civil war of 1341−7 and became his prime minister, despite his aversion to the doctrine of Gregory *Palamas and the Hesychasts which John favoured. He learnt Latin, probably from the Dominicans in Constantinople, and translated the works of Thomas Aquinas into Greek, as well as some of St Augustine and Anselm of Canterbury. He was converted to the Roman church and retired for a while in 1354. *John V invited him back to court; and for thirty years he was again prime minister. He accompanied John V to Rome in 1369. He spent his last years mainly in Venice and Crete. His influence as a unionist and a convert was considerable. He wrote three *Apologies* explaining the reasons for his conversion. His brother Prochoros, who helped him with his Latin translations, seems not to have followed his example. About 450 of his letters survive, as well as a number of orations, all of which are important for their historical content.

BIBL. Loenertz 1956, 1960; *PLP* no. 13876

L

Leo I Emperor 457−74

When *Marcian died in January 457 Leo was proclaimed Emperor by Aspar, the commander of the soldiers in Constantinople, who hoped to wield power through his nominee. Leo was crowned in February, the first Emperor on record to have received his crown from a Patriarch of Constantinople, *Anatolius. He was a Thracian by origin and therefore less of an outsider than his commander Aspar, who was an Alan. Aspar had picked the wrong man for his own purposes. He was murdered in 471. But to neutralize the alarming influence in the army of non-Romans, especially Germans, Leo recruited large numbers of Isaurians, half-tamed mountaineers from Taurus in southern Anatolia. The Isaurians were in fact more barbarous than the Germans. But they fulfilled their function of counteracting the dangerous German monopoly in the army of the capital; and Leo gave his daughter Ariadne as wife to one of their chieftains, who changed his foreign name to *Zeno. In 468 Leo launched a grandiose expedition to liberate North Africa from the Vandals, commanded by his brother-in-law *Basiliscus. It was a dismal failure and almost bankrupted the imperial treasury. In religion Leo was a firmly Orthodox supporter of the rulings of the Council of Chalcedon in 451. He died in February 474 having nominated as Emperor his infant grandson *Leo II.

BIBL. Bury 1923, I: 314−23, 335−7

Leo II Emperor 474

He was the son of *Zeno, the Isaurian leader who had married Ariadne, daughter of *Leo I. He was barely six years old when he succeeded his grandfather and he survived for only a few months. He died in November 474, leaving the throne to his father Zeno.

BIBL. Bury 1923, I: 389

Leo III Emperor 717−41

Known as the 'Isaurian', Leo probably came from northern Syria. From lowly origins he rose to become *strategos* or commander of the Anatolikon Theme or military district in Asia Minor. His troops there proclaimed him Emperor in place of the feeble *Theodosios III; and on 25 March 717 Leo was crowned in Constantinople. Six months later a vast Arab army and fleet besieged the city. The danger had been anticipated and, after a year-long siege, the Arabs were repulsed. Leo complemented his victory at Constantinople by driving them back in Asia Minor and defeating their army at Akroinon in Phrygia in 740.

As a soldier-emperor Leo III had few equals. But he also instituted important reforms and innovations in the law, the administration and the church. In 741 he issued an abridged code of law known as the *Ecloga*

(*Eklogē* or Selection), a revision in Greek, and in accord with Christian principles, of *Justinian's *Corpus* of civil law. Wise from his own experience, he divided the enormous theme of Anatolikon into two. But he acquired most notoriety from his enforcement of iconoclasm or destruction of religious images. The reasons for his opposition to the traditional veneration of icons, first expressed in 726 and then proclaimed as imperial policy in 730, have been much debated. But Leo was a sincerely religious man and his convictions were shared by many eastern bishops and by many of his soldiers who respected him for his leadership. The iconoclast controversy which he aroused lasted for over a hundred years and contributed to the alienation of the Byzantine church from the papacy and western Christendom. The Patriarch *Germanos I refused to support his Emperor and was deposed. Other opponents of iconoclasm, notably the monks, were persecuted. Leo III was the founder of the Isaurian or Syrian dynasty (717–97). He died in June 741 and was succeeded by his son *Constantine V.

BIBL. Ostrogorsky 1968: 156–65; Jenkins 1966: 61–8, 74–89

Leo IV Emperor 775–80

Leo was the son of *Constantine V and his Khazar wife and came to the throne when his father died in 775. In foreign affairs he aimed to continue his father's work. He fought three successful campaigns against the Arabs and scored a diplomatic victory over the Bulgars by welcoming their deposed ruler as a refugee in Constantinople. In other matters, however, he was dominated by his overbearing wife *Eirene. Like his father and grandfather, *Leo III, he was an iconoclast; but Eirene, who was of the opposite persuasion, prevailed upon him to be more tolerant of his adversaries. He died in September 780 when his son and heir *Constantine VI was only ten years old.

BIBL. Ostrogorsky 1968: 175–7

Leo V Emperor 813–20

Leo V was an Armenian who had a successful military career under the Emperors *Nikephoros I and *Michael I. He became *strategos* or commander of the Anatolikon Theme, whose troops proclaimed him as their Emperor after the defeat of Michael I by the Bulgars in 813, in the hope that he might revive the heroic days of the soldier-emperors *Leo III and *Constantine V. Their success seemed to show that God was on the side of the iconoclasts. Leo V's reign therefore ushered in a second era of iconoclasm and the banning of religious imagery. First, however, he had to face the crisis of a determined attack on Constantinople by the victorious Bulgars led by their ambitious ruler Krum. Providence came to Leo's aid by causing the sudden death of Krum in April 814; and his son Omurtag was persuaded to sign a thirty-year treaty of peace, by which the boundaries between Bulgaria and Byzantium were defined. The revival of iconoclasm was secured at a council in St Sophia which Leo arranged at Easter 815. The Patriarch *Nikephoros, who had crowned him as Emperor, refused to approve its decrees. He was dismissed and replaced by a more amenable

Patriarch, *Theodotos. The council of 815 reaffirmed the rulings of the first iconoclast council summoned by the Emperor *Constantine V in 754. Leo's life was cut short on Christmas Day 820. He was assassinated by conspirators working for his erstwhile friend Michael the Amorian, whom he had arrested on an evidently justifiable suspicion of treachery, and who at once ascended the throne as *Michael II.

BIBL. Ostrogorsky 1968: 200—3; Jenkins 1966: 130—9; Treadgold 1988: 196—225

Leo VI Emperor 886—912

Leo succeeded his father *Basil I in August 886 when he was twenty years of age. Basil had been illiterate, though he had a great respect for learning and he saw to it that his son had a sound education. As a result Leo became more of an intellectual than a man of action and his father turned against him. In 883 he was imprisoned for three years on a charge of treason. When he came to the throne he chose his own ministers of state, chief among whom was Stylianos Zaoutzes. He dismissed the Patriarch *Photios and replaced him with his own nineteen-year-old brother *Stephen, thus assuring his control over the church. Leo accomplished much solid and lasting administrative and legal work which gave his Empire an even firmer basis and structure. He completed his father's project of revising the laws in the compilation known as the *Basilika* in sixty books. He also issued 113 Novels or new laws of his own. The *Book of the Eparch* or Prefect, regulating the conditions of commerce and trade in Constantinople, was also composed in his reign. His legislation laid a new emphasis on the absolute autocracy of the Emperor as the fount and origin of all law and order in the world.

In foreign affairs Leo was less forceful and less successful. The Arabs completed their conquest of Sicily in 902. In 904 they captured Thessalonica and massacred its inhabitants. An attempt to recover from them the island of Crete failed in 911. In the same year Leo made a trade agreement with the Russians. But the worst threat came from the Bulgars whose ruler Symeon defeated the imperial army in 896, forced Leo to pay him tribute and began to fancy himself as Emperor of Constantinople. This was a problem that Leo bequeathed to his successor, as also was the scandal of his private life. In his determination to produce a male heir he contracted a fourth marriage, which was uncanonical. The lady, *Zoe Karbounopsina, daughter of his minister Stylianos Zaoutzes, gave him the son he had been wanting. The Patriarch *Nicholas I Mystikos baptized him as Constantine but refused to sanction the marriage. There was thus some doubt about the legitimacy of the future Emperor *Constantine VII. Leo VI died in May 912 and was succeeded by his brother *Alexander. In later times he was known as Leo the Wise or the Philosopher and oracles and prophecies were attributed to him.

BIBL. Vasiliev 1968: 115—216; Ostrogorsky 1968: 241—60; Jenkins 1966: 198—211.

Leo the Deacon (end 10th century) historian

Born about 950 in Kaloē in Asia Minor, Leo studied in Constantinople as a young man. Ordained as a deacon, he joined the ranks of the palace clergy on the accession of the Emperor *Basil II, for whom he wrote a panegyric. He went with Basil on his Bulgarian campaign in 986. His major work is his *History* of the years 959 to 976 in ten books, written in the richly contrived Greek of a self-conscious scholar. Much of it is based on eye-witness accounts; and it deals in some detail with the careers of Basil's predecessors from *Nikephoros II to *John I and their wars against the Arabs in Crete and Asia Minor and against the Bulgars and Russians in Europe.

BIBL. Hase 1828; Hunger 1978, I: 369−71

Leo the Mathematician (*c*. 790−*c*. 869) scholar

Leo the Mathematician or Philosopher was a cousin of the learned Patriarch *John VII Grammatikos and a leading light in the revival of scholarship in Byzantium in the ninth century. His erudition was so well known that the Arab Caliph tried to lure him to his court at Baghdad. To prevent this brain-drain the Emperor *Theophilos secured Leo's appointment as Bishop of Thessalonica in 840. He was an iconoclast by conviction, a fact which cost him his bishopric when Orthodoxy was restored in 843. He was none the less allowed to continue his researches and in the 850s became head of the new school of higher education in Constantinople. Among his technical inventions was a beacon system of early warning stations running from east to west across the Empire. He is said also to have had a hand in the construction of the mechanical toys and contrivances which so impressed visitors to the Emperor's throne room in the palace. He knew, and may have taught, *Constantine-Cyril, the apostle of the Slavs, and *Photios, the later Patriarch.

BIBL. Wilson 1983: 79−84; Hunger 1978, II: 237−8

Leontios Emperor 695−8

Governor (*strategos*) of the newly-created Theme of Hellas in central Greece, Leontios was proclaimed Emperor by the revolutionaries who overthrew *Justinian II in 695. His short reign was marked by the Arab conquest of Carthage and the province of North Africa. The Byzantine fleet sent to avert this disaster rebelled and proclaimed the *droungarios* or admiral Apsimar as Emperor. He came to the throne as *Tiberius II. Leontios was imprisoned and executed when Justinian II came back to Constantinople in 705.

BIBL. Ostrogorsky 1968: 140−1

Leontios of Neapolis (*c*. 590−*c*. 650) Bishop

Leontios was Bishop of Neapolis in Cyprus and a friend of the Cypriote Patriarch of Alexandria, John the Almsgiver (610−19), whose *Life* he wrote. Written in a popular style, it is a valuable source for the social and economic life of the seventh century. He also composed theological and hagiographical works.

BIBL. Dawes and Baynes 1948; Beck 1959: 485–6

Leontios Theotokites Patriarch of Constantinople 1189 *See* **Niketas II Mountanes** Patriarch

Luke Chrysoberges Patriarch of Constantinople 1157–70

   Little is known about his career. He had to concur with the opinion of his Emperor, *Manuel I Komnenos, in a controversy which broke out about 1160 over the meaning of the passage 'My Father is greater than I' (John 14: 28). In 1166 Manuel presided over a council at which he forced his own interpretation on the church. The decrees of the council were inscribed on stone and have been preserved. Luke was succeeded as Patriarch by *Michael III.

BIBL. Grumel 1947: 110–42; Beck 1959: 661–2; Mango 1963: 315–30

M

Macedonius II Patriarch of Constantinople 496–511

Macedonius was appointed by the Emperor *Anastasius I to succeed the banished Patriarch *Euphemius. He too fell out with the Emperor over his theological opinions and was deposed and exiled in August 511. He was replaced by Timotheus whose Monophysite views were acceptable to Anastasius.

BIBL. Grumel 1972: 137–42; Bury 1923, I: 437–8

Makarios Patriarch of Constantinople 1377–9; 1390–1

Makarios was appointed by the usurper *Andronikos IV, whose coronation as Emperor he performed in October 1377. He fled when Andronikos's father, *John V, re-entered Constantinople in 1379; but he was reinstated by John in 1390.

BIBL. *PLP* no. 16310

Makrembolites, Alexios (first half 14th century) writer

Little is known about his career save for what can be gleaned from his own writings. He was a layman and in the service of one Patrikiotes, a wealthy business-man and loyal friend of *John (VI) Kantakouzenos. Makrembolites became a teacher, possibly of the Scriptures and the Psalter. His literary works are not very distinguished by their style; but some of them are of unusual interest because of their author's concern, rare among Byzantine writers, for the social injustices of his day, as revealed particularly in his *Dialogue between the Rich and the Poor*. His other compositions include a historical account of the war between John VI and the Genoese in 1348–9, and an essay on the destruction by earthquake in 1346 of part of the church of St Sophia in Constantinople. Many of his other works remain to be published.

BIBL. Ševčenko 1960: 187–228; *PLP* no. 16352

Malalas, John (*c*. 491–*c*. 578) chronicler

A Syrian by birth, Malalas wrote a *World Chronicle* of events from the Creation to the year 565 which is the oldest Byzantine chronicle of its kind. Written in simple and almost colloquial Greek, it is a naive and uncritical compilation of biblical, mythological and historical material bound together in a Christian framework and directed at a monastic audience. It was extremely popular and was used by all subsequent Byzantine chroniclers. It was also translated into Slavonic and Georgian.

BIBL. Dindorff 1831; Jeffreys, Jeffreys and Scott 1986

Manasses, Constantine (*d*. *c*. 1187) chronicler

Manasses was a government official who entered the church and is said, not very plausibly, to have died as Metropolitan of Naupaktos, where his nephew and pupil, John *Apokaukos, was to succeed him about 1200. He composed a *World Chronicle* from the Creation to 1081. Its only originality is that it is in verse, though its language and style lend it some charm. He also wrote letters, speeches and a long account in verse of a diplomatic mission which he undertook to Antioch, Jerusalem and Cyprus in connection with the second marriage of the Emperor *Manuel I.

BIBL. Bekker 1837; Hunger 1978, I: 419−22

Maniakes, George (*d*. 1043) general

Maniakes was a man of humble birth from the eastern provinces who worked his way to the top as a soldier and became one of the ablest Byzantine generals. In 1032 he conquered Edessa from the Arabs. He was then posted to Sicily, which the Emperor *Basil II had been planning to invade when he died in 1025. Maniakes seemed on the point of recovering the island, with the help of the Scandinavian hero Harald Hardraada who was in his service. In 1040, however, he was recalled by the Emperor *Michael IV on suspicion of treason. The Normans were thus encouraged to invade and occupy southern Italy; and Maniakes was sent back to restore order. He then rebelled; his troops proclaimed him Emperor; he crossed over from Otranto to Epiros and was marching towards Thessalonica in 1043 when he was killed.

BIBL. Jenkins 1966: 345−6

Manuel I Komnenos Emperor 1143−80

Manuel was the fourth son of *John II Komnenos who nominated him as his heir in April 1143. He was then with his father in Cilicia, while his elder brother Isaac, who no doubt expected to be Emperor, was in Constantinople. The matter was resolved without bloodshed and Manuel was crowned in St Sophia by a Patriarch of his own creation *Michael II Oxeites. He was a less austere figure than his father and he looked for ways of co-operation rather than confrontation with the emerging powers of western Christendom. His mother was Hungarian; his first wife, Bertha of Sulzbach, was related to the German Emperor Conrad III; his second wife, Mary of Antioch, was of Norman blood; and he was personally attracted by many aspects of Latin culture. He had no doubts, however, about the oecumenical authority invested in him as Emperor of the Romans. It was a myth not shared by the Holy Roman Empire in Germany, by the Norman Kingdom of Sicily, by the Kingdom of Hungary, the papacy or the Republic of Venice.

The failure of the Second Crusade, which passed through Constantinople in 1147, was blamed on him. He had got on well with the western Emperor Conrad III, but he could reach no understanding with Conrad's successor Frederick I Barbarossa, against whom he was driven to making friends with the Normans and ultimately to relinquishing any further claim to a foothold in Italy. In Serbia and in Hungary he had more success. But he antagonized the Venetians. In 1171 he had all resident Venetian traders throughout his Empire arrested and their goods impounded. They were not set free until after Manuel's death. In the Christian east he completed his father's work by restoring Byzantine rule over the crusader principality of Antioch. But in the Muslim world he misjudged the strength of his adversaries, the Seljuq Turks, whose Sultan, after a series of defeats, was ready to be the Emperor's vassal. Manuel wanted nothing less than unconditional surrender; and in 1176 he led his army to total defeat by the Turks at the battle of Myriokephalon. He died four years later, in September 1180. In the minds of the western Christians, whose friendship he had cultivated, his humiliation at Myriokephalon demonstrated what Frederick Barbarossa had rudely observed, that Manuel was not Emperor of the Romans but merely King of the Greeks. In the minds of his own people his favouritism towards the Latins had gone too far. He left a legacy of resentment and racial prejudice which was soon to erupt in violence fostered by his cousin *Andronikos Komnenos.

BIBL. Chalandon 1912; Angold 1984: 164–242

Manuel II Palaiologos Emperor 1391–1425

Manuel was the second son of the Emperor *John V, whom he succeeded in February 1391. He had been governor of Thessalonica in 1368 and from there went to rescue his father from his detention in Venice. In 1373 he was crowned as co-Emperor after the revolt of his eldest brother *Andronikos IV; though he was imprisoned, with his father, when Andronikos took his revenge in 1376. Three years later he escaped and helped to reinstate his father. In 1383 he left Constantinople and returned to Thessalonica as Emperor in his own right. For nearly five years, in defiance of his father's wishes, he worked to make Thessalonica a centre of resistance to the Turks. It was constantly under siege and in April 1387, disappointed by the apathy of its citizens, he abandoned it and left them to surrender. Like his father, he became a vassal of the Sultan. When his nephew *John VII staged a coup d'état in 1390, Manuel again came to his father's rescue. Five months later he became Emperor.

In 1394 the Sultan Bajezid laid siege to Constantinople. Manuel maintained a passive defiance. But in 1399 he travelled to the west to seek help, particularly from Charles VI of France. From Paris he crossed to England and spent Christmas 1400 as the guest of King Henry IV. He was much honoured on his travels but they brought him little practical comfort. During his absence, in 1402, the Sultan Bajezid was defeated and captured by the Mongols and the Ottoman dominions were shattered. Manuel returned in 1403 to find that the siege of Constantinople had been lifted and Thessalonica and other places had been restored to his Empire by Bajezid's eldest son Suleiman. Suleiman and his brothers fought over their inheritance until Mehmed I emerged as Sultan in 1413. Manuel had assisted Mehmed and he had his reward. For eight years the Turks left him alone and gave him time to see to the defence of his remaining provinces. When Mehmed died in 1421, however, and Murad II became Sultan the respite was over. Murad resumed the siege of Constantinople in 1421; and Manuel was forced to make a humiliating treaty.

He died in July 1425, much mourned by his people. He had gained little military or economic aid from the westerners and only a few years' peace from the Turks. But he was respected by all as a man of courage, dignity and culture. He wrote a number of literary, ethical and rhetorical works, including a Dialogue with a Turk; and many of his letters have survived. In 1392 he had married Helena, daughter of the Serbian prince Constantine Dragaš. She bore him six sons, one of whom came to the throne as *John VIII.

BIBL. Barker 1969; Dennis 1977

Manuel I Sarantenos Patriarch of Constantinople 1217–22
Manuel was appointed Patriarch at Nicaea after the short reign of Maximos II. In 1220 he consecrated St Sava as Archbishop of Serbia; and he challenged as uncanonical the unauthorized ordinations of bishop being permitted by *Michael I Komnenos Doukas, the independent ruler of Epiros.

BIBL. Laurent 1971a: 27–39

Manuel II Patriarch of Constantinople 1244–54
His predecessor, Methodios, held the patriarchate at Nicaea for only three months in 1240. There was then no Patriarch for three years since the Emperor *John III Batatzes could find no acceptable candidate. Manuel was appointed in 1244 and died almost simultaneously with the Emperor, in November 1254. He was succeeded by *Arsenios Autoreianos.

BIBL. Laurent 1971a: 111–32

Manuel III Komnenos Emperor of Trebizond 1390–1417
The son of *Alexios III Komnenos of Trebizond, Manuel became Emperor in 1390. His reign coincided with the Mongol invasion of Asia Minor which resulted in the defeat of the Ottoman Turks in 1402. He saved his Empire from extinction by siding with the Mongols. In 1396 he married a lady of the Byzantine family of Philanthropenos, who became the mother of the Emperor *Alexios IV of Trebizond.

BIBL. Miller 1926: 70–9

Manuel Kantakouzenos Despot of the Morea 1349–80
Manuel was the second son of the Emperor *John VI Kantakouzenos who, in 1349, sent him to govern the Morea (Peloponnese) with the title of Despot. He was a talented soldier and administrator and he made the Despotate of the Morea, with its capital at Mistra, the most flourishing province of the late Byzantine Empire. He married Isabelle of Lusignan and died, without issue, in April 1380. He founded two of the churches at Mistra.

BIBL. Nicol 1968: no. 25

Marcian Emperor 450–7
Marcian had served the Emperor *Theodosius II as a general and

succeeded him as Emperor at Constantinople in August 450, taking his sister Pulcheria to wife. His short reign was one of comparative peace and recuperation. He refused to pay any more bribes to the Huns; and by judicious economic measures he built up a healthy surplus in his treasury. It was not his fault that the western part of the Empire continued to totter to its fall. The most memorable event of his reign was the Council of Chalcedon, the Fourth Oecumenical Council of the church, which he convened in 451. The assembled bishops there upheld the traditional doctrine on the issue of the nature of Christ which had for long troubled and divided church and state. They condemned as heretics the Monophysites and the misguided followers of *Nestorius; and they defined once and for all the impenetrable relationship of consubstantiality between the divinity and the humanity in the Son of God. The definition gratified Marcian and his pious wife Pulcheria. But those denounced for rejecting it were to cause endless trouble in the future. The 28th Canon of the Council admitted the political realities of the time by declaring that, while the Bishop of Rome might enjoy a primacy of honour in the church universal, the Bishop of Constantinople, the evident capital of what was left of the Roman Empire, was his equal in authority. Marcian died in January 457. He was the last Emperor of the dynasty founded by *Theodosius I. His successor was *Leo I.

BIBL. Bury 1923, I: 235—9

Matthew Kantakouzenos Emperor 1353—7
Matthew was the eldest son of *John VI Kantakouzenos who became Emperor in 1347. He was induced to serve his father loyally; but he was resentful that his brother-in-law, *John V Palaiologos, had been designated and crowned as heir to the throne. Fighting broke out and Matthew was proclaimed Emperor in 1353 in place of John V. He was crowned in February 1354. When his father had to abdicate in December of that year and John V became Emperor, Matthew again took to arms. In December 1357, however, he was persuaded to renounce his claim to the throne; and in 1361 he went to join his brother *Manuel Kantakouzenos in the Morea (Peloponnese). There he died in 1383, leaving two sons, John and Demetrios, and three daughters by his wife Eirene Palaiologina, a grand-daughter of the Emperor *Andronikos II.

BIBL. Nicol 1972: no. 24

Matthew I Patriarch of Constantinople 1397—1410
In 1387 Matthew held a number of appointments, as abbot of a monastery in Constantinople, Bishop of Kyzikos, and Bishop-elect of Chalcedon. After his election as Patriarch in October 1397 he was accused of pluralism. He was deposed in 1402, though the Emperor *Manuel II recalled him in June 1403. He was also wrongfully accused of treacherous dealings with the Turks. He died in August 1410. Among his surviving writings are his rules for the cathedral clergy of St Sophia and his last will and testament.

BIBL. *PLP* no. 17387

Maurice Emperor 582–602

Maurice (Mauricius) was the greatest of the immediate successors of *Justinian I. He served the Emperor *Tiberius I as commander in the war against the Persians. Tiberius crowned him as Emperor and gave him his daughter Constantina in marriage just before his own death in August 582. For eight years he waged war on the Persians and was able to take advantage of their own internal disputes. The heir to the Persian throne, Chosroes II, was exiled in 590. Maurice gave him asylum in Constantinople and in 591 sent him with an army to recover his kingdom. The result was a lasting treaty between Byzantium and Persia.

In the west Maurice strengthened his hold on what was left of Justinian's conquests by imposing a form of martial law. At Ravenna he appointed a military governor with the title of Exarch who combined civil and military authority as a viceroy of the Emperor. A similar Exarchate was set up at Carthage. This was a departure from Justinian's principle of centralized government. But it helped to save Ravenna from the Lombards for another century and more. Against the Avars and the Slavs in the north Maurice took the offensive, sending his armies into enemy territory north of the Danube. He had some successes but only in isolated battles which made little impact on such enormous numbers of barbarians. The cost of continuous warfare had to be met by harsh taxation; and the conditions of fighting were hard. In 602 his troops mutinied and proclaimed a junior officer, *Phokas, as their Emperor. He led them to Constantinople where the revolt was supported by the over-taxed citizens. Maurice was thrown out and executed. His name was later given to a handbook of strategy called the *Strategikon*.

BIBL. Goubert 1971; Dennis 1984; Whitby 1988

Mavropous, John (11th century) scholar and bishop

Born in Paphlagonia, he was educated in Constantinople, where he became a teacher of great renown. His brightest pupil was Michael *Psellos, his lifelong friend. In the 1030s he became a monk in Constantinople, though continuing to teach. He was then counsellor and orator of the Emperor *Constantine IX. About 1049 he was appointed Metropolitan of Euchaita in the Pontos, a distant region which he much disliked. He was there until 1075 when he came back to his monastery in the capital. He died there soon after 1081. His literary works include epigrams, funeral orations and other speeches, some of great historical interest, and seventy-seven letters to Psellos, to *John (VIII) Xiphilinos, to *Michael (I) Keroullarios and others. Some of his epigrams are official, set pieces; but others are more personal and original, revealing a personality of great culture and learning with a wit and irony unusual in a Byzantine writer. He was a man of the spirit without being fanatical, a man of sincere piety without being priggish.

BIBL. Karpozilos 1990; Beck 1959: 555–6; Moravcsik 1983: 334–5

Maximian Patriarch of Constantinople 431–4

He was appointed in place of *Nestorius, who had been damned as a heretic at the Council of Ephesos in 431. He was a monk with a reputation for holiness. He died in April 434, to be succeeded by *Proclus.

BIBL. Grumel 1972: 55—60

Maximos the Confessor (580—662) theologian
Born in Constantinople, he served as secretary of state to the Emperor *Heraclius until in 613 he became a monk, first in Chrysopolis (Skutari) and then in North Africa and Rome. In 653 the Emperor *Constans II, whose theology Maximos had denounced, summoned him back to Constantinople. He was exiled to Thrace, then mutilated and banished to Lazika on the Black Sea, where he died in August 662. He was, and is, revered by the church as a Confessor (*Homologētēs*) and a saint for his witness in writing as in speech to the truths of Orthodoxy in the matter of the nature and the will of Christ, as against the heretical Monophysites and Monotheletes. His many writings are too abundant to enumerate. They include dogmatic and polemical works, exegetical and ascetic works, and letters. He was the greatest theologian of the seventh century and one of the Fathers of the church universal.

BIBL. Works *in MPG*, vols. 90—1; Beck 1959: 436—42

Mazaris (early 15th century) satirical writer
Little is known of the life and career of Mazaris. He seems to have served at the court in Constantinople before 1399, then in Lemnos, and to have fallen out of favour and settled in the Morea (Peloponnese). There he composed a satirical work entitled *Journey to Hades* which, on internal evidence, can be dated to 1414—15.

BIBL. Barry, Share *et al.* 1975

Melissenos, Nikephoros (11th to 12th century) Caesar
Born into one of the great landowning military families of Asia Minor, he was a brother-in-law of the Emperor *Alexios I Komnenos and one of his rivals for the throne. Once Alexios had been crowned, however, in 1081, Nikephoros submitted and accepted the rank and title of Caesar and the governorship of Thessalonica. He was later to be found fighting on the Emperor's side against the Seljuq Turks.

BIBL. Ostrogorsky 1968: 349—50

Menander Protector (second half 6th century) historian
Menander (Menandros) was born in Constantinople where he studied law. After a hedonistic youth, he entered the service of the Emperor *Maurice with the honorary title of Protector or court dignitary. He wrote his *History* as a sequel to that by *Agathias; and it covers the years from 558 to 582. Only parts of it have survived, but it is clear that it was based on official documents of the time and on eye-witness accounts. It is the only historical narrative of the last years of the reign of *Justinian I and of his immediate successors.

BIBL. Dindorf 1871: 1—131; Hunger 1978, I: 309—12

Menas Patriarch of Constantinople 536—52

Menas was consecrated as Patriarch by Pope Agapetus when he was in Constantinople in 536, after the deposition of the heretical *Anthimus. He was, however, later excommunicated by Pope Vigilius for supporting the theological aberration of his Emperor *Justinian I. He died in August 552 and was succeeded by *Eutychius.

BIBL. Grumel 1972: 169—76

Mesarites, John (1161—1207) monk

His father had intended him for the civil service, but in 1185 he became a monk in a monastery in Constantinople and a professor of exegesis of the Scriptures. After the capture of Constantinople by the crusaders in 1204 he became a leader of the opposition to the Roman church. As such he and his brother Nicholas *Mesarites defended the Orthodox faith in dialogues with papal legates, in 1204, when John confronted the legate Peter Capuano, and again in August and September 1206. He also signed a letter to Pope Innocent III on the problems facing the Greek clergy under Latin rule.

BIBL. *see under* Nicholas *Mesarites

Mesarites, Nicholas Bishop of Ephesos *c*. 1212—20

The younger brother of John *Mesarites, he was a priest at St Sophia in Constantinople. Soon after the conquest of the city by the crusaders in 1204 he went to Nicaea, where he served the Patriarch in exile, *Michael IV Autoreianos. He was made Metropolitan of Ephesos about 1212 and died about 1220. Like his brother, he was a champion of Orthodoxy against the claims of the Roman church. He wrote accounts of his disputations with the Cardinal legate Benedict and the Latin Patriarch of Constantinople, Thomas Morosini, in 1206 and of the fruitless discussions with Cardinal Pelagius on the union of the churches held at Constantinople and Nicaea in 1214. The long epitaph which he wrote for his brother John, who died in 1207, is of interest for its historical information.

BIBL. Works *in* Heisenberg 1973; Beck 1959: 665—7

Mesopotamites, Constantine (*c*. 1170—*c*. 1230) Bishop of Thessalonica

Constantine came to the fore as a civil servant under the Emperor *Isaac II whose administrative power he sought to usurp. Banished by the Emperor *Andronikos I, he was recalled through the influence of the Empress *Euphrosyne Doukaina and became the power behind the throne of her husband *Alexios III Angelos. He secured her return from exile after she had been accused of a love affair. The Patriarch *George II Xiphilinos loaded him with ecclesiastical honours and in 1197 appointed him Metropolitan of Thessalonica. By then he was the most powerful man in affairs of state and church and able to promote members of his own family to high office. He was brought low by his political and ecclesiastical enemies and went into exile. About 1225 he was reinstated as Bishop of Thessalonica after *Theodore Komnenos Doukas of Epiros had liberated the city from the Latins; but he refused to perform the coronation of Theodore as Emperor, preferring once again to go into exile.

BIBL. Brand 1968: 99, 110, 114, 144−6; Nicol 1957: 65, 74, 95

Methodios I Patriarch of Constantinople 843−7
Methodios was a monk who suffered for his convictions in the reign of the iconoclast Emperor *Michael II and for a time took refuge in Rome. The Emperor *Theophilos, however, admired his erudition and allowed him to return and live in peace in Constantinople. When in 843 the Empress *Theodora restored the veneration of icons, she picked on Methodios as successor to the Patriarch *John VII who refused to change his views. He was a moderate and tolerant man, yet he felt bound to excommunicate the leaders of the extreme monastic faction in the church who longed for vengeance on the iconoclasts. He died in June 847 and was succeeded by *Ignatios. He wrote a number of saints' lives.

BIBL. Grumel 1936: 42−64; Beck 1959: 496−8

Methodios (c. 825−85) saint and missionary
St Methodios was the elder brother of *Constantine-Cyril, whom he accompanied on his mission to the Slavs in Moravia to spread the Gospel among them in their own language. Born in Thessalonica, he held a government post in one of the Slav provinces before becoming a monk on Mount Olympos in Asia Minor. When his brother died in Rome in 869 Methodios obeyed his death bed instruction to continue the good work of christianizing the Slavs. A change of rulers in Moravia, however, coupled with the jealousy of western missionaries there led to his being arrested and imprisoned for two years. Released on the intervention of the Pope in 873, Methodios struggled on with his sacred but lonely mission in the face of political instability and ecclesiastical rivalry. The popes too soon turned against the use of the vernacular and of the Slavonic script invented by Constantine-Cyril. In 881 Methodios visited Constantinople and was warmly received by the Emperor *Basil I and the Patriarch *Photios, who gave him badly-needed encouragement. He went back to Moravia and spent much of his last few years industriously adding to the corpus of Slavonic translations of Greek texts, religious and secular. He died there in April 885 and his disciples were imprisoned or exiled. He was soon canonized by the Orthodox church and, in 1880, by the church of Rome.

BIBL. see *Constantine-Cyril

Metochites, Demetrios Palaiologos (d. 1453) soldier and statesman
Soldier, civil servant, ambassador and governor of the island of Lemnos, Demetrios was appointed commander of the city of Constantinople in 1449. He and his sons were killed when the Turks broke in in 1453. He was the last Greek governor of the city.

BIBL. *PLP* no. 17981

Metochites, George (*d.* 1328) archdeacon and writer

George was the father of the more famous Theodore *Metochites. He was in favour of the union of the eastern and western churches and an active negotiator for the Emperor *Michael VIII with the papacy after the union was proclaimed at Lyons in 1274. When it was denounced in 1283 and 1285 George, along with his friends Constantine Meliteniotes and the Patriarch *John XI Bekkos, was arrested and exiled. He died after a long imprisonment in 1328. Some of his pro-Latin dogmatic writings survive.

BIBL. *PLP* no. 17979

Metochites, Theodore (1270–1332) statesman and scholar

Theodore was the son of George *Metochites. He was educated in Constantinople, and in his middle years he studied astronomy under Manuel Bryennios. He rose to the highest ranks of the civil service as Grand Logothete (Chancellor) and *mesazon* or prime minister of the Emperor *Andronikos II. Earlier he had acted as the Emperor's ambassador to Cyprus and to Serbia, about which he wrote an interesting account. Between 1316 and 1321 he commissioned the restoration and adornment with mosaics and frescoes of the monastery of the Saviour in Chora (Kariye Djami) in Constantinople. When *Andronikos III came to the throne in 1328 Theodore was banished and his property was confiscated. He was allowed to return when his health declined; and he died in the Chora monastery as a monk in March 1332.

His many compositions include speeches, poems, encomia of saints, astronomical treatises, paraphrases of Aristotle and 120 philosophical and historical essays. He was renowned as a polymath. His pupil Nikephoros *Gregoras called him 'a living library'; and he housed a large collection of manuscripts in the Chora monastery. He was particularly proud of his knowledge of astronomy. Though not an editor of classical texts, he was widely read in ancient Greek literature and philosophy. The encyclopaedic range of his learning is shown in his essays, which also reveal his freshness of mind in reflecting on the parlous state and uncertain future of his society. He was unusually disinterested in theology, perhaps because of his father's unhappy experiences; though he was careful to distinguish between the merits of the truths of the Christian revelation and the speculations of pagan scholars. He had five sons, two of whom, Alexios Laskaris Metochites and Demetrios Angelos Metochites, served as army officers in the later fourteenth century; while one, Nikephoros Laskaris Metochites, was Grand Logothete in 1355–7.

BIBL. Ševčenko 1975: 19–91; Wilson 1983: 256–64; *PLP* no. 17982

Metrophanes II Patriarch of Constantinople 1440–3

As Bishop of Kyzikos Metrophanes attended the Council of Ferrara-Florence in 1438–9 and supported the union of the eastern and western churches there proclaimed. He was made Patriarch in April 1440 and died in August 1443.

BIBL. *PLP* no. 18069

Michael I Rangabe Emperor 811—13

Michael was a son-in-law of the Emperor *Nikephoros I. He was probably a Slav and he was elected as Emperor to succeed Nikephoros's dying son *Stavrakios in October 811. His short reign was marked by one diplomatic success and one military disaster. In 812 his ambassadors to Aachen agreed to recognize Charlemagne's title as Emperor in return for the restitution of Venice and other places which he had occupied on the Dalmatian coast. In June 813 Michael's armies, by no means wholly loyal to him, were routed by the Bulgars at Versinikia near Adrianople (Edirne). The defeat cost him his crown and two weeks later he relinquished it to a greater ruler, *Leo V. He retired to a monastery where he died about 843.

BIBL. Treadgold 1988: 177—89

Michael II Emperor 820—9

He was born of humble parentage at Amorion in Phrygia and was thus known as Michael the Amorian. The dynasty which he founded lasted until 867. Michael was a soldier by profession and for long a comrade-in-arms of the Emperor *Leo V. In 820, however, he was arrested for treason; and in December of that year he contrived Leo's murder and ascended his throne. The Patriarch *Theodotos crowned him as Emperor immediately after the crime. His succession was challenged by another of his army colleagues, *Thomas the Slav, a revolt which Michael repressed with difficulty in 823. The consequences were serious. The Arabs of Baghdad, who had supported Thomas, gained little from his bid for power. Arabs from Spain and North Africa, however, seized the chance to strike by sea and occupied Crete in 826 and Sicily in 827. Crete was to become a base for Arab raids all over the coastline and islands of the Empire. In religion Michael II was an iconoclast, though inclined to tolerance and ambivalence. He died in his bed in October 829 and was succeeded by *Theophilos, son of his first wife Thecla. His second wife Euphrosyne was a daughter of *Constantine VI.

BIBL. Jenkins 1966: 140—6; Treadgold 1988: 225—62

Michael III Emperor 842—67

Michael, son of the Emperor *Theophilos, was two years old when his father died in January 842. His mother *Theodora acted as regent, assisted by a council headed by her favourite minister of state, *Theoktistos. Her first concern was to put an end to iconoclasm and to restore the icons to their rightful place in the church; and this she achieved in 843. Not until 856 was the young Michael able to assert his own imperial authority. He disposed of Theoktistos and replaced him by his own uncle *Bardas, whom he honoured with the title of Caesar. This was the beginning of Michael III's reign.

It was an era of success in military and diplomatic terms. The campaigns of his general *Petronas in the east ensured that the initiative in the long conflict with the Arabs passed to Byzantium. A start was made on the christianization of the Slavs and Bulgars, prompted by the Emperor and

87

by the Patriarch *Photios, whom he appointed in 858. The Russians too began to enter the Byzantine orbit, making their first appearance in a vain attack on Constantinople in 860. The Caesar Bardas revived and reformed the school of higher education which had lapsed during the iconoclast period, encouraging the renaissance of scholarship in which Photios also played a leading part. Latterly Michael fell under the spell of the upstart *Basil (I) the Macedonian and in May 866 nominated him as co-Emperor. It was Basil who contrived the murder first of Bardas and then of Michael himself, in September 867. Later Byzantine historians, committed to the glorification of the Macedonian Emperors beginning with Basil I, played down the achievements of Michael III and mocked him as a drunkard. They did him an injustice. He may have had a dissolute youth. He shocked his mother by his affair with a lady called Eudokia Ingerina. But the golden age that dawned for the Byzantine Empire in the ninth century was inaugurated as much by Michael III as by his murderer and successor Basil I.

BIBL. Ostrogorsky 1968: 217−32; Jenkins 1966: 153−67

Michael IV Emperor 1034−41

Michael, called the Paphlagonian, came from the eastern provinces to Constantinople and made his fortune there largely through the influence in high places of his brother, *John the Orphanotrophos. John introduced him into court circles. Michael became the playboy of the Empress *Zoe; and when her husband, *Romanos III, died in 1034, she married him and made him her Emperor. He had his enemies who conspired against him, among them the future Patriarch *Michael Keroullarios and the future Emperor *Constantine IX. Although he was an epileptic, Michael was a competent ruler and a brave soldier. He had little time for Zoe once she had brought him to the summit of power; and he relied on his ruthless brother John to run the administration. His armies won some temporary victories over the Arabs in Sicily; and he made a favourable treaty with the Fatimid Caliph of Egypt about 1037. The Slavs in the Balkans rebelled against the burden of taxes that they had to pay to Constantinople. Michael managed to suppress the uprising in Bulgaria, led by Peter Deljan; but the neighbouring Slav rulers in Serbia proved less tractable. On returning from his Bulgarian campaign, Michael succumbed to his illness and died, in December 1041. Zoe outlived him and named his nephew, *Michael V, as his successor.

BIBL. Ostrogorsky 1968: 323−6

Michael V Kalaphates Emperor 1041−2

He was a nephew of the Emperor *Michael IV and had been adopted by the Empress *Zoe, his uncle's widow. He came to the throne in December 1041 and reigned for one disastrous year. His greatest mistake was to try to disembarrass himself of his benefactress Zoe by shutting her up in a convent. The people rioted in her favour. Michael was thrown out and blinded and Zoe was reinstated in April 1042. His name Kalaphates meant 'ship's caulker', which had been his father's trade.

BIBL. Angold 1984: 34—5

Michael VI Stratiotikos Emperor 1056—7
The Empress *Theodora, the last of the Macedonian dynasty, nominated Michael to succeed her as she lay dying. He was an elderly civil servant who had held a position in the war office, from which he derived his name of Stratiotikos. The Patriarch *Michael I Keroullarios disapproved of him. But so, more effectively, did the army leaders whom he seems deliberately to have antagonized. A military junta led by the general *Isaac (I) Komnenos finally disposed of him. He abdicated and became a monk in August 1057.

BIBL. Angold 1984: 48—51

Michael VII Doukas Parapinakes Emperor 1071—8
Michael was a child when his father *Constantine X died in 1067. His mother *Eudokia Makrembolitissa was regent for a while until she married *Romanos IV. When Romanos was defeated by the Seljuq Turks at Manzikert in 1071, Michael, who had been a pupil and protégé of Michael *Psellos, was proclaimed Emperor at Constantinople His reign was punctuated by a series of rebellions mounted by pretenders to his throne. One was led by the Norman mercenary Roussel de Bailleul, who put up the Caesar John *Doukas for Emperor. He was captured with the help of the Turks. Two other pretenders from the military aristocracy were Nikephoros Bryennios at Adrianople (Edirne) and *Nikephoros (III) Botaneiates. The latter proclaimed himself Emperor in Asia Minor in January 1078 and was crowned as such in Constantinople soon after. Michael VII abdicated and died as a monk about 1090. In domestic affairs he had been dominated by the eunuch Nikephoritzes, who had come to office under Constantine X, and who provoked rioting by trying to make the corn trade a state monopoly, a policy which worsened the prevailing economic crisis. The Byzantine gold coin, which had been stable for some 500 years, had to be devalued with an alloy of base metal. This earned Michael VII his nickname of *parapinakes*. A gold coin which had formerly bought a bushel of wheat would now buy only a bushel minus a quarter (or *pinakion*). Michael married a Caucasian princess, Maria, who gave him one son, Constantine *Doukas.

BIBL. Polemis 1968: no. 14; Ostrogorsky 1968: 345—8

Michael VIII Palaiologos Emperor 1259—82
Michael Palaiologos was born about 1225. He had a mercurial career of brilliance and treachery in the military service of the Emperors in exile at Nicaea. He was made Grand Constable or commander of the Latin mercenaries by *John III Batatzes. John's successor *Theodore II Laskaris mistrusted him and not without reason. When Theodore died in 1258, Michael skilfully worked his way to becoming regent for the infant heir-apparent, *John IV Laskaris. Early in 1259 he assumed the imperial title. In July 1261 Constantinople was liberated from the Latins; and in August Michael entered the city and was crowned Emperor. John IV was blinded

and banished. The dynasty of Laskaris, which had steered the Empire through fifty-seven years of exile, was thus replaced by that of Palaiologos whose members, with one exception, were to hold the throne in Constantinople until its conquest by the Turks in 1453.

Michael was never free of political and religious opponents who regarded him as a usurper and a criminal. But his worst enemies were the Christians of the west, notably the papacy and the Venetians. Baldwin II, the last of the Latin Emperors, fled to Italy where his relative Charles of Anjou, brother of Louis VII of France, posed as leader of a crusade to restore the Latin regime in Constantinople. Michael believed that this could be prevented only by convincing the Pope that the Byzantine church was no longer in schism from Rome. After long negotiations he sent a delegation to the west to announce his obedience to the Roman church; and in 1274 union between the eastern and western churches was proclaimed at the Second Council of Lyons. Charles of Anjou was forbidden to attack the Byzantine Empire. In Constantinople, however, the reaction was violent; and succeeding popes saw that the union was a sham. In 1281 Charles was allowed to launch his crusade. His first attempt was beaten back by the Byzantine army. His second attempt, by sea from Sicily, was thwarted by the revolt known as the Sicilian Vespers. Michael later declared that the liberation of the Sicilians from their French oppressors had been the work of his agents. He died a few months later, in December 1282.

Michael VIII did much to revive the glory and prestige of his Empire. He was an accomplished diplomat. He arranged the marriages of his son *Andronikos II first to a Hungarian princess and then to a lady from Montferrat; and he married off his five daughters to Greek, Bulgarian and Mongol potentates. He liked to be known as the New Constantine. He might have been hailed as the saviour of his people. But his political and religious opponents were united in their aversion to his pretended union with the Roman church; and he died condemned by most of his subjects as a traitor and a heretic. In the longer term the greatest charge against him is that, by concentrating all his military resources on the western approaches, he neglected the defence of his eastern frontiers and so facilitated the advance of the Turks into his Empire. He was succeeded by his son *Andronikos II.

BIBL. Geanakoplos 1959; Nicol 1972: 45−96

Michael IX Palaiologos Emperor 1294−1320

Michael was the son and heir-apparent of *Andronikos II. He was born in 1277, nominated as co-Emperor with his father and crowned as such in 1294. It had been hoped that he would marry Catherine of Courtenay, the Latin claimant to the throne of Constantinople. But in 1295 he married Rita (Maria), a sister of the King of Armenia, by whom he had two sons and two daughters. He fought unsuccessfully against the Turks in southern Asia Minor; and he fell foul of the Catalan Company of mercenaries whose services his father had rashly enlisted. He never came into possession of the throne for he died at Thessalonica in October 1320. His early death was reputedly hastened by the misdemeanours of his eldest son *Andronikos (III).

BIBL. Nicol 1972: 122−4, 131−9, 146−7, 159−65

Michael I Keroullarios Patriarch of Constantinople 1043−58

Michael Keroullarios (Cerularius) is celebrated for his altercation with Cardinal Humbert, the Pope's legate to Constantinople in 1054, which provoked a technical schism between the eastern and western churches. Born and educated in Constantinople, Michael was a civil servant driven to become a monk for his part in a conspiracy against the Emperor *Michael IV. He was made Patriarch in March 1043 by *Constantine IX, who had been party to the same plot. He was a vain and ambitious prelate with an exaggerated idea of his unique status as Patriarch of Constantinople. He was an embarrassment to the Emperor who had appointed him and to his three successors. His responsibility for breaking with the church of Rome is probably no greater than that of Cardinal Humbert, for both were arrogant and intolerant men. Michael's bigotry caused him to close the Latin churches in Constantinople; he obstinately refused to co-operate with his Emperor in the diplomatic negotiations which had brought Humbert and his mission to Byzantium; and he excited the people to harrass the Pope's legates. When Humbert lost patience and excommunicated him in July 1054, he was quick to reply in kind.

The elderly Empress *Theodora, who succeeded Constantine IX in 1055, detested Keroullarios. Her successor, *Michael VI, was his victim. Only *Isaac I Komnenos stood up to him; and when he took to boasting that his authority was greater than that of the Emperor and to wearing imperial regalia, he was sent into exile pending trial on a number of charges including heresy as well as treason, for it was alleged that he had dabbled in the occult. He died on the way to his trial, in November 1058. Michael *Psellos, who had drafted the accusation against him, also composed his Epitaph. He was more of a politician than a churchman and he was no great theologian or scholar. This did not deter him from writing anti-Latin polemics.

BIBL. Grumel 1947: 1−16; Michel 1925, 1930; Runciman 1955: 28−54; Hussey 1986: 129−38

Michael II Kourkouas Oxeites Patriarch of Constantinople 1143−6

Michael was abbot of the monastery of Oxeia, one of the Princes' Islands in the Sea of Marmora. His surname of Kourkouas (Curcuas) implies an Armenian origin. He was made Patriarch by the Emperor *Manuel I Komnenos in July 1143 in succession to Leo Stypiotes who had been Patriarch since 1134; and he performed Manuel's coronation. He was reluctantly called upon to give judgment in a case of suspected heresy involving a monk called Niphon and a deacon called Kosmas. The effort exhausted him and he resigned in March 1146 and withdrew to the tranquillity of his monastery. The deacon Kosmas succeeded him as the Patriarch *Kosmas II Attikos.

BIBL. Grumel 1947: 88−97; Angold 1984: 229; Beck 1959: 661

Michael III Patriarch of Constantinople 1170−8

Michael was a pupil of the Bishop of Anchialos on the Bulgarian coast who entered the service of the patriarchate in Constantinople. He was appointed Professor of Philosophy and then, in January 1170, Patriarch in succession to *Luke Chrysoberges. He was noted for his rejection of any compromise with the Latins; and he committed his views to writing in a Dialogue with the Emperor *Manuel I, who had proposed discussions with the church of Rome. He was no less hostile to the Armenians. His inaugural lecture as Professor has survived and is informative about philosophical studies at the time as well as about Byzantine relations with Hungary. Michael *Choniates delivered a speech to him as Patriarch. He died in March 1178 and was succeeded by *Theodosios I.

BIBL. Grumel 1947: 143−69; Browning 1961: 174−214; Beck 1959: 267

Michael IV Autoreianos Patriarch of Constantinople 1208−14

Michael Autoreianos was the first of the Patriarchs in exile at Nicaea after the Latin conquest of Constantinople in 1204. He was elected by a synod set up by *Theodore I Laskaris after the Patriarch *John X Kamateros, who had fled from Constantinople, declined an invitation to leave his refuge in Bulgaria and come to settle at Nicaea. Michael crowned Theodore as Emperor in 1208 and died in August 1214.

BIBL. Laurent 1971a: 1−22

Michael I Komnenos Doukas (Angelos) ruler of Epiros 1204−15

After the Fourth Crusade and the capture of Constantinople by the Latins in 1204, Michael fled to north-western Greece; and there, safe behind the barrier of the Pindos mountains, he took command of the provinces of Epiros and Akarnania and saved them from conquest by the crusader armies. He was a cousin of the Emperors *Isaac II and *Alexios III Angelos. He had relatives in Epiros and he took over the provincial administration centred on the city of Arta. There is no evidence for the assumption that he held the Byzantine title of Despot. He was no more than a local dynast, though evidently hailed as leader of the local resistance to the Latin invaders of Greece. *Theodore I Laskaris, the leader of the other resistance movement in Asia Minor, had himself crowned Emperor at Nicaea in 1208 and claimed political as well as ecclesiastical sovereignty over Epiros. Michael Komnenos Doukas ignored the claim. The rivalry between the successor states of Epiros and Nicaea prolonged the existence of the Latin regime in Constantinople. Michael was as unscrupulous as he was daring. By a combination of successful warfare and broken agreements, first with the Venetians and then with the crusaders, he extended his dominions into Thessaly on the east and up to Durazzo and the island of Corfu in the north. He died about 1215, allegedly murdered, leaving his lands and his ambitions to his half-brother *Theodore Komnenos Doukas.

BIBL. Nicol 1957 and 1984

Michael II Komnenos Doukas (Angelos) Despot in Epiros *c*. 1230–67

He was an illegitimate son of *Michael I of Epiros, founder of the separatist state in north-western Greece after the Fourth Crusade. His early career is obscure; but by about 1230 he had established himself as his father's heir at Arta with the imperial title of Despot. After Thessalonica was incorporated into the Empire of Nicaea in 1246, Michael was encouraged by his uncle *Theodore Komnenos Doukas to fight back. Peace between the rival states of Epiros and Nicaea was supposed to be confirmed by the marriage of Michael's son *Nikephoros to the daughter of *Theodore II Laskaris in 1256, but the conditions were such that Michael went to war. His first objective was Thessalonica; his second was no doubt Constantinople. He gathered an impressive coalition of allies. Manfred of Sicily, son of Frederick II, had his own designs on Constantinople and had occupied parts of the coast of Epiros. He threw in his lot with Michael, who gave him a daughter in marriage. Michael's other ally was William of Villehardouin, the French Prince of Achaia in the Peloponnese, to whom he gave another daughter in marriage. The long rivalry between Epiros and Nicaea was finally fought out at Pelagonia in Macedonia in 1259. Michael's grand alliance broke up; and the victorious army of Nicaea, commanded by the Emperor's brother John Palaiologos, went on to invade Thessaly and Epiros. Michael fled to the island of Cephalonia.

The battle of Pelagonia was the prelude to the liberation of Constantinople from the Latins, which was achieved two years later. The Emperor of Nicaea, *Michael VIII Palaiologos, was *de facto* as well as *de jure* Emperor of Constantinople. Michael of Epiros, who was soon back in his capital at Arta, refused to recognize him as such. Not until 1264 did he come to terms. His son Nikephoros, whose first wife had died, married Anna Palaiologina, the Emperor's niece, and was confirmed in his right to the rank and title of Despot. But another seventy years were to pass before the spirit of independence in Epiros was broken. Michael II died about 1267 having divided his Despotate between his sons, *Nikephoros and *John Doukas. His widow, Theodora of the family of Petraliphas, had suffered much from him. She died as a nun in Arta, where her tomb is still to be seen and where she is revered as a local saint. Michael built a number of churches and monasteries in Epiros, some in atonement for his ill-treatment of Theodora.

BIBL. Nicol 1957 and 1984

Moschos, John (*c*. 550–619) monk

John Moschos, also known as Eukratas, became a monk in the monastery of St Theodosius near Jerusalem. He later opted for the vagrant eremitical life and travelled, in company with Sophronius, later Patriarch of Jerusalem, in Palestine, Egypt, Sinai and Cyprus. In 614 they went to Rome, where John died in 619. His best known work is his *Spiritual Meadow* (*Pratum Spirituale* or *Leimonarion*), a collection of edifying tales of monks written in a simple, popular style. It had a great influence and wide circulation, being translated into Latin and Arabic.

BIBL. Baynes 1955; Beck 1959: 412–13

N

Narses (*c.* 480–574) general

A eunuch of the imperial bodyguard of *Justinian I, Narses helped to quell the riot in Constantinople which nearly unseated the Emperor in 532. In 538, as the Emperor's treasurer, he was sent to Italy to support *Belisarius in his war against the Goths. The distrust and jealousy between the two men was such that Narses had to be recalled in 539. But in 551, when Belisarius had been summoned home, he was sent back to Italy with 30 000 troops to stifle the resurgence of the Goths under their leader Totila; and it was Narses who completed the reconquest of Italy by defeating Totila in battle in 552. He remained as civil and military governor of Italy until Justinian's death in 567. *Justin II relieved him of his command and he retired, a very wealthy man, to live in Naples. Legend has it that he took his revenge on Justin by inviting the Lombards into Italy.

BIBL. *see under* *Justinian I

Nectarius Patriarch of Constantinople 381–97

Nectarius was the first Bishop of Constantinople to be called Patriarch. The title was conferred on him and his successors at the Second Oecumenical Council of the church held at Constantinople in 381 under the Emperor *Theodosius I. The same council decreed that the see of Constantinople should rank next to that of Rome, since Constantinople was the New Rome. Nectarius was appointed in default of the great theologian *Gregory of Nazianzus. He had been in government service and was himself no great theologian; but he knew the will of his Emperor. He died in September 397 and was succeeded by *John (I) Chrysostom.

BIBL. Grumel 1972: 1–12

Neilos Kerameus Patriarch of Constantinople 1380–8

Neilos was a Hesychast monk and abbot of a monastery in Constantinople before becoming Patriarch. He had been a pupil of Gregory *Palamas, whose devoted follower he was and of whom he wrote an encomium. He corresponded with Demetrios *Kydones and also with Pope Urban VI.

BIBL. *PLP* no. 11648

Nestorius Patriarch of Constantinople 428–31

Nestorius came from Antioch where he gained fame as an eloquent presbyter, monk and theologian. The Emperor *Theodosius II appointed him Patriarch of Constantinople in 428 to settle the dissension in the church following the death of the Patriarch *Sisinnius I. He quickly made matters worse by propounding the ideas that he had acquired from the Antiochene school of theology. In particular he scandalized Orthodox

Christians by preaching that the Virgin Mary was not the Mother of God (Theotokos) but only the Mother of Christ, thereby appearing to deny the divinity of Christ and to divide Him into two Persons. He was accused of heresy by *Cyril, Patriarch of Alexandria, whose motives, while sincere theologically, were also political, in that he was out to belittle the upstart see of Constantinople and to aggrandize the apostolic see of Alexandria. Cyril called on the Pope and the Emperor to join him in condemning Nestorius; and in August 430 Pope Celestine denounced him at a council in Rome. The Emperor summoned a council at Ephesos, the Third Oecumenical Council of the church, at which Nestorius was again anathematized in the presence of Roman legates. He was exiled first to his monastery near Antioch and then to Egypt, where he died some twenty years later. The influence of his thought and teaching was profound and pervasive; Christianity in its Nestorian form spread in the east from Persia into central Asia and India. His only extant literary work, a defence of his career, survives in a Syriac version under the pseudonym of Heracleides of Damascus. His successor as Patriarch was *Maximian.

BIBL. Driver and Hodgson 1925; Grumel 1972: 41−53; Quasten 1960: 514−19

Nicholas I Mystikos Patriarch of Constantinople 901−7; 912−25
Born in 852, Nicholas was a friend and perhaps a pupil of the Patriarch *Photios. In 867, when Photios was deposed, he became a monk and then private secretary (*mystikos*) of the Emperor *Leo VI. In March 901, after the death of *Antonios II Kauleas, he was made Patriarch. As such he was deeply involved in the rights and wrongs of the scandalous fourth marriage of Leo VI and crossed swords over the matter with his friends *Arethas of Caesarea and the monk *Euthymios. His refusal to pardon the Emperor led to his dismissal in January 907. Euthymios took his place, but only for a few years; for Nicholas was reinstated in May 912, just before Leo died. For some months he then acted as regent for the young *Constantine VII. In this capacity he had to contend with the threats and demands of Symeon, Tsar of the Bulgarians, who coveted the title of Emperor of the Romans. Nicholas appeased Symeon for a time by placing a crown on his head outside the walls of Constantinople, a diplomatic blunder which caused his downfall as regent. In February 914 Leo VI's widow, *Zoe Karbounopsina, whom Nicholas had denounced as a harlot, assumed the regency for her son. Nicholas continued to be Patriarch, however, until he died in May 925. His greatest achievement was to unite the warring factions in his church behind the new Emperor *Romanos I, who came to power in 920. His Letters, many of them addressed to Symeon of Bulgaria, survive.

BIBL. Jenkins and Westerink 1973; Westerink 1981; Grumel 1936: 133−46, 148−221; Hussey 1986: 102−10; Beck 1959: 550

Nicholas III Kyrdiniates Grammatikos Patriarch of Constantinople 1084−1111
He was a reformer of abuses in the church, especially those arising from

lay control of monasteries. Rather unwillingly, he pursued his Emperor's suggestions for re-opening the question of union with the Roman church, but to no avail. Among his written works is a series of responses to various questions put to him by the monks of Mount Athos on matters of canon law.

BIBL. Grumel 1947: 40—79; Beck 1959: 660

Nikephoros I Emperor 802—11

Nikephoros served as minister of finance under the Empress *Eirene and came to the throne in the revolution that caused her downfall in 802. Having dashed the hopes of two rival pretenders, he nominated his son *Stavrakios as his co-Emperor. In 806 he appointed as Patriarch the historian *Nikephoros, like himself a civil servant. Both were Orthodox in faith and pledged to uphold the rulings of the anti-iconoclast council of 787. None the less, the Emperor had an authoritarian view of his position as head of the church. He did much to repair the damage done during Eirene's administration, revoking the tax reductions and exemptions with which she had courted popularity, and finding new sources of revenue, for which purpose he conducted a census of the entire taxable population of the Empire. His foreign policy was less successful. He antagonized the Arabs by refusing to pay the tribute with which Eirene had kept them at bay. He achieved the reconquest of the Greek peninsula from the Slavs who had overrun it two hundred years before; and he consolidated the new Theme or military district of Hellas in central Greece, reinhabiting it with settlers forcibly transported from other regions of the Empire. He also created new Themes in the neighbouring districts of the Peloponnese, Cephalonia and Thessalonica. But in the Bulgars he met his match. In July 811, during a massive invasion of Bulgaria, Nikephoros and his army were ambushed and butchered. The Bulgarian ruler, Krum, had the Emperor's head fashioned into a drinking cup. His son Stavrakios escaped and took over as Emperor.

BIBL. Ostrogorsky 1968: 186—200; Jenkins 1966: 117—29; Niavis 1987; Treadgold 1988: 127—95

Nikephoros II Phokas Emperor 963—9

Nikephoros was born into one of the great aristocratic military families of Asia Minor. His grandfather, Nikephoros the elder, had served the Emperors *Basil I and *Leo VI as a commander in Italy and in Bulgaria. His father, Bardas Phokas, had been commander-in-chief under *Constantine VII. His uncle, Leo Phokas, served in the same capacity during the regency of the Empress *Zoe; and Nikephoros held the same position when *Romanos II came to the throne in 959. He prepared the great armada which set out in 960 to reconquer Crete from the Arabs. After a siege lasting all winter he captured the island's capital city of Chandax (Candia), in March 961. It was a momentous victory. For 135 years Crete had been under Arab occupation. Now it was again a Byzantine island and the Aegean Sea was a Byzantine lake. Nikephoros was then posted to the east, where his brother Leo had been keeping the Arabs at bay. Here too his strategy brought notable victories, culminating in his capture of Aleppo. In March 963, however, Romanos II died, leaving his widow Theophano in charge of his two little sons. The army in the east proclaimed Nikephoros as their Emperor. The Patriarch *Polyeuktos also favoured him and was ready to crown him as Emperor when he entered Constantinople on 16 August 963. A few weeks later he married the dowager Empress *Theophano and became co-Emperor with and protector of the legitimate heirs of the Macedonian dynasty, *Basil II and *Constantine VIII.

Once crowned, Nikephoros gave his brother Leo the title of Caesar and made him commander of the western forces. The eastern forces he entrusted to the Armenian soldier *John (I) Tzimiskes; and he appointed Basil, a bastard son of *Romanos I, as his chamberlain (*parakoimomenos*). The war against the infidel Arabs, however, he regarded as his own divine mission; and every year from 965 to 969 he took personal charge of the offensive against them. In 965 he drove them out of Cyprus and in 969 out of Antioch. The way to Jerusalem seemed open. The prestige of Byzantium had never stood higher. Yet this was the moment chosen by the German king Otto, whom the Pope had crowned as Emperor in 963, to propose a division of the Roman Empire between east and west. Nikephoros responded with contempt. His major diplomatic blunder was to invite the Russians as his allies to invade Bulgaria from the north. The consequences had to be faced by his successor; for in December 969 Nikephoros was killed. His wife Theophano had soon found him to be an austere and melancholic husband with a taste for monastic deprivation. She had turned for comfort to his general John Tzimiskes; and it was to him that she opened the path to the throne by arranging the brutal murder of Nikephoros.

BIBL. Schlumberger 1890; Ostrogorsky 1968: 283−93; Jenkins 1966: 269−95

Nikephoros III Botaneiates Emperor 1078−81

Discontent with the economic and military mismanagement of the Emperor *Michael VII provoked rioting in Constantinople. A number of pretenders to his throne emerged, among them Nikephoros Botaneiates. He was one of the military aristocracy in Asia Minor and had been governor-general of the Anatolikon district. His troops proclaimed him Emperor at Nicaea in January 1078 and in March he entered Constantinople. Michael VII was deposed. He became a monk and Nikephoros married his thus spiritually widowed wife. Rival claimants to the throne continued to come forward: Nikephoros Bryennios and then Nikephoros Basilakes in the west, and in the east Nikephoros Melissenos, who sought help from the Turks, as Botaneiates himself had done. The youngest and the most able of them, however, was *Alexios (I) Komnenos, who finally gained control of Constantinople. Nikephoros III, elderly and outwitted, was persuaded to abdicate and became a monk in April 1081.

BIBL. Angold 1984: 102−4

Nikephoros I Patriarch of Constantinople and historian 806—15

He was a layman and a colleague in the higher civil service of the Patriarch *Tarasios, with whom he attended the anti-iconoclast Council at Nicaea in 787. When Tarasios died in 806, the Emperor *Nikephoros I persuaded him to accept the patriarchate. He was tonsured as a monk, ordained as deacon and priest, and installed as Patriarch at Easter 806, much to the disgust of the extremist party in the church led by *Theodore of Stoudios. When iconoclasm was revived under the Emperor *Leo V, Nikephoros was deposed in March 815. He died in exile. He was the author of a number of theological tracts in defence of the icons. But his major works were historical: a *Chronicle* or list of secular and ecclesiastical rulers from the Creation to 829, and a more connected historical account of events in the years 602 to 769 called the *Breviarium*, which is an invaluable source for events in the seventh and eighth centuries. It was translated into Latin about 870 by the Pope's librarian Anastasius.

BIBL. Grumel 1936: 23—40; Hunger 1978, I: 344—7; Alexander 1958; Mango 1990

Nikephoros Doukas Despot in Epiros 1267—96

When *Michael II of Epiros died about 1267 his dominions were divided between his eldest son Nikephoros and his natural son *John Doukas. Nikephoros inherited Old Epiros, extending from Ioannina in the north to Naupaktos in the south, with its capital at Arta. His title of Despot had been confirmed in 1265 by the Emperor *Michael VIII, whose niece he married. But he was not inclined to pay allegiance to any Emperor in Constantinople; and his aversion was strengthened by Michael's policy of union with the Roman church. He gave asylum to the Emperor's ecclesiastical and political opponents and encouraged Charles of Anjou to use Epiros as his base for his invasion of the Byzantine Empire. Charles's plans were frustrated in 1282; but his son Charles II revived the alliance between Epiros and his Kingdom of Naples. In 1294 his son Philip of Taranto married Thamar, daughter of Nikephoros; and her dowry included several places in southern Epiros, which consequently passed under French colonial rule. Nikephoros died in 1296 leaving his wife Anna Palaiologina as regent for her son *Thomas. The major monument of his reign is the church of the Paregoritissa in Arta, which was completed just before he died.

BIBL. Nicol 1984

Niketas I Patriarch of Constantinople 766—80

A Slav eunuch, Niketas was appointed Patriarch by the fanatically iconoclast Emperor *Constantine V in place of the disgraced Patriarch *Constantine II. He contrived to hold office for the rest of his Emperor's reign and for five years thereafter until his death in February 780. He was succeeded by *Paul IV.

BIBL. Grumel 1936: 11

Niketas II Mountanes Patriarch of Constantinople 1186−8

He was an old and saintly man, chosen to succeed *Basil II Kamateros as Patriarch in February 1186. The Emperor *Isaac II, however, preferred a favourite of his own called Dositheos, then titular Patriarch of Jerusalem. He engaged the canon lawyer Theodore *Balsamon to find legal grounds for transferring Dositheos to Constantinople. Niketas resigned in 1188. But the synod protested at the appointment of Dositheos and the Emperor had to nominate another Patriarch of Constantinople, a monk called Leontios. Dositheos, however, was reinstated in 1189 and only in September 1191 did he resign from both of his patriarchates. His successor in Constantinople was *George II Xiphilinos.

BIBL. Grumel 1947: 177−9; Brand 1968: 77−8, 100

Niketas Stethatos (*c*. 1000−*c*. 1090) monk and theologian

Niketas, nicknamed Stethatos for his outspoken condemnation of the love life of the Emperor *Constantine IX, was a monk in the monastery of Stoudios in Constantinople and a disciple of *Symeon the New Theologian, whose *Life* he wrote. He was deeply involved in defending the Orthodox position against the Roman delegation to Constantinople in 1054; and in the last years of his long life, as abbot of his monastery, he composed a series of anti-Latin polemics.

BIBL. Hausherr and Horn 1928; Beck 1959: 535−6

Nikon (*c*. 930−98) missionary and saint

St Nikon was a monk from the Black Sea area. His mission was evangelization, first in Asia Minor, then in Crete after the reconquest of the island from the Arabs in 961, and then on the mainland of Greece among the Slavs and Greeks. He earned his nickname of Metanoeite ('repent') from his constant calls to repentance. He died about 998 in the monastery at Lakedaimon (Sparta) which he and the local residents had built in gratitude for his many miracles. His *Life* is a unique source for the study of Greek society in the tenth century.

BIBL. Beck 1959: 577, 589−90

Niphon Patriarch of Constantinople 1310−14

Formerly Bishop of Kyzikos, he was elected after the second resignation of the Patriarch *Athanasios I in 1309. Niphon takes the credit for ending the Arsenite schism which had divided the Byzantine church since the deposition of the Patriarch *Arsenios in 1264. He was accused of simony and resigned in 1314.

BIBL. *PLP* no. 20679

Notaras, Luke (*d*. 1453) Grand Duke

Luke (Loukas) Notaras came of a wealthy aristocratic family in Constantinople. He was connected with the Emperors *John VIII and *Constantin XI Palaiologos, whom he served as interpreter, Grand Duke (High Admiral) and prime minister. He was made a citizen of Venice and

99

of Genoa and he had considerable investments in Italy. He played a leading and heroic part in the last defence of Constantinople against the Turks in 1453. After the conquest he and two of his sons were executed on the Sultan's orders. His daughter Anna Notaras, who had already settled in Italy, became a patroness of the Greek refugees in Venice.

BIBL. Runciman 1965: 69–71, 93–4, 226–30; *PLP* no. 20730

O

Orphanotrophos *see* **John the Orphanotrophos**

Ouranos, Nikephoros (10th to 11th century) soldier and writer

Ouranos (Uranus) was a professional soldier in the service of the Emperor *Basil II who promoted him to the rank of commander-in-chief of the western forces. As such he inflicted a notable defeat on the Bulgarians in 997. From 999 to about 1006 he was governor of Antioch. He wrote a work on strategy (*Taktika*) as well as lives of saints and letters.

BIBL. Dain 1957; Hunger 1978, II: 337

P

Pachymeres, George (1242–1310) historian and scholar

Born in the Empire in exile at Nicaea, Pachymeres moved to Constantinople in 1261 and quickly rose to prominence as a civil servant and official of the church. He is best known for his *History* of the reigns of the Emperors *Michael VIII and *Andronikos II Palaiologos from 1261 to 1308. It is not easy to read for it was consciously composed in the archaizing style of what he took to be classical Greek; but it is singularly important as the only narrative source for the period. Pachymeres was a scholar of many parts. He also wrote rhetorical and theological treatises; a summary of Aristotelian philosophy; and a Handbook of the Four Sciences (*Quadrivium*).

BIBL. Bekker 1835; Failler and Laurent 1984; Tannery 1940; Hunger 1978, I: 447–53

Pakourianos, Gregory (*d.* 1086) Grand Domestic

He was a professional soldier who helped pave the way to the throne for the Emperor *Alexios I Komnenos and was rewarded with the rank of Grand Domestic or commander-in-chief. He was of Georgian birth and founded the monastery of Petritzos (now Bačkovo) in Bulgaria in 1083. He personally composed its *typikon* or charter in Greek, though deliberately limiting its intake of monks to Georgian speakers. He died in battle against the Pechenegs in 1086.

BIBL. Beck 1959: 646

Palamas, Gregory (1296–1359) Bishop of Thessalonica and saint

Born and educated in Constantinople, Palamas came of an aristocratic family who originated from Asia Minor. After his father's death in 1303 he continued his studies as a ward of the Emperor *Andronikos II. Under the influence of *Theoleptos of Philadelphia, however, he soon rejected profane scholarship as irrelevant to the spiritual life and became a monk on Mount Athos. There he was instructed in the Hesychast method of solitary prayer and contemplation whose goal was the transfiguration and deification of man. Ordained in 1326, he became abbot of the monastery of Esphigmenou on Mount Athos; but he preferred a more solitary life and retired to his hermitage near Berroia in Macedonia. While there he corresponded with *Barlaam of Calabria about the nature of the Trinity. Barlaam, whom Palamas distrusted as a western scholastic, took to ridiculing the theology and practices of the Hesychast monks. Palamas replied with a manifesto (*Tomos*) signed by many of the leading monks on Athos, followed by his own *Defence of the Holy Hesychasts*, in which he formulated their doctrine. Barlaam was condemned in 1341. But some Byzantine theologians who had joined in his condemnation had doubts about the orthodoxy of Palamas. Gregory *Akindynos, his former friend, turned against him, as did Nikephoros *Gregoras. In the circumstances of civil war between 1341 and 1347 the issue acquired political overtones. Palamas supported the right to the throne of *John (VI) Kantakouzenos. The Patriarch *John XIV therefore arrested and excommunicated him. In 1347, when John VI became Emperor, the tables were turned. The Patriarch was denounced by his bishops and Palamas was restored to favour. In 1350 he was appointed Metropolitan of Thessalonica; and in 1351 a council in Constantinople, presided over by the Emperor and the Patriarch *Kallistos I, reaffirmed that his doctrine of Hesychasm was theologically sound. In 1354 he was taken prisoner by the Turks and spent many months in Asia Minor, an experience which he recorded in letters and in a debate with a Muslim theologian. He returned to Thessalonica in 1355 and died there in November 1359. He was officially canonized by the Orthodox church in 1368. His teaching was quickly condemned as heretical by the western church; but in the east it had a lasting effect on the development of Orthodox theology and spirituality.

BIBL. Meyendorff 1973; Chrestou 1962, 1966, 1970; Meyendorff 1959; Lawrence 1964

Panaretos, Michael (14th century) chronicler of Trebizond
He wrote a *Chronicle* which is a unique source for events in the independent Empire of Trebizond between the years 1204 and 1390. He is otherwise unknown. The extension of the *Chronicle* from 1390 to 1426 appears to be by another author.

BIBL. Lampsides 1958; Hunger 1978, I: 480−1

Paul II Patriarch of Constantinople 641−53
Paul became Patriarch when *Pyrrhos was removed and exiled in October 641, though he too subscribed to the doctrine of the single will of Christ (Monotheletism). *Maximos the Confessor alerted the Pope to this fact, which Paul freely admitted, and the Pope excommunicated him.

BIBL. Grumel 1972: 227−9; Beck 1959: 432−3

Paul IV Patriarch of Constantinople 780−4
Paul came from Cyprus. He was appointed Patriarch by the iconoclast Emperor *Leo IV in February 780 and reluctantly swore to uphold the Emperor's policy. When Leo died, however, and his widow *Eirene assumed the regency, Paul recanted, publicly denounced iconoclasm and urged the convocation of a council of the church. He then abdicated and retired to a monastery in August 784. His successor was *Tarasios.

BIBL. Grumel 1936: 11−12

Paul the Silentiary (6th century) poet
Paul was a contemporary and friend of *Agathias and a member of the literary circle at the court of *Justinian I, where he served as an usher (*silentiarius*). His poetic works are mainly short, occasional pieces, many of them mildly erotic in content. The best known is his Description

(*Ekphrasis*) of the church of St Sophia in Constantinople, with an appendix on its pulpit, written in 1000 hexameter verses.

BIBL. Friedländer 1912; Veh 1977; Hunger 1978, II: 166–74

Peter Patriarch of Constantinople 654–66

In theology Peter adhered to the Monothelete doctrine of the single will of Christ, for all the efforts of Pope Vitalian to bring him round to Orthodox belief; and he went so far as to denounce the pillar of Orthodoxy, *Maximos the Confessor. He was succeeded as Patriarch by Thomas II (667–9).

BIBL. Grumel 1972: 231–3; Beck 1959: 432–3

Petronas (mid 9th century) general

Petronas was a brother of the Empress *Theodora and, together with her other brother *Bardas Caesar, one of her chief counsellors during the minority of her son *Michael III in the years of her widowhood after the death of the Emperor *Theophilos in 842. Petronas was an accomplished soldier and held office as *strategos* or commander of the Thrakesion Theme in western Asia Minor. His triumphant campaigns against the Arabs between the years 856 and 859 turned the tide in favour of Byzantium in the long drawn-out struggle with the Muslims on the eastern frontier.

BIBL. Ostrogorsky 1968: 218, 227

Philanthropenos, Alexios (end of 13th century) general

The Philanthropenos family came to prominence in the middle of the thirteenth century and its members intermarried with other noble families of the time. Alexios was in fact a son of Michael Tarchaneiotes, a nephew of the Emperor *Michael VIII, but he preferred his mother's surname. Born about 1270, he distinguished himself as a soldier, especially in his victorious campaigns against the Turks in western Asia Minor. In 1295 his troops proclaimed him Emperor, enthusiastically supported by the local inhabitants who felt that the government of *Andronikos II in Constantinople had neglected them. The rebellion was suppressed and Alexios was blinded. His experience and reputation were such that in 1324 he was brought out of retirement to help relieve the Turkish blockade of Philadelphia; and ten years later he was sent to besiege Mitylene on Lesbos. He was a friend and correspondent of many of the scholars of his day, among them Nikephoros *Gregoras and Maximos *Planoudes. His wife was a granddaughter of George *Akropolites.

BIBL. Nicol 1972: 131–3, 166; Polemis 1968: 169

Philes, Manuel (*c.* 1275–1346) poet

Philes was for a time court poet of Constantinople and served also on diplomatic missions to Russia and Persia. Later he was disgraced and spent a while in prison. He was more of a versifier than a poet of original talent and his many works are of interest mainly because of their prosopographical and historical content.

BIBL. Miller 1855, 1857; Martini 1900

Philippikos-Bardanes Emperor 711–13

Bardanes was an Armenian general who was proclaimed Emperor on the overthrow of *Justinian II in December 711 and adopted the name of Philippikos. He gained some fame by reviving the heresy of Monotheletism (the single will of Christ) which had been condemned by *Constantine IV in 681, thus antagonizing the Pope. Both Arabs and Bulgars made further inroads into the Empire during his brief reign. Finally the army rebelled and Philippikos was deposed and blinded in June 713. *Anastasios II became Emperor in his place.

BIBL. Jenkins 1966: 59–62

Philostorgius (c. 368–c. 433) church historian

He was born in Cappadocia but spent most of his life in Constantinople. He was a layman and wrote a *Church History* in twelve books, covering the years from 300 to 425. Intended as a continuation of the *Ecclesiastical History* by *Eusebius, it is none the less different in tone. For Philostorgius was of the Arian persuasion and his work is in large measure an apology for Arianism, which had been defined as a heresy at the Council of Nicaea in 325.

BIBL. Quasten 1960: 530–2

Philotheos Kokkinos Patriarch of Constantinople 1353–4; 1364–76

As Bishop of Herakleia Philotheos prepared the document excommunicating the theological opponents of Gregory *Palamas in 1351; and he wrote a vivid description of the sack of Herakleia by Genoese marauders in the same year. He was elected Patriarch in November 1353 and performed the coronation of *Matthew Kantakouzenos as Emperor in February 1354. He was dismissed after the change of rulers in that year, but reinstated in 1363 following the death of the Patriarch *Kallistos I. Although a Hesychast monk and disciple of Gregory Palamas, he had an exalted view of the oecumenical status of his office; and he promoted the idea of a pan-Orthodox alliance of Byzantines and Slavs against the Turks. He was a prolific author, especially of saints' lives.

BIBL. Psevtongas 1981; Kaimakis 1983; Tzamis 1985; Beck 1959: 723–7

Phokas Emperor 602–10

Proclaimed Emperor on the Danube frontier by the mutinous soldiers of *Maurice in November 602, Phokas marched on Constantinople and was crowned over the dead body of his predecessor. He was a cruel tyrant with little talent for government or defence. The Persian king, whom Maurice had befriended, declared war and sent his armies into Asia Minor, reaching Chalcedon on the Bosporos in 608. The withdrawal of Maurice's army from the Danube left the way clear for the Avars and Slavs to descend into Thrace, Macedonia and Greece, though Phokas agreed to pay tribute to the Avars in 604. He antagonized the eastern

105

provinces by his savage persecution of the Monophysite heretics and of the Jews, whom he accused of siding with the Persians. Almost his only friend was Pope Gregory the Great, who enjoyed being told that the church of Rome was the head of all the churches. A column was erected in Rome in honour of Phokas in 608. In Constantinople, however, his reign of terror provoked rioting and rebellion. Deliverance from the tyrant came after an appeal to the Exarch of Carthage, who sent his son *Heraclius with a fleet to the rescue of Constantinople in October 610. Phokas was murdered and Heraclius was crowned as Emperor.

BIBL. Ostrogorsky 1968: 83–6

Phokas, Bardas (*d.* 989) pretender

Bardas Phokas was a nephew of the Emperor *Nikephoros II Phokas, on whose death in 969 he had himself proclaimed Emperor at Caesarea. He was for a time imprisoned by *John I Tzimiskes who had succeeded Nikephoros as Emperor. He came forward again as one of the two chief contenders for the throne when John I died in 976. The other was Bardas *Skleros; and it was against him and his troops that Phokas took command of Constantinople. Skleros was beaten off and took refuge with the Arabs. In 987 the military aristocracy of Asia Minor declared Phokas to be their Emperor in opposition to the young *Basil II. In the same year Skleros also declared himself to be Emperor. But Phokas outwitted him and incarcerated him in a castle on the eastern frontier. He then marched on Constantinople to substantiate his own claim to the crown. He died in the attempt, struck down by a seizure in April 989.

BIBL. Jenkins 1966: 297, 303–7, 309–10

Photios Patriarch of Constantinople 858–67; 877–86

Photios came of an aristocratic Constantinopolitan family and was related to the Patriarch *Tarasios. He was a friend if not a pupil of the learned *Leo the Mathematician and acquired a profound and encyclopaedic knowledge of all branches of scholarship. His parents had suffered under the iconoclast Emperors; but after Orthodoxy had been restored in 843, Photios busied himself as a secretary of state and a teacher. In December 858 he was appointed Patriarch in place of the less tolerant *Ignatios, a move that scandalized the Pope, for Photios was a layman. One consequence was the first official schism between the churches of Rome and Constantinople. The estrangement was aggravated by the rivalry between the churches over the evangelization of the Slavs and Bulgars; for Photios found that Roman missionaries were spreading an adulterated form of the Christian creed which, by the unauthorized addition of a word (*Filioque*), made a muddle of Trinitarian theology. With the change of Emperors in 867, Photios was deposed and excommunicated at a council in 869 attended by the Pope's legates and Ignatios was reinstated. Eight years later, when Ignatios died, the Emperor *Basil I restored Photios to the patriarchate, this time with the consent of Rome; and in 879 another council was held at Constantinople to clear the air. Basil's son *Leo VI reversed this decision and Photios finally ended his days in exile about 893. In later times he was revered as an apostle of the Slavs and Russians and as a champion of Orthodoxy against the extravagant claims and the aberrant theology of the popes. The Orthodox church today regards him as a saint for these reasons. But in a wider world he is remembered as one of the greatest scholars of the Middle Ages.

His main literary compositions are his *Bibliotheca* (*Myriobiblon*) and his *Lexikon*. The former reveals the extent of his famous library, consisting of notes and comments on 280 books which he had read on subjects as diverse as philosophy, theology, history, literature and medical and scientific matters. His *Lexikon* is a dictionary of rare words and phrases in classical Greek literature; for he claimed to have read it all. His other works include homilies, commentaries, polemics, letters and his *Amphilochia*, a collection of 300 chapters on numerous topics, notably theology. He was probably part author of the passage in the *Epanagogē* drawn up by *Basil I which sets forth the ideal relationship of harmonious co-operation between Emperor and Patriarch. It was an ideal that did not commend itself to the extremists in the church and hardly worked with Photios himself.

BIBL. Works *in MPG*, vols. 101–4; Henry 1959–65; Grumel 1936: 72–95, 100–29; Hergenröther 1867–9; Dvornik 1948; Wilson 1983: 89–119

Planoudes, Maximos (*c.* 1255–1305) monk and scholar

He was born at Nikomedia with the name Manuel and studied at Constantinople after 1261. He was a friend of Nikephoros *Choumnos and of the later Patriarch *John XIII Glykys. He became a monk with the name Maximos and ran a school in Constantinople. He also served as secretary to the Emperor *Andronikos II, for whom he went on a diplomatic mission to Venice in 1296. Planoudes was a born scholar with a very wide range of academic expertise, from philology to theology, mathematics and astronomy. Particularly important was his work on editing classical Greek texts, among them Plutarch and Ptolemy. He was also one of the first Byzantine scholars of his day to master Latin; and he translated into Greek many works of St Augustine, Boethius, Caesar, Cato, Cicero and Ovid. He assembled a collection of ancient epigrams, known as the Planudean Anthology. His letters are informative about their author and about a scholar's life in thirteenth-century Byzantium.

BIBL. Treu 1890; Wilson 1983: 230–41

Plethon *see* **Gemistos, George**

Polyeuktos Patriarch of Constantinople 956–70

He was appointed by the Emperor *Constantine VII in succession to the indolent Patriarch *Theophylact. He was an elderly monk and, unlike his predecessor, a stickler for the rigid moral principles of canon law. In August 963 he performed the coronation of Nikephoros II Phokas; but he made the Emperor do penance for his uncanonical marriage to *Theophano, widow of *Romanos II. He disagreed with Nikephoros over the question of church property; and he refused to adopt the Emperor's suggestion that Christian soldiers killed in battle against the infidel should be classed as

martyrs. He imposed strict conditions before he would accept and crown
*John I Tzimiskes as Emperor in 969. He died in February of the following
year. His successors were Basil I Skamandrenos (970–4) and then Antonios
III Stoudites (974–9).

BIBL. Grumel 1936: 225–8

Proclus Patriarch of Constantinople 434–46
Proclus was elected as Patriarch after *Maximian, the successor of the
heretic *Nestorius, died in 434. He had formerly been Bishop of Kyzikos.
He had played no active part in the Council of Ephesos in 431 at which
Nestorius was anathematized, though he was clearly on the side of received
Orthodox belief in the matter of Christ's divine and human natures. He
preached a sermon in the presence of Nestorius praising the Virgin Mary
as the Mother of God (*Theotokos*). He died in July 446.

BIBL. Grumel 1972: 61–74; Quasten 1960: 521–5

Procopius (first half 6th century) historian
Procopius (Prokopios) was born about 500 in Caesarea in Palestine,
where he was thoroughly grounded in rhetoric and then in law, probably
at the law school at Berytus (Beirut). In 527 he became legal adviser and
secretary of *Belisarius, *Justinian's general, and accompanied him on his
victorious campaigns against the Persians in the east, against the Vandals
in North Africa and against the Goths in Italy. By 542, when Belisarius
had fallen out of imperial favour, Procopius was back in Constantinople,
for he describes the plague which then decimated its inhabitants. It is said
that he ended his career as Prefect of the City in 562.
His literary works are: 1. *History of the Wars of Justinian* (*Polemon*; *De
bellis*) in eight books covering the years from 527 to 553, based on his own
observations in the various fields of battle in east and west and on official
documents to which he had access; 2. *The Buildings* (*Peri ktismaton*; *De
aedificiis*), an account of the many public works and monuments erected
throughout the Empire on Justinian's initiative, possibly written at the
Emperor's request; 3. *The Secret History* (*Anekdota*; *Arcana*), published
after his death, a work in marked contrast to his other compositions,
purporting to tell the unvarnished truth about the private lives and public
policies of Justinian and his wife *Theodora, and of Belisarius and his
wife Antonina. As a piece of scurrilous invective and character assassination it has few equals. The identification of the author of the *Secret
History* with the author of the *Wars* and the *Buildings* begs credulity but
leaves no room for doubt. As a serious historian, however, and a literary
stylist modelling himself on Thucydides, Procopius ranks with some of the
greatest writers of Greek antiquity.

BIBL. Haury 1905–13; Dewing and Downey 1914–40; Williamson 1966;
Cameron 1985; Hunger 1978, I: 291–300

Prodromos, Theodore (*c.* 1100–*c.* 1165) poet
Prodromos was the court poet of the Empress *Eirene Doukaina, her

son *John II Komnenos and her grandson *Manuel I, under whom he lost imperial patronage. He became a monk with the name of Nicholas. His literary output was very large. It includes a verse romance in the Hellenistic style called *Rhodanthē and Dosikles*; the *Katomyomachia* or War of the Cats and Mice, a verse drama; a long astronomical poem; some satirical verses; and many occasional poems addressed to his actual or potential patrons and benefactors. A number of begging poems written in vernacular Greek are attributed to Ptochoprodromos, though it remains uncertain whether he and Theodore Prodromos are the same person. Also under the name of Prodromos are several works in prose on philosophy and grammar as well as letters and speeches.

BIBL. Kazhdan 1984c: 87−114; Hunger 1978, II: 127−33

Psellos, Michael (1018−78 or 1096) philosopher and statesman
Born with the name Constantine in Constantinople, Psellos was taught and greatly influenced by John *Mavropous. He rapidly rose to prominence as a gifted intellectual in the secretariate of the Emperors *Michael V and *Constantine IX who, in 1045, made him Professor of Philosophy in the refounded imperial university. When Constantine IX died in 1055 Psellos became a monk with the name of Michael; but he was soon back at court, where he acted as secretary, counsellor, diplomat and sometimes king-maker. He served as prime minister for his former pupil *Michael VII Doukas, at the end of whose dismal reign he was forced to retire to his monastery in Asia Minor.

Psellos owed his success as a power behind the throne to his duplicity and his talent as a courtier. But his learning was prodigious and his literary output enormous, ranging from theology and law to grammar, mathematics, medicine, astrology and demonology. It was in philosophy, however, that he made his greatest contribution, not least to the revival of platonic and neoplatonic studies, a pursuit which he carried almost too far. He was suspected of heresy for subjecting the revealed truths of Christianity to philosophical inquiry, though he was able to refute the charge. He is best known for his *Chronicle* (the *Chronographia*) narrating the reigns of the fourteen Emperors and Empresses from *Basil II in 976 to the accession of *Nikephoros III in 1078 − a work that is more memoirs than history, larded with court gossip and scandal and enlivened with vivid character sketches, but factually reliable and a masterpiece of literature. Among his friends and correspondents were his teacher John Mavropous and the Patriarchs *John VIII Xiphilinos and *Michael I Keroullarios, for each of whom he wrote Epitaphs.

BIBL. Renauld 1926−8; Sewter 1966; Hussey 1937; Wilson 1983: 156−66; Hunger 1978, I: 372−81

Pyrrhos Patriarch of Constantinople 638−41; 654
He succeeded *Sergios I as Patriarch and espoused the creed of Mono-theletism which Sergios had formulated with the approval of the Emperor *Heraclius in 638 in his so-called *Ekthesis*, to the effect that Christ had a single will. Pyrrhos enjoyed the favour of the Empress Martina, widow of

Heraclius, but he was not popular. He was accused along with her of poisoning the Emperor *Constantine III and was banished to North Africa in September 641. In Carthage he held a theological debate with *Maximos the Confessor. He was recalled to the patriarchate in Constantinople for a few months in 654.

BIBL. Grumel 1972: 223–6; Beck 1959: 432

R

Raoulaina, Theodora (*d.* 1300) princess

By birth a Kantakouzenē, Theodora was also connected by descent or by marriage with the families of Palaiologos and Raoul. The Raouls were originally of Norman blood but through intermarriage with noble Byzantine families had become completely hellenized and Orthodox by faith in the thirteenth century. Theodora was an Arsenite, staunchly loyal to the memory of the Patriarch *Arsenios, and an active opponent of the Emperor *Michael VIII's policy of union with the Roman church, for which she suffered persecution. She died as a nun in December 1300. She was a woman of exceptional culture and learning, well read in ancient Greek literature, and possessed of a rich library where she copied manuscripts in her own hand. She refounded the monastery of St Andrew in Krisei in Constantinople and gave shelter to the Patriarch *Gregory II after his resignation in 1289. She was acquainted with many of the leading scholars of her time, such as Nikephoros *Choumnos, Manuel *Holobolos and Maximos *Planoudes.

BIBL. Nicol 1968: no. 14; Fassoulakis 1973: no. 11

Romanos I Lakapenos Emperor 920–44

Romanos was the only son of an Armenian peasant from Lakapē in eastern Anatolia who, like *Basil I, rose to the top through his native ability. Following the death of the Emperor *Alexander and during the regency of the Patriarch *Nicholas (I) Mystikos and the Empress *Zoe, Romanos was *droungarios* or admiral of the fleet. The Empire was in mortal danger from attack by Symeon of Bulgaria. It needed a man of action. Romanos resolved to make himself regent for the young *Constantine VII. He had the approval of the Patriarch and in 919, having led a squadron into the palace harbour at Constantinople, he evicted Zoe, posed as the protector of the lawful Emperor Constantine and gave him his own daughter Helena as a child bride. In September 920 he was made Caesar and in December he was crowned, ostensibly as junior Emperor until his son-in-law came of age. For the next seven years Symeon of Bulgaria devastated Byzantine territory and vainly assaulted Constantinople. Romanos, secure behind the city's impregnable walls, allowed him to exhaust himself and encouraged his other enemies to attack Bulgaria from the rear. He won the contest not by war but by patience, cunning and diplomacy; and in May 927 Symeon died leaving his country bankrupt and ruined. His son Peter signed a treaty with Romanos and married his granddaughter, Maria Lakapenē.

Romanos nominated three of his four sons as his co-Emperors; his fourth he made Patriarch when Nicholas Mystikos died. But he held to the principle that the senior Emperor of all was the heir of the Macedonian dynasty, Constantine VII. On his eastern frontier his armies, led by the gifted Armenian general John *Kourkouas, continued the reconquest of territory from the Arabs, capturing Melitene and advancing across the Euphrates as far as Nisibis. In 944 he made a new commercial agreement with Prince Igor of Kiev after the Russians had attacked Constantinople. He was the first Emperor to detect a spreading cancer in his own society which was partly a result of its growing prosperity. Wealthy landowners were buying out the small farmers on whom the military and economic structure of the provinces depended. He sought to arrest this dangerous development by legislation.

Romanos was brought to a tragic end through the machinations of his sons, Stephen and Constantine, who resented his preference for Constantine VII as heir-presumptive. In December 944 they had their father arrested and deported to an island, where he died as a monk four years later. Public opinion, however, was wholly on the side of the true heir of the Macedonian house, Constantine VII, who had little difficulty in rounding them up and sending them into exile.

BIBL. Runciman 1929; Ostrogorsky 1968: 264–79

Romanos II Emperor 959–63

Aged twenty-one when his father *Constantine VII died in November 959, Romanos II inherited an Empire that was strong and flourishing. His father had left him abundant advice on how to administer and protect it. But he was a pleasure-loving young man who preferred, as Edward Gibbon put it, to consume his time 'in strenuous idleness'. He was fortunate to be surrounded by statesmen and soldiers of talent. He dismissed his father's counsellor, the chamberlain Basil, and gave that office to another able if unscrupulous eunuch, Joseph Bringas. As commander-in-chief of his armed forces he relied upon the experience of the great general *Nikephoros (II) Phokas, the future Emperor; and it was Nikephoros who brought glory to his master's reign by reconquering Crete and capturing Aleppo from the Arabs. Three years before his accession Romanos had defied his father's wishes by marrying a lady of lowly origin called *Theophano. When he died prematurely in March 963, Theophano was left in charge of his two young sons, the legitimate heirs of the Macedonian dynasty, *Basil (II) and *Constantine VIII.

BIBL. Diehl 1906a: 217–43; Jenkins 1966: 268–77

Romanos III Argyros Emperor 1028–34

Born in 968, Romanos came of a well-established senatorial family in Constantinople. In 1028 he was Prefect of the City. In the same year he was obliged by the dying Emperor *Constantine VIII to divorce his wife and to marry the Emperor's sister *Zoe. He thus became Emperor as Romanos III. Zoe, though in her fifties, soon found him to be a pompous and pedantic old man and amused herself with a peasant boy called *Michael (IV). Romanos died in his bath in April 1034, assisted on his way by Zoe's servants. He had delusions of grandeur which were not substantiated by two military campaigns in Syria. In the civil administration he perverted the economic reforms of his predecessors by farming out the taxes, thus making life easier for the large landowners who could afford to keep the taxmen at bay and harder for the small holders who turned for protection to the rich and powerful.

BIBL. Vannier 1975: no. 12

Romanos IV Diogenes Emperor 1068−71

After the ineffectual reign of *Constantine X the Empire badly needed a soldier on the throne, a fact which the military quickly made clear. Constantine's widow *Eudokia Makrembolitissa was persuaded to marry one of their number, Romanos Diogenes, who was crowned Emperor in January 1068. Romanos was an experienced general; but the rot had gone too far and his reign was marked, and terminated, by two of the worst military disasters that Byzantium had ever suffered. Rightly judging the Seljuq Turks to be the greatest threat, Romanos went to war against them. But his army was scratched together from heterogeneous mercenaries; and his third campaign ended in overwhelming defeat at Manzikert in Armenia in August 1071. His army was annihilated. He himself was taken captive by the Turkish Sultan. He bought his freedom and returned to Constantinople only to find that he had been deposed *in absentia* and that his throne had been usurped by the son of Constantine X, *Michael VII, the protégé of Michael *Psellos. Romanos was arrested, blinded and sent into exile where he died in 1072. The other disaster of his reign occurred in the same year as that at Manzikert. In April 1071 the Normans captured Bari, the last Byzantine stronghold in Italy. Neither of these defeats was the fault of Romanos IV. They, and the disintegrating state of the Empire, could be blamed on the civil aristocracy of the capital, who were brought back to power in the person of his successor, Michael VII.

BIBL. Jenkins 1966: 368−74; Ostrogorsky 1968: 344−6

Romanos Melodos (first half 6th century) hymnographer

Romanos was the son of a Jewish family in Syria. He became a deacon at Berytus (Beirut) and, in the reign of the Emperor *Anastasius I, came to Constantinople as a priest. He was a prolific hymn-writer; and he perfected if he did not invent the form of hymn-sermons with refrains, known as *kontakia*, which came to him allegedly through divine inspiration. The most famous are his Christmas Hymn to the Virgin and the *Akathistos Hymn*, which is still sung in the Orthodox church. Because of his fame many hymns were falsely attributed to him. He was canonized by the Byzantine church.

BIBL. Maas and Trypanis 1963 and 1970; Grosdidier de Matons 1964−81; Beck 1959: 425−8

S

Sergios I Patriarch of Constantinople 610—38

When the Emperor *Heraclius, in despair, contemplated moving his capital from Constantinople to Carthage, it was the Patriarch Sergios who dissuaded him. When the Emperor went off to his Persian wars in 622 he appointed Sergios as regent; and during the combined Avar and Persian siege of Constantinople in 626—7 Sergios kept up the morale of the citizens. He sought to bring peace in the church by proposing another compromise between the errors of the Monophysites and the truth of Orthodoxy, to the effect that the human and divine natures of Christ had one energy. This he later modified to a 'single will' (Monotheletism) and formulated it in a document issued by Heraclius under the name of the *Ekthesis*. It was approved by Pope Honorius I and taken up by the Patriarch *Pyrrhos who succeeded when Sergios died in December 638. In 680—1, however, the Sixth Oecumenical Council called by the Emperor *Constantine IV found the doctrine enshrined in the *Ekthesis* to be false; and Sergios, along with Pope Honorius, was anathematized.

BIBL. Grumel 1972; 211—22; Ostrogorsky 1968: 107—9

Sergios II Patriarch of Constantinople 1001—19

Sergios succeeded *Sisinnios II after a short interval. During his patriarchate the Pope's name ceased, perhaps inadvertently, to be commemorated in church services in Constantinople; and it was later supposed that the origin of the schism between the eastern and western churches dated to the year 1009, the year of the death of Pope John XVIII. Sergios was succeeded by the Patriarch *Eustathios.

BIBL. Grumel 1936: 239—44; Runciman 1955: 32—4

Sisinnius I Patriarch of Constantinople 426—7

Sisinnius was a priest of Constantinople who was raised to the patriarchate in February 426. His only known act as Patriarch was to consecrate as Bishop of Kyzikos, *Proclus, who was later to succeed him. His immediate successor was *Nestorius.

BIBL. Grumel 1972: 37—9

Sisinnios II Patriarch of Constantinople 996—8

The Emperor *Basil II set little store by his Patriarchs. Indeed, after the death of Nicholas II Chrysoberges (979—91), the patriarchal throne was vacant for more than four years. In April 996, however, Sisinnios was appointed. He was a layman and a physician, but he was also interested in canon law. In 997 he issued a statement on the legal impediments to marriage; and he composed some eulogies of saints.

BIBL. Grumel 1936: 231—9; Beck 1959: 88—9, 554

Skleros, Bardas (*c*. 920−91) pretender

Skleros came of a distinguished Armenian family of soldiers and was a leading light of the military aristocracy of Asia Minor in the tenth century. He proved himself as a commander under the Emperor *John I Tzimiskes in battle against the Russians who had invaded Thrace in 970−1. When John died and the young *Basil II came to the throne in 976, Skleros was commander-in-chief of the eastern armies. His sister, Maria Skleraina, had been the first wife of John Tzimiskes. Skleros saw himself as successor to the throne. He was not alone. A rival contender was Bardas *Phokas and it was he who commanded Constantinople. In 979 Skleros, though acknowledged as Emperor by his troops, was driven back from the capital and took refuge with the Arab Caliph. In 987 he made a second bid for power and was again proclaimed Emperor. But Phokas outwitted him by proposing to divide the Empire with him and then having him arrested and confined to a castle on the eastern frontier. When Phokas died during his march on Constantinople in 989, Skleros found his freedom. But he was elderly and going blind. The Emperor Basil II, whom he had tried to dislodge, treated him with tactful clemency, allowing him to retain all his properties and privileges, save for the title of Emperor. He died in March 991.

BIBL. Seibt 1976: 29−58; Jenkins 1966: 297, 303−7, 310−11

Skylitzes, John (second half 11th century) historian

He was the author of a *Historical Synopsis* covering the years from 811 to 1057, a chronicle of events rather than a narrative history, though derived from some sources that are now lost. It was for long known only from the copy of its later stages made by George *Kedrenos. Skylitzes seems to have written it while still holding public office as *droungarios* or commander of the watch, which he occupied in 1092. A twelfth-century manuscript of his work, now in Madrid, is profusely illustrated. A sequel known as *Scylitzes Continuatus*, chronicling events from 1057 to 1079, is probably from his own pen.

BIBL. Thurn 1973; Tsolakis 1968; Grabar and Manoussacas 1979

Socrates (*c*. 380−*c*. 450) church historian

Socrates, called Scholasticus, was a lawyer in Constantinople who wrote an *Ecclesiastical History* in seven books, covering political as well as religious events from 305 to 439. Each book is devoted to the reign of one Emperor, from *Constantine I to *Theodosius II. He was the first layman to attempt a history of the church and, though he was much indebted to his predecessor *Eusebius, the later part of his work is based on many ecclesiastical and imperial documents as well as eye-witness accounts.

BIBL. Bright 1878; Quasten 1960: 532−4

Sozomen (*c*. 400−*c*. 450) church historian

Born near Gaza in Palestine, Sozomen (Sozomenus) became a lawyer in Constantinople and composed a *History of the Church* in nine books

115

from its origins to the year 439. He dedicated it to the Emperor *Theodosius II. The first and last parts are lost and the existing text covers the years from 324 to 425. He clearly drew on the *Ecclesiastical History* of his older contemporary *Socrates; but his literary style is self-consciously superior and he was more aware of western sources. He is a unique authority for many events in early church history.

BIBL. Bidez and Hansen 1960; Quasten 1960: 534–6

Sphrantzes, George (1401–*c*. 1478) historian

Sphrantzes (not Phrantzes) was a civil servant in Constantinople from 1418 and a much experienced imperial ambassador. He became prime minister of the Emperor *Constantine XI Palaiologos and was captured by the Turks when they fought their way into Constantinople in 1453. He escaped to the Morea and then to Corfu, where he died as a monk. The *Chronicle* which he wrote (known as the *Chronicon minus*) covers the years from 1401 to 1477 and is very informative about events leading up to the fall of Constantinople and the aftermath. He was inclined to blame the union of the eastern and western churches as a major factor in the tragedy. An expanded version of the work, known as the *Chronicon maius* and running from 1258 to 1481, was composed under the name of Phrantzes by one Makarios Melissenos in the sixteenth century.

BIBL. Grecu 1966; Philippides 1980; Hunger 1978; 494–9

Stavrakios Emperor 811

Stavrakios was the son and co-Emperor of *Nikephoros I and married Theophano, a relative of the Empress *Eirene. He was mortally wounded in the Bulgarian campaign in July 811 when his father was killed. He escaped from the battlefield but reigned as Emperor in Constantinople for only a few weeks before handing over to his brother-in-law *Michael I. He died in January 812.

BIBL. Treadgold 1988: 174–7

Stephen I Patriarch of Constantinople 886–93

Stephen was the fourth and youngest son of the Emperor *Basil I. His brother *Leo VI made him Patriarch in December 886 as soon as he had disposed of the Patriarch *Photios. Stephen was then nineteen years of age. He died in May 893 after a not very memorable tenure. His successor was *Antonios II.

BIBL. Grumel 1936: 130–1

Strategopoulos, Alexios (13th century) general

As an officer in the army of the Emperor *Michael VIII Palaiologos, he took part in the battle against the Despot *Michael II of Epiros and his allies at Pelagonia in 1259. He was celebrated for his opportunistic entry into Constantinople in July 1261 and the consequent liberation of the city from the Latins. He was less successful in his later campaigns in Greece where he was taken prisoner and shipped as a hostage to Italy.

BIBL. Nicol 1972: 37–40, 45; Nicol 1957: 186–92

Symeon Archbishop of Thessalonica 1416–29

Appointed Metropolitan of Thessalonica in 1416 or 1417, Symeon was there during the difficult years from 1423 when the city was controlled by the Venetians and constantly under siege by the Turks, although he died before the Turks conquered it in 1430. His writings on liturgical and theological themes have long been known. He was also the author of homilies, letters and a uniquely informative work on events in Thessalonica in the years from 1387 to 1427 in the form of an oration to the city's patron Saint Demetrios.

BIBL. Balfour 1979

Symeon Metaphrastes (second half 10th century) hagiographer

Symeon served as Logothete (Chancellor) under the Emperors *Nikephoros II, *John I and *Basil II and became a monk towards the end of his life. He died before the close of the tenth century. He was celebrated and later canonized for his long and painstaking labour as a translator (*metaphrastēs*) of hagiographical texts. For he converted the homely and popular versions of numerous martyrologies and saints' lives from colloquial into classical Greek, sometimes rewriting them in the process and making them sophisticated literary compositions more acceptable to educated readers. His version of the Menologion or Calendar of feasts month by month became the standard hagiographical text of the Orthodox church.

It is possible, though not proven, that he was the author, or part author, of a *Chronicle* attributed to one Symeon Magistros and Logothete, about whom nothing else is known.

BIBL. Beck 1959: 570–5; Hunger 1978; I: 354–7

Symeon the New Theologian (949–1022) monk and saint

Symeon came of a wealthy Paphlagonian family who intended that he should serve at the imperial court. But he came under the influence of a monk, Symeon Stylites, in the monastery of Stoudios in Constantinople, and he was greatly taken by the mystical writings of *John Climax. He became a monk and then abbot of the monastery of St Mamas in Constantinople, which he restored and where he gained fame as a disciplinarian, a reformer and a mystic. His reforms seemed too rigid for his monks. His emphasis on the individualism of the holy man and his personal relationship with God seemed dangerous to the church authorities with whom, for all his sanctity, Symeon was frequently at odds. He was exiled to a little monastery on the Asiatic side of the Bosporos which he restored and where he died in 1022. Thirty years later the Patriarch *Michael Keroullarios approved the transfer of his relics to Constantinople and he was canonized by the Byzantine church.

Symeon's many writings were collected by his disciple *Niketas Stethatos, who also wrote his *Life*. They include his *Catecheses* or addresses to his monks, his *Hymns* and his *Theological* and *Ethical Treatises*. They are perhaps the most significant and formative works of Byzantine mystical literature and profoundly affected the later development of Orthodox Christian thought.

BIBL. Krivocheine and Paramelle 1963−5; Darrouzès 1966−7; Kambylis 1976; Hausherr and Horn 1928

Synadenos, Theodore (*d.* 1345) soldier

From 1320 Synadenos was one of the chief partisans of *Andronikos III Palaiologos in his conflict with his grandfather *Andronikos II. He was a friend of *Michael IX and of *John (VI) Kantakouzenos. After 1328, when the conflict ended, Andronikos III made him Prefect of the city of Constantinople. In 1330 he was governor of Mesembria on the Black Sea; and in 1337 he was appointed to govern Arta in Epiros, where he was imprisoned by rebels. In 1340 he was made governor of Thessalonica, from where he was evicted by the revolutionaries known as the Zealots in 1342. He changed sides in the civil war between John Kantakouzenos and the regency in Constantinople and died probably in 1345. His mother, Theodora Palaiologina, founded the convent of Good Hope (*Bebaia Elpis*) in Constantinople, in whose charter Synadenos is portrayed.

BIBL. Polemis 1968: nos. 193, 196; Nicol 1972; 163−8, 185−7, 200−1

Syrgiannes Palaiologos Philanthropenos (*d.* 1334) soldier and politician

Syrgiannes was the son of a Mongol who had entered the service of the Emperor *Michael VIII. His mother was Eugenia Palaiologina, a cousin of the Emperor *Andronikos II, and related to the family of Kantakouzenos. He was a devious and ambitious man. Having been a friend and supporter of *Andronikos III at the start of the civil war that broke out in 1321, he went over to the enemy camp. He was suspected of plotting and put in prison. When the war was over in 1328 *John (VI) Kantakouzenos secured his release and sent him to govern Thessalonica, where again he was accused of intrigue and detained. He escaped and, after many adventures, gained the ear of the King of Serbia, who encouraged him to attack Thessalonica. The danger was averted by an officer of Andronikos III who murdered Syrgiannes in August 1334.

BIBL. Nicol 1984: 77−9, 83−92, 102−4

Syropoulos, Sylvester (15th century) churchman and writer

A deacon and official of the Great Church in Constantinople, Syropoulos went with the Patriarch *Joseph II to the Council of Ferrara-Florence in 1438−9, at which the union of the eastern and western churches was proclaimed. His *Memoirs* of that Council, though hardly impartial, form one of the principal sources for its day-to-day proceedings.

BIBL. Laurent 1971b

T

Tarasios Patriarch of Constantinople 784—806

He was a layman of moderate views, head of the imperial chancery and secretary of state to the widowed Empress *Eirene. It was she who persuaded him to take over the patriarchate when *Paul IV resigned in 784. As Patriarch he presided over the Council at Nicaea in 787 at which iconoclasm was declared to be a heresy, in accordance with the plans of the Empress. The Pope sent delegates to the Council; and the Orthodox church to this day regards it as the Seventh and last truly Oecumenical Council of the church. The statesmanship of Tarasios was tested again in the matter of the scandalous divorce and remarriage of Eirene's son *Constantine VI, which he countenanced despite the fanatical opposition of the less tolerant churchmen and monks led by *Theodore of Stoudios. He died in February 806 and was succeeded by the Patriarch *Nikephoros I. His *Life* was written by his pupil, *Ignatios the Deacon, later Bishop of Nicaea; and the church honoured him as a saint.

BIBL. Grumel 1936: 12—22; Hussey 1986; 44—52; Beck 1959: 489, 511—12

Tarchaneiotes, Michael Glabas (*d. c.* 1305) general

The houses of Glabas and Tarchaneiotes were prominent among the landowning military families that came to the fore in the thirteenth century. Michael belonged to both. As a soldier in the service first of the Emperor *Michael VIII and then of *Andronikos II he fought in Bulgaria and in Serbia, rose to the rank of *protostrator* or commander, and was made governor of the western provinces with his headquarters at Thessalonica. His military exploits were extolled in a long poem by his friend Manuel *Philes, the court poet of Andronikos II. Michael advertised his piety by the endowment or restoration of several charitable institutions; and his name is especially associated with the monastery of the Virgin Pammakaristos in Constantinople, in whose side chapel he was buried about 1305.

BIBL. Belting, Mango and Mouriki 1978; 11—19

Tatikios (11th to 12th century) soldier

Of humble birth, Tatikios was the son of a Turkish servant of John Komnenos, father of the Emperor *Alexios I, in whose service he became a trusted military commander. He was detailed to conduct the armies of the First Crusade across Asia Minor and to ensure that their leaders respected the oaths that they had sworn to the Emperor. He led them as far as Antioch; but during the siege of the city in February 1098 he left them, taking his troops with him, an action which the crusaders later condemned as calculated treachery.

BIBL. Runciman 1951: 188—93, 300—1; Angold 1984: 140—1

Theodora Empress 527–48

Theodora was the wife of *Justinian I who became Emperor in 527 when she was about twenty-seven years old. She is said to have been the daughter of a bear-keeper in the Hippodrome at Constantinople. She led a colourful life as an actress before going to Libya and Alexandria, where she seems to have come under Christian influence. She certainly had an illegitimate child. Most of the lurid tales of her early life, however, derive from the poison pen of *Procopius in his *Secret History*; and there was the added scandal that she was and remained a Monophysite by faith and so a heretic. She was physically attractive and mentally astute; and as an actress she enjoyed playing the part of a *grande dame*. She added drama to the court ceremonial of Constantinople. Justinian was infatuated with her and promoted her in social rank so that, from being his mistress, she could become his wife. Two years later, when he came to the throne, she was crowned as his Augusta or Empress. Thenceforth her name appeared along with that of her husband in nearly all the laws enacted during her lifetime. Her influence on him was enormous. During the Nika riot in Constantinople in 532, when Justinian panicked and was about to leave the city, Theodora shamed him into staying. Her hand is to be seen in the disgrace of *John of Cappadocia, whom she loathed; and she befriended Antonina, the wife of *Belisarius, when he was in trouble. She never abjured her Monophysite belief and even sheltered her persecuted co-religionists in the palace. She was also noted for her championship of the legal rights of women, especially in the matters of under-age prostitution and divorce. When she died of cancer in June 548, Justinian degenerated into a lonely old man incapable of new ideas.

BIBL. Diehl 1904; Browning 1971

Theodora Empress 830–57

Theodora married the Emperor *Theophilos and was crowned as his Empress in June 830. After his death in 842 she headed a council of regents for her infant son *Michael III. Its leading members were her favourite minister of state, the Logothete *Theoktistos, and her brother *Bardas. Theodora was convinced that her late husband's policy of icono-clasm was wrong and that the veneration of sacred images must be restored without delay. The Patriarch *John VII Grammatikos would not agree and had to be dismissed. His place was taken by *Methodios. A council of bishops was then convened in Constantinople at which it was simply proclaimed that iconoclasm was over and that the rulings of the Seventh Oecumenical Council of 787 were reaffirmed. On the first Sunday of Lent in March 843 the end of heresy and the Feast of Orthodoxy were celebrated in St Sophia. This was Theodora's major achievement; but it was her adviser Theoktistos who saw to it that the triumph of Orthodoxy was not accompanied by a wave of retribution and persecution of the heterodox. As an act of devotion to the memory of her husband Theophilos, Theodora persuaded the hierarchy to omit his name from the list of anathematized iconoclast Emperors. When her son Michael came of age he found ways of asserting his own imperial authority by undermining the power of her counsellors. Theoktistos was murdered in 855. Two years later Theodora retired from the palace with her daughters and entered a convent, where she died in February 867. She was canonized as a saint by the Orthodox church.

BIBL. Diehl 1906a: 133—56; Ostrogorsky 1968: 219—21; Jenkins 1966: 154—60

Theodora Empress 1042; 1055—6

She was a daughter of the Emperor *Constantine VIII and sister of the Empress *Zoe. She became a nun and kept out of the limelight until 1042, when she was called upon to share the throne with her twice-widowed sister following the deposition of the Emperor *Michael V. The sisters were elderly and they hated the sight of each other. Their joint rule lasted only until Zoe found herself a third husband, *Constantine (IX) Monomachos. Zoe died in 1050; and when Constantine IX died five years later, Theodora, who had never married, reigned as sole ruler and last of the line of the Macedonian dynasty which had been founded by the Emperor *Basil I in 867. She died in August 1056 aged about seventy, having named as her successor a member of the civilian aristocracy of Constantinople, *Michael VI.

BIBL. Jenkins 1966: 339, 344, 361—3, 371

Theodore I Laskaris Emperor at Nicaea 1208—22

Theodore was born about 1175 and married Anna, daughter of the Emperor *Alexios III Angelos. With his brother Constantine Laskaris he played a notable part in the defence of Constantinople against the Fourth Crusade in 1204. But when the city was taken by the Latins he fled across the Bosporos to Asia Minor. There he assembled the nucleus of a resistance movement which developed into a Byzantine government in exile based on the city of Nicaea. In 1208 he was crowned as Emperor by the Patriarch *Michael IV. His Empire in exile had to fight to survive, against the Seljuq Turks, against the crusaders and against *Alexios Komnenos, who had set up a rival Greek Empire at Trebizond on the Black Sea. In 1211 Theodore defeated the Seljuq Sultan and captured the ex-Emperor *Alexios III Angelos, who had incited the Sultan to war against his upstart son-in-law. In 1214 he coerced the Latin Emperor of Constantinople, Henry of Flanders, to respect the frontiers and the autonomy of the Empire of Nicaea. He went on to annex parts of the rival Empire of Trebizond.

The liberation of Constantinople from the Latins was always Theodore's objective. To gain a foothold in the door of the city he took as his third wife Mary of Courtenay, sister of the Latin Emperor Robert; and, to win the confidence of the popes, he initiated discussions at Nicaea about the reunion of the eastern and western churches. He offered his daughter Eudokia in marriage to the Emperor Robert; and in 1219 he arranged a five-year commercial agreement with the Venetians granting their merchants free trade in his dominions. He died in 1222. He had no sons but by general consensus he was succeeded by his son-in-law *John III Doukas

Batatzes. Theodore left a stable economy, administration and defence on which his successors at Nicaea could build pending the return of the Byzantine government to Constantinople.

BIBL. Gardner 1912; Angold 1975

Theodore II Laskaris Emperor at Nicaea 1254—8

Theodore II was the only child of *John III Doukas Batatzes whom he succeeded as Emperor at Nicaea in November 1254. He married Helena, daughter of the Bulgarian Tsar John Asen II. He was more of a scholar and a theologian than a soldier or statesman, and his health was poor. He was morbidly suspicious of the aristocracy of Nicaea whom his father had enriched; and he chose his officers of state from men of lower rank whom he could trust. He made his peace with the Seljuq Turks and with the Bulgarians; but he antagonized his enemy in Greece, *Michael II, Despot in Epiros, whose son married one of his daughters. The Despot Michael saw himself as a rival claimant for the possession of Constantinople, which was still in Latin hands; and Theodore's hesitancy and misjudgment gave Michael the scope to plan the revival of the Empire at Thessalonica, the first step on the way to Constantinople. Theodore II died in August 1258 leaving his successor to contend with this problem. His son, *John IV Laskaris, was only eight years old and the appointment of a regent led to bloodshed, out of which *Michael VIII Palaiologos emerged as Emperor. In his short reign, however, Theodore did much for Greek scholarship. He founded a school of higher education at Nicaea and wrote theological, philosophical and rhetorical works. Scholars such as George *Akropolites and Nikephoros *Blemmydes were among his friends and protégés; and his extensive correspondence survives.

BIBL. Pappadopoulos 1908; Angold 1975

Theodore II Eirenikos Patriarch of Constantinople 1214—16

A teacher of philosophy in Constantinople before the Latin conquest in 1204, he became the second of the Patriarchs in exile at Nicaea after the death of *Michael IV Autoreianos in 1214.

BIBL. Laurent 1971a: 23—5

Theodore Komnenos Doukas Emperor at Thessalonica 1224—30

Theodore was a half-brother and successor of *Michael I Komnenos Doukas, independent ruler of Epiros in north-western Greece after the Fourth Crusade in 1204. Theodore's ambition was to make Epiros a base for the reconquest from the Latins first of Thessalonica and then of Constantinople. In 1217 he attracted notoriety by capturing the Latin Emperor Peter of Courtenay who was marching east overland through Epiros. Then in a series of victorious campaigns he drove the Latins out of Thessaly, beat back the Bulgarians in western Macedonia and encircled Thessalonica. In December 1224 his troops entered the city; and there, about 1227, Theodore was crowned as Emperor of the Romans by the Archbishop of Ochrida, Demetrios *Chomatianos. His coronation was a direct challenge to the Emperor in exile at Nicaea; but he was fully supported by all the bishops and administrators whom he had created in Epiros. Another Byzantine Empire in exile had been born at Thessalonica. It remained to expel the Latins from Constantinople. Theodore was on his way to achieving this when he was defeated and captured by the Bulgarians in March 1230. Much of his infant Empire was overrun, though his brother Manuel was left to act the part of Emperor in Thessalonica.

Theodore was blinded during his captivity in Bulgaria but he was allowed to return to Thessalonica in 1237, where he evicted Manuel and installed his own son John as Emperor. He was finally humiliated by his rival at Nicaea, *John III Batatzes, who marched on Thessalonica in 1242 and forced John to renounce his imperial title. Four years later he annexed Thessalonica to the Empire of Nicaea. Theodore, blind and elderly, was not yet beaten. He fired the ambition of his nephew *Michael II, who had inherited Epiros, to return to the attack and revive the lost Empire of Thessalonica. Not until 1253 did the Emperor of Nicaea bring Michael to terms. His troops then arrested Theodore and took him away to end his tumultuous career in prison in Asia Minor.

He married Maria of the family of Petraliphas and had two daughters and two sons, John entitled Emperor and Demetrios entitled Despot.

BIBL. Nicol 1957 and 1984

Theodore I Palaiologos Despot of the Morea 1393—1407
Theodore I was the fourth son of the Emperor *John V Palaiologos who appointed him as Despot at Mistra when *Manuel Kantakouzenos died in 1380. His appointment was contested by one of the two sons of *Matthew Kantakouzenos and not secured until 1383. Theodore extended the frontiers of the Despotate of the Morea at the expense of the Latin Principality of Achaia; and he was in alliance with the Florentine Duke of Athens, Nerio Acciajuoli, whose daughter he married. But he incurred the wrath of the Turks who twice devastated the Morea. He died childless in 1407; and his brother *Manuel (II) composed an eloquent funeral oration for him.

BIBL. Zakythinos 1975; Runciman 1980: 56—66; Chrysostomides 1985

Theodore II Palaiologos Despot of the Morea 1407—43
He was the second son of the Emperor *Manuel II who appointed him to succeed his uncle *Theodore I Palaiologos as Despot at Mistra in 1407. It was during his reign that his father, on a visit to Greece in 1415, ordered the construction of the Hexamilion wall across the Isthmus of Corinth in a vain attempt to keep the Turks out of the Morea. In 1421 he married Cleope Malatesta of Rimini, who shared his enthusiasm for making his court at Mistra a centre for scholars and philosophers, among them George *Gemistos Plethon. The last of the Latins were driven out of the Morea while he was Despot; but it was ravaged by the Turks who broke through the Hexamilion wall in 1423. In 1443 Theodore exchanged his Despotate for a principality in Thrace, where he died in June 1448. His place at Mistra was taken by his brother *Constantine (XI) Palaiologos.

BIBL. Zakythinos 1975; Runciman 1980: 66–76

Theodore of Stoudios (759–826) monk, theologian and saint

Theodore Stoudites was born and educated in Constantinople before becoming a monk in the monastery of Sakkoudion in Bithynia, where he succeeded his uncle Plato as abbot in 794. In 798 he and his monks moved to the then deserted monastery of Stoudios in Constantinople, which he transformed into a model for others to imitate. He expressed his view on the ideals and the practice of the monastic life in his *Catecheses* or precepts addressed to his monks, of whom there were about 700. He was a fervent and outspoken adversary of iconoclasm and of imperial interference in ecclesiastical affairs. He was banished for a while for condemning the marriage of the Emperor *Constantine VI to his mistress in 795. When the Emperor *Leo V reintroduced iconoclasm in 815, Theodore, who had suffered a second term of exile for defying his Patriarch, was banished for a third time. Yet nothing could prevent him from pouring out propaganda for what he believed to be the truth of Orthodox belief and he died in exile in November 826. About 550 of his letters survive and are exceptionally informative about the ecclesiastical, political and social life of his day. He died before his theological cause had triumphed. His political cause, the freedom of the church from dictation by the state, was never fully won in Byzantium. But his monastic reforms had a lasting effect; and the Stoudite ideal of coenobitic monasticism was adopted by many later foundations, not least on Mount Athos. He is revered as a saint by both eastern and western churches.

BIBL. Works *in MPG*, vol. 99; Gradner 1905; Beck 1959: 491–5

Theodoret of Cyrus (*c.* 393–*c.* 458) theologian and church historian

Theodoret was a monk who in 423 became Bishop of Cyrus (Kyros or Cyrrhus) near his birthplace of Antioch. In his theology he was suspected of over-emphasizing the humanity of Christ and of being a follower of his colleague *Nestorius. In 449 at a council at Ephesos he was accused of heresy and exiled. The council, which was packed with his opponents, was later known as the 'Robber Synod'. Theodoret appealed to Pope Leo the Great in Rome and was recalled to his see by the Emperor *Marcian. The Council of Chalcedon in 451 reinstated him on certain conditions; and he died about 458. He was in a sense a mediator between the extreme theological positions of his contemporaries. He wrote thirty-five works, mostly apologetic and dogmatic in nature, but including an *Ecclesiastical History* in five books. It covers the period from 325 to 428 and, in part, up to 434, in continuation of the similar work by *Eusebius.

BIBL. Scheidweiler 1954; Quasten 1960: 536–54

Theodosius I Emperor 379–95

After the disastrous defeat of the army by the Visigoths at Adrianople in August 378 and the death of the Emperor *Valens, Theodosius was raised to the purple. He was a Spaniard with a proven record as a military commander; and in January 379 the western Emperor Gratian appointed him as his co-Emperor to govern the eastern part of the Empire. He made a treaty with the Goths on his northern frontier and enlisted them as *foederati* or allies, settling them on imperial territory and granting them autonomy and tax exemption in return for their military service. Himself a Christian who accepted the creed defined at the Council of Nicaea in 325, Theodosius exercised his prerogative as a Roman Emperor by declaring that no other form of Christian belief was permissible. In 381 the church upheld his definition of right belief or Orthodoxy at a council of Bishops which he convened at Constantinople, later called the Second Oecumenical Council of the Christian church. Orthodox Christianity was henceforth the state religion of the Roman Empire. Pagan cults, which Theodosius had once tolerated, had to be proscribed. The reaction in Italy and the west was political as well as religious. When the western Emperor Valentinian died in May 392 a pagan usurper was put up to succeed him. Theodosius had to take an army to Italy. He succeeded in asserting his authority and so became sole ruler of a reunited Empire. He died at Milan in January 395, having nominated his elder son *Arcadius as Emperor in the east and his younger son Honorius in the west. His mortal remains were transferred from Italy to rest in the church of the Holy Apostles in Constantinople.

BIBL. King 1961; Lippold 1968

Theodosius II Emperor 408–50

Theodosius was barely seven years old when his father *Arcadius died in January 408. At first he was under the regency of Anthemius, his father's Praetorian Prefect, but after 414 under that of his sister Pulcheria, who assumed the imperial title of Augusta. He was a scholarly man, content to leave government to his ministers and warfare to his generals. He was also dominated by his forceful wife Athenais-Eudocia, daughter of a pagan professor at Athens. His armies successfully held their own against the Persians; but they could not prevent the Vandals from occupying North Africa. During his reign the structure of the Roman Empire in the west broke down irretrievably. Rome was sacked by Alaric and his Goths in 410. In the east total collapse before the barbarian incursions was only averted with difficulty. The Huns led by Attila wrought havoc in the Balkan peninsula in the 440s despite Theodosius's attempts to mollify them by appeasement and bribery. Only when they could find no more plunder in eastern Europe did they turn their attentions to Italy. To defend Constantinople from the fate that had befallen Rome Theodosius commissioned Anthemius to build the massive land and sea fortifications generally known as the Theodosian walls. He left his own marks on education and the law. In 425 he established a new centre of higher education in Constantinople; and he supervised the collection of all imperial edicts since the reign of *Constantine I, which he promulgated as the *Codex Theodosianus* in 438. His reign was marked and marred by continuing religious dissension fomented by *Nestorius whom he had appointed as Patriarch of Constantinople in 428 and who was anathematized as a heretic at the Council of Ephesos in 431.

Theodosius died in July 450 after a hunting accident. He had no sons and he was succeeded by one of his loyal officers, *Marcian.

BIBL. Bury 1923, I: 212−35; Jones 1964, I

Theodosios III Emperor 715−17

A tax-collector in Asia Minor, Theodosios was reluctantly raised to the throne by the army in place of the Emperor *Anastasios II towards the end of 715, after six months of civil war. He had neither the will nor the talent to be Emperor and was perhaps relieved to be dethroned by *Leo III in March 717. He ended his days as a monk at Ephesos.

BIBL. Ostrogorsky 1968: 154−6

Theodosios I Boradiotes Patriarch of Constantinople 1179−83

He succeeded Chariton Eugeniotes as Patriarch in 1179, and acted as guardian of the young *Alexios II Komnenos when his father *Manuel I died in 1180. He then had the unenviable task of giving his blessing to the usurpation of the throne by *Andronikos I Komnenos in 1182. He preferred to retire and leave the task to his successor, *Basil II Kamateros.

BIBL. Grumel 1947: 170−4

Theodotos Melissenos Kassiteras Patriarch of Constantinople 815−21

He was the first Patriarch to be appointed by the Emperor *Leo V after the revival of iconoclasm, taking the place of the Patriarch *Nikephoros on 1 April 815. He presided over the council in St Sophia which reversed the rulings of the Council at Nicaea in 787 and reaffirmed those made in 754. He died in January 821 and was followed by *Antonios I.

BIBL. Grumel 1936: 40−1

Theoktistos (*d.* 855) Logothete

Theoktistos loyally served the Emperors *Michael II and *Theophilos as a minister of state and rose to the high rank of Logothete of the Dromos or Postmaster General. When Theophilos died in 842 he became chairman of the council of advisers to the dowager Empress *Theodora, whose favourite he was. Theoktistos was a eunuch and therefore posed no personal threat to the throne; and he was a gifted and cultured statesman as well as a soldier. When the iconoclasts were outlawed and Orthodoxy was restored in 843, his tactful handling of the situation ensured that there were no reprisals or recriminations. Later in the same year he led a naval expedition to Crete which drove the Arabs out of the island for a short time. As a financial administrator Theoktistos managed to build up a healthy reserve of gold in the imperial treasury. As a scholar he helped the cause of higher education in Constantinople which Theophilos had fostered; and he encouraged the work of *Constantine-Cyril, the later apostle of the Slavs. His power and his influence in high places, however, made him enemies. Foremost among them was the Caesar *Bardas, brother of the Empress Theodora; and it was he who engineered the murder of Theoktistos in November 855. He was honoured as a martyr in the Byzantine church.

BIBL. Ostrogorsky 1968: 219–23; Jenkins 1966: 154, 157–60

Theoleptos Bishop of Philadelphia 1283–1322

When the Emperor *Michael VIII Palaiologos tried to impose union with the Roman church on his people after the Council of Lyons in 1274, Theoleptos organized the opposition in and around his native city of Nicaea. He was imprisoned but later released and, despite the protests of his wife, became a monk. After the union had been abjured he was elected Metropolitan of Philadelphia, in 1283. He was active in repairing the defences of his city against the encroaching Turks. But he was chiefly known and revered as a spiritual leader. He had a great influence on Gregory *Palamas, one of whose forerunners he was. In 1285 he was among those who questioned the theological judgment of the Patriarch *Gregory II and caused him to resign. He was the author of homilies, ascetical, liturgical and polemical tracts, and notably of a treatise *On the Life in Christ*. Nikephoros *Choumnos, whose daughter became a nun under the spiritual guidance of Theoleptos, wrote an epitaph for him.

BIBL. *PLP* no. 7509

Theophanes (c. 760–818) chronicler

Born into a well-known Constantinopolitan family, Theophanes was a godson of the Emperor *Leo V, under whose care he was brought up. He was married at the age of eighteen but, with his wife's consent though against the Emperor's wishes, he soon became a monk. He settled in the monastery which his father had founded at Sigrianē on the south coast of the Sea of Marmora but later founded his own monastery on the island of Kalonymos nearby. He was an outspoken adversary of Leo V's revival of iconoclasm and as a result was imprisoned and then exiled to the island of Samothrace where he died in March 818. He is revered in the Orthodox church as a Confessor (*Homologētēs*) and a saint.

Theophanes is best known for his *Chronicle* (*Chronographia*) which he composed between 810 and 814 as a continuation of that written by his friend *George Synkellos. It covers the years from 284 to 813 in the form of strictly chronological annals, though his chronology is not always reliable. It is a naive, pious, theocentric and uncritical compilation, intended for the edification of monks. But its author had access to many sources that are now lost; and his work was much consulted by Greek historians of later times. A Latin translation made about 875 by the Pope's librarian, Anastasius Bibliothecarius, made it available to western historians in the Middle Ages. The *Chronicle* was carried forward by a number of anonymous Greek historians in the tenth century under the patronage of the Emperor *Constantine VII. The six books which they wrote cover the years from 813 to 961 and go by the title of Theophanes Continuatus, or the *Scriptores post Theophanem*.

BIBL. de Boor 1883; Bekker 1938a; Hunger 1978, I: 334–43

Theophano Empress 959–69

Theophano was the wife and Empress of *Romanos II. He married her in 956 against the wishes of his father *Constantine VII; for she was no better than an inn-keeper's daughter. She was, however, very beautiful and, as it turned out, very ambitious. She became Empress when her husband was crowned in 959. She presented him with two sons, *Basil II and *Constantine VIII, and one daughter, Anna; and when he died aged twenty-four in March 963, Theophano was left as guardian of her sons, the legitimate heirs of the Macedonian dynasty.

In August of that year *Nikephoros II Phokas, the conquering hero in the war against the Arabs, whose troops had proclaimed him Emperor, entered Constantinople and was crowned by the Patriarch *Polyeuktos. Theophano, fearful for the safety of her children, talked him into marrying her, on the understanding that he would protect their lives and their dynastic rights. They were married in September 963, despite the objections of the Patriarch on grounds of canon law, for which he made Nikephoros do penance. Theophano was then twenty-two. Nikephoros was over fifty, ugly in looks and austere in temperament, although he was infatuated by her beauty. She turned for comfort to his nephew, the dashing and handsome soldier *John (I) Tzimiskes; and it was he who contrived the murder of Nikephoros in December 969. If she had hoped for a reward as an accomplice in the crime she was disappointed. John Tzimiskes obeyed the Patriarch's command that Theophano must be sent away. She was immured in a convent on one of the Prince's Islands and then, after one brief and dramatic re-appearance in Constantinople, exiled to Armenia. Her sons recalled her when Tzimiskes died in 976 and she lived out her days in obscurity in the palace. Her daughter Anna married Vladimir, Prince of Kiev.

BIBL. Diehl 1906a: 217–43; Jenkins 1966: 270, 276–8, 289–93

Theophilos Emperor 829–42

Theophilos was the son of *Michael II and the second in line of the Emperors of the Amorian dynasty. Educated by the learned *John (VII) Grammatikos, he acquired a taste for scholarship and culture. He admired the art and civilization of the Arab world and sent a magnificent embassy to the Caliph at Baghdad in 830. He was none the less obliged to defend his eastern frontiers against Arab attacks for most of his reign. In 838 they destroyed Amorion, his father's birthplace. To secure the most vulnerable mountain passes he created three new military zones known as *kleisourai*. He also established new Themes or military and administrative districts, one in the Crimea and one at Dyrrachion (Durazzo) in Albania. He maintained a strong but ineffective naval and military presence in Sicily. But the Arabs there captured Taranto in southern Italy in 839. He proposed an alliance with the western Emperors against the common enemy, suggesting that his daughter should marry Louis II, son of Lothair. His revival of education and learning in Constantinople was encouraged by John Grammatikos, whom he appointed as Patriarch, and by the polymath *Leo the Mathematician, whose fame was such that the Caliphs tried to lure him to Baghdad. Both men were, like their Emperor, iconoclasts, though by intellect rather than by faith. Theophilos was the last of the iconoclast Emperors and the last to persecute those who persisted in the veneration of sacred images. He died in January 842 and iconoclasm as an imperial policy died with him. His widow *Theodora became regent for her infant son *Michael III.

BIBL. Ostrogorsky 1968: 206–9; Jenkins 1966: 146–52; Treadgold 1988: 263–329

Theophylact Patriarch of Constantinople 933–56
Theophylact (Theophylaktos) was the fourth son of the Emperor *Romanos I Lakapenos, who had him ordained while still young with a view to his becoming Patriarch. He had to wait his turn. The Patriarch *Nicholas I Mystikos died in 925 and was replaced first by Stephen II (925–8) and then by Tryphon (928–31). Theophylact was made Patriarch two years later, although he was only sixteen years of age. The fact that he did his father's bidding ensured harmonious co-operation between church and state, though he was no great churchman and preferred hunting to theology. He survived his father's downfall in 944 until he was incapacitated by a riding accident which hastened his death in 956. His successor was *Polyeuktos.

BIBL. Grumel 1936: 222–4; Hussey 1986: 111–12

Theophylact Archbishop of Ochrida c. 1090–c. 1108
Born in Euboia, Theophylact was educated in Constantinople, partly by Michael *Psellos. Ordained as a deacon, he became a teacher of rhetoric in a school attached to the patriarchate. Among his pupils was Constantine *Doukas, co-Emperor with *Alexios I, to both of whom he addressed treatises on kingship. About 1090 he was appointed Archbishop of Ochrida (Ohrid) or Bulgaria. There he remained until his death some time after 1108. His many letters reveal much about the military, social and economic life of a remote but important Byzantine province in Macedonia; and also about Theophylact's real or pretended distaste for his boorish Bulgarian flock and his nostalgia for the sophisticated Greek world of Constantinople. He was none the less a tolerant and capable administrator as well as a scholar; and one of his greatest literary works is his *Life* of his saintly predecessor, St Clement of Ochrida, who was a Slav and not a Greek. He also wrote commentaries on the Bible and on the Pauline Epistles, sermons, poems and theological works.

BIBL. Gautier 1980 and 1986; Obolensky 1988: 34–82

Theophylact Simokattes (first half 7th century) historian
Theophylact Simokattes (or Simocatta: so-called from his likeness to a snub-nosed cat) came from Alexandria and went to Constantinople to study law at the start of the reign of the Emperor *Heraclius in 610. He held several offices of state. Little else is known about his career. His major surviving work is his *History* covering the reign of the Emperor *Maurice (582–602), a sequel to the work of *Menander Protector. His literary style is ornate but his facts are generally reliable.

BIBL. Whitby and Whitby 1986

Thomas Komnenos Doukas Despot in Epiros 1296—1318

Thomas was the son of *Nikephoros of Epiros who died in 1296 leaving him under the care of his mother. The Emperor in Constantinople, *Andronikos II, had conferred the title of Despot on him in 1294 and he married the Emperor's granddaughter, Anna Palaiologina. He was assassinated in 1318 and was the last of the line of separatist Greek rulers directly descended from *Michael I of Epiros. The so-called Despotate of Epiros thereafter passed by marriage to the Italian family of Orsini, Counts of the offshore islands of Cephalonia and Zante, before being briefly reincorporated into the Byzantine Empire by the Emperor *Andronikos III in 1340.

BIBL. Nicol 1984

Thomas Magistros (*c*. 1275—*c*. 1347) scholar and monk

Thomas Magistros (or Magister) was a native of Thessalonica. He became a monk with the name Theodoulos and was a friend of Nikephoros *Gregoras. His pupils included the Patriarch *Philotheos Kokkinos, Gregory *Akindynos and Demetrios *Triklinios. He was primarily a philologist, author of a lexikon of Greek prose and of commentaries on Aeschylus, Euripides, Sophocles and Pindar.

BIBL. *PLP* no. 16045; Wilson 1983: 247—9

Thomas Palaiologos Despot of the Morea 1430—60

The sixth son of the Emperor *Manuel II, Thomas was appointed Despot at Mistra in 1430. In 1449 he agreed to rule the Morea jointly with his brother *Demetrios Palaiologos. The arrangement proved to be unworkable and hastened the Turkish conquest of Mistra in 1460. Thomas fled to Rome taking with him the head of St Andrew which he presented to Pope Pius II. He died in Rome as a pensioner of the Pope in May 1465. Of his four children, Zoe (or Sophia) married Ivan III of Russia in 1503.

BIBL. Runciman 1980: 72—5, 82—92

Thomas the Slav (*d*. 823) pretender

Thomas, a Slav from Asia Minor, had been an officer in the eastern army of the Emperors *Nikephoros I and *Leo V and a comrade-in-arms of Leo's son *Michael II. When Michael came to the throne in 820 Thomas was simultaneously proclaimed Emperor by his troops in Anatolia. He claimed to be the avenger of the deposed Emperor Leo V and he fostered the myth that he was the Emperor *Constantine VI *redivivus*. He had a huge following and controlled most of Asia Minor. He won the support of the Arab Caliph of Baghdad and had himself crowned Emperor by the Patriarch of Antioch. At the head of a vast army and navy he crossed the Hellespont and marched on Constantinople in 821. For more than a year he laid siege to the city. The Emperor Michael II, with help from his Bulgarian neighbours, finally won the day. Thomas was captured and put to death in October 823. His followers dispersed. There is much that is obscure about the affair of Thomas the Slav. But it was more of a civil war than a revolt; and its causes were probably political rather than social or economic. Its consequences are easier to discern. Much of Thrace had been devastated in the fighting for the possession of Constantinople; but above all, the foreign enemies of Byzantium had been given the opportunity to strike while the Emperor's hands were tied.

BIBL. Ostrogorsky 1968: 204—5; Lemerle 1965: 255—97; Treadgold 1988: 225—45

Tiberius I Emperor 578—82

Tiberius Constantine was an officer in the army of *Justin II who adopted him and gave him the title of Caesar in December 574, and whom he succeeded as Emperor in October 578. Tiberius made heroic efforts to stem the tide on all fronts. The Slavs continued to penetrate into the Balkans; their masters, the Avars, whom Tiberius tried to buy off with an annual tribute, captured Sirmium on the Sava river in 582. In Italy the Lombards laid siege to Ravenna in 578. They too had to be bought off. In the east the Persians rose to the attack in the same year and invaded Armenia. Here Tiberius was fortunate to have a talented general to lead his army in the person of *Maurice, who succeeded him as Emperor when he died in August 582.

BIBL. Barker 1966: 218—21

Tiberius II Emperor 698—705

Tiberius, originally known as Apsimar, was an admiral (*droungarios*) who was proclaimed Emperor by the fleet after the Arabs had conquered Carthage. He took over Constantinople from the feeble *Leontios who had ousted *Justinian II in 695. Tiberius made no attempt to recover Carthage or North Africa; but he scored some victories over the Arabs in Asia Minor and took steps to reinforce the navy there. He was rightly apprehensive that the deposed Justinian II, who had taken refuge with the Khazars, might come back, and he hoped to get him extradited or murdered. When his fears were realized and Justinian re-entered Constantinople in 705, Tiberius tried to escape; but he was caught and executed along with his predecessor Leontios.

BIBL. Ostrogorsky 1968: 141—3

Tornikes, Demetrios (*d.* 1200) statesman.

Demetrios was the younger brother of George *Tornikes. He was a judge in Constantinople who rose to become Logothete of the Dromos (Postmaster General) about 1190. He wrote homilies and letters and corresponded with Michael *Choniates, though he is better known for his career as a public servant than for his literary output. He was much involved in diplomatic exchanges with the west between 1190 and 1200, when he died. His cousin, Euthymios Tornikes, Metropolitan of Patras, wrote his epitaph.

BIBL. Darrouzès 1970

Tornikes, George (12th century) Bishop of Ephesos

George, elder brother of Demetrios *Tornikes, was a priest who taught the Psalter and the Gospels in Constantinople before being made Metropolitan of Ephesos about 1157. Much of his correspondence survives, some of it with Michael *Choniates, Bishop of Athens; and he wrote a eulogy of the historian *Anna Komnenē. The date of his death is unknown.

BIBL. *see under* *Tornikes, Demetrios

Tornikes, Leo (mid 11th century) pretender

Leo Tornikes, or Tornikios, was a relative of the Emperor *Constantine IX, against whom he rebelled after a quarrel. The soldiers in Thrace, who had their own grievance against Constantine, supported the rebellion and proclaimed Leo as Emperor at Adrianople (Edirne) in 1047. He marched on the capital and all but captured it. It was saved by the arrival of the imperial armies from the east; and on his second attempt to usurp the throne Leo was taken prisoner and blinded.

BIBL. Angold 1984: 37−8

Tribonian (*d.* 545) lawyer

Born in Sidē in Pamphylia, Tribonian was a formidably erudite lawyer who became Quaestor of the Sacred Palace or Chancellor of the Emperor *Justinian I in 529. As head of a commission of legal experts he was responsible for the codification of Roman law which was one of the major achievements of Justinian's reign. The first edition of the *Codex*, a collection of all the valid edicts of the Roman Emperors since Hadrian, came out in 529. Tribonian then supervised the preparation of the *Digest* (or *Pandects*), a collection and revision of all the rulings and precedents of classical Roman lawyers, in fifty books, which appeared in 533. In the same year a smaller version of the *Codex* and *Digest* was produced called the *Institutes*; and in 534 the definitive edition of the *Codex Justinianus* was published. Tribonian was unique among Justinian's collaborators in that he was a pagan, even though it was he who adapted Roman law for the conditions of a Christian Empire.

BIBL. Honoré 1978

Triklinios, Demetrios (14th century) scholar

Triklinios was born and lived in Thessalonica. He was a pupil of *Thomas Magistros and a friend of Maximos *Planoudes. He was interested in astronomy but was primarily a philologist. He was one of the first properly to understand the principles of ancient Greek metre in poetry and was perhaps the greatest of all Byzantine editors of classical Greek texts. He edited and commented on Aeschylus, Aristophanes, Sophocles and Euripides.

BIBL. Wilson 1983: 249−56

Tzetzes, John (*c.* 1110−*c.* 1180) scholar

When a young man Tzetzes lost his job as secretary to a provincial governor due to some indiscretion with his employer's wife. Thereafter he made a bare living as a teacher and writer in Constantinople, though under the patronage of distinguished families, who sent their sons to his school. His poverty was such that he had to sell all his books. He was, however, blessed with a prodigious, if not always dependable, memory. An exceptionally erudite and prolific scholar, he wrote about sixty books. His works include commentaries on Homer, Hesiod and Aristotle; poems on the Trojan War; a mythological poem called the *Theogony*; 107 letters, many of them fictitious; and a huge poem called the *Historiae* or *Chiliads* consisting of extended footnotes to his own letters, explaining the historical, mythological, geographical and literary allusions in them. Vain, tetchy and rather tiresome though he was, John Tzetzes merits attention not least because he had access to some classical Greek texts which are now lost.

BIBL. Wilson 1983: 190−6; Hunger 1978, II: 59−63, 117−18; Moravcsik 1983: 342−4

V

Valens Emperor 364–78

On the premature death of the Emperor *Jovian in February 364, his troops proclaimed one of their officers, Valentinian I, as Emperor at Nicaea. He at once designated his younger brother Valens as his co-Emperor to rule over the eastern part of the Empire with his capital at Constantinople. Valentinian governed the west. Valens was a Christian, though of the Arian persuasion which had been denounced as heretical at the Council of Nicaea in 325. Valentinian supported the Nicene creed. Both Emperors were beset by new waves of Germanic invaders. Valens had to make peace with the Persians, the perennial enemies of the Empire in the east, to man the defences of the Danube frontier against the Visigoths: and it was they who caused his downfall and his death in August 378 in a great battle at Adrianople (Edirne) in Thrace in which the entire Roman army of the east was annihilated. His successor was *Theodosius I.

BIBL. Jones 1964, I

X

Xanthopoulos, Nikephoros Kallistos (*c*. 1256–*c*. 1335) church historian
A priest of St Sophia in Constantinople in the time of the Emperor
*Andronikos II Palaiologos, he taught rhetoric and theology and became
a monk with the name of Neilos before he died. He made his name with
his *History of the Church* which he wrote about 1330 and dedicated to
the Emperor. Its eighteen books cover the period from the origins of
Christianity to the reign of the Emperor *Phokas in 610. He derived his
information from earlier church historians such as *Eusebius, *Sozomen
and *Evagrius. He also composed hymns, poems, lives of saints and
commentaries on *Gregory of Nazianzus; and he was the author of a
catalogue of early bishops and patriarchs of Constantinople in prose and a
list of church Fathers in verse. His church history was translated into
Latin in the sixteenth century.

BIBL. Works *in MPG*, vols. 145–7; Beck 1959: 705–7

Z

Zeno Emperor 474–91

Zeno, originally known as Tarasicodissa, was one of the barbarous Isaurian soldiers introduced to Constantinople by the Emperor *Leo I to counteract the dangerous influence of the German soldiery. He married Leo's daughter Ariadne and claimed the throne when her son *Leo II died as a child in November 474. He made a treaty with the Vandals in North Africa whom Leo I had vainly tried to dislodge and secured peace on that front for nearly sixty years.

He was not popular. A plot against him was hatched by his mother-in-law Verina, whose brother *Basiliscus was proclaimed Emperor. Zeno fled to Isauria; though he came back in August 476 and took his revenge. His position was never secure. Other pretenders of his own race conspired against him, notably his former commander Illus. But it was Zeno who found a way of disembarrassing the eastern Empire of the troublesome Goths. The western Empire had been formally terminated in 476 when Odoacer dethroned the last Emperor, Romulus Augustulus. The two most powerful Germanic leaders in the eastern provinces were Theodoric Strabo and Theodoric the Amal. The former died in 484; and in 488 Zeno proposed that Theodoric the Amal should relieve Odoacer of his Italian dominions, thereby relieving Byzantium of his presence. After a fierce struggle Theodoric killed Odoacer and set up the Gothic Kingdom of Italy.

Bitter religious discord continued to split the Empire in Zeno's reign. The Monophysites, who believed that Christ's human and divine natures were one, had been anathematised at the Council of Chalcedon in 451. But they had strong support in the east. In 482, with the approval of the Patriarch *Acacius, Zeno issued a document called the *Henotikon* which presented a compromise formula acceptable to both sides in the dispute. It was never a long-term solution and it was rejected by the Pope, who excommunicated the Patriarch. The churches of Rome and Constantinople were thereafter in schism until 518, when the Emperor *Justin I disclaimed the *Henotikon*. Zeno died in April 491 and was succeeded by *Anastasius I.

BIBL. Brooks 1893: 209–38; Bury 1923, I: 389–404; Jones 1964, I

Zoe Karbounopsina Empress 906–19

Zoe was a daughter of Stylianos Zaoutzes, chief minister of the Emperor *Leo VI. She was renowned for her beauty and Leo took her as his mistress. When she had borne him a son, *Constantine VII, he took her as his fourth wife, thus causing the celebrated scandal of the 'tetragamy'. Byzantine canon law forbade a fourth marriage. The Patriarch *Nicholas (I) Mystikos baptized the infant Constantine, but only on condition that Zoe was turned out of the palace. Four months later, in April 906, Leo recalled her, went through a form of marriage with her and crowned her as his Empress. The extremists in the church protested loudly. The Emperor appealed to the Pope, for the canon law of the Roman church was more flexible in the matter. Nicholas Mystikos was dismissed and a new Patriarch was found in the person of *Euthymios, who gave his approval to the marriage in 907. When Leo VI's brother and successor *Alexander died in 913 Zoe came forward as regent for her son Constantine (VII). She was at first outwitted by Nicholas Mystikos, who had come back as Patriarch. He had her removed to a convent. But in 914 she returned and reigned as Empress-regent with a council of advisers. In March 919, however, *Romanos (I) Lakapenos, with the Patriarch's support, assumed the regency. Zoe was accused of trying to poison him and was sent back to her convent. Her dark eyes, which gave her the name Karbounopsina, were thereafter hidden from the world. She ended her days as a nun with the name of Anna.

BIBL. Jenkins 1966: 215–16, 220–2, 228–36

Zoe porphyrogenita Empress 1028–50

The Emperor *Basil II had no offspring. His brother *Constantine VIII succeeded him in 1025; and when he died three years later the throne passed to his two daughters, Zoe and *Theodora, as the only remaining descendants of the Macedonian dynasty. On his deathbed, Constantine arranged that Zoe should marry the elderly senator *Romanos (III) Argyros, who thus became Emperor. She was then in her fifties. At a much earlier age she had been betrothed to the heir to the western imperial throne. Otto III of Germany. He died before she reached him and she returned to Constantinople. Romanos III was a pompous old man and Zoe soon tired of him. She took as her lover a peasant lad, Michael the Paphlagonian. In April 1034 Romanos was found dead in his bath and on the same day Zoe married her lover, who was then crowned as the Emperor *Michael IV. Having achieved his ambition through marrying Zoe, Michael neglected her. She adopted his nephew, also called Michael; and when her husband died in 1041 she made him Emperor as *Michael V, who thanked her by relegating her to a convent. Zoe, however, still held the affection of the people. There was rioting in Constantinople. Michael V was deposed and she was recalled to the throne, this time with her slightly younger sister Theodora as her co-Empress, although they detested each other. In June 1042, however, Zoe, then aged sixty-four, took as her third husband *Constantine Monomachos, whose extravagant tastes she shared, and who ascended the throne as her Emperor, Constantine IX. Zoe died in 1050.

BIBL. Diehl 1906b

Zonaras, John (first half 12th century) chronicler

Zonaras was an official at court in Constantinople who later became a monk. He composed a *World Chronicle* from the Creation to the year 1118, a work rather more sophisticated than others of its genre. Since he made use of sources that are now lost, he provides some unique information;

and he is a valuable check on the *Alexiad* of *Anna Komnenē. His other writings include a *Lexikon* of rare Greek words and an important treatise on canon law.

BIBL. Pinder and Büttner-Wobst 1841−97; Tittmann 1808; Hunger 1978, I: 416−19; Beck 1959: 655−7

Zosimus (first half 5th century) historian

Little is known about his career. He seems to have been a civil servant in the age of the Emperor *Theodosius II and his immediate successors. He was a pagan and the author of a *New History* in six books covering the years from 295 to 410. Its tone is often virulently anti-Christian, for his major theme is that the Roman Empire has declined because it has turned its back on the old Roman religion. It has therefore a unique interest.

BIBL. Mendelssohn 1887; Kaegi 1968

Index of Other Persons

Family Names of Emperors, Patriarchs and other Dignitaries

Angelos *see* Alexios III, Alexios IV, Isaac II, Emperors
Argyros *see* Romanos III Emperor
Autoreianos *see* Arsenios Patriarch; Michael IV Patriarch
Batatzes *see* John III Emperor
Bekkos *see* John XI Patriarch
Boradiotes *see* Theodosius I Patriarch
Botaneiates *see* Nikephoros III Emperor
Boucheiras *see* Isidore I Patriarch
Chamaetos *see* Kabasilas, Nicholas
Chrysoberges *see* Luke Patriarch
Diogenes *see* Romanos IV Emperor
Doukas *see* Alexios V, Constantine X, John III, Michael VIII, Emperors; Eirene Doukaina, Euphrosyne Doukaina, Empresses; John *sebastokrator*; Michael I, Michael II of Epiros; Nikephoros of Epiros; Theodore and Thomas of Epiros
Eirenikos *see* Theodore II Patriarch
Garidas *see* Eustratios Patriarch
Glabas *see* Isidore, Bishop of Thessalonica; Tarchaneiotes, Michael
Glykys *see* John XIII Patriarch
Kalekas *see* John XIV Patriarch
Kamateros *see* Basil II Patriarch; John X Patriarch
Kantakouzenos *see* John VI Emperor; Manuel Despot; Matthew Emperor
Kassimatas *see* Antonios I Patriarch
Kassiteras *see* Theodotos Patriarch
Kauleas *see* Antonios II Patriarch
Kerameus *see* Neilos Patriarch
Keroullarios *see* Michael I Patriarch
Kokkinos *see* Philotheos Patriarch
Komnenos *see* Alexios I, Alexios II, Emperors; Alexios IV, Basil, David, John IV, Manuel III, Emperors of Trebizond; Andronikos I, Isaac I, John II, Manuel I, Emperors; Michael I, Michael II, Theodore, Thomas of Epiros; Anna Komnenē
Kosmas *see* John XII Patriarch
Kourkouas *see* Michael II Patriarch
Kourtesis *see* Gennadios II Patriarch
Kyrdiniates *see* Nicholas III Patriarch
Lakapenos *see* Romanos I Emperor
Laskaris *see* John IV, Theodore I, Theodore II, Emperors
Leichoudes *see* Constantine III Patriarch
Makrembolitissa *see* Eudokia Empress
Mammē *see* Gregory III Patriarch
Melissenos *see* Theodotos Patriarch
Monomachos *see* Constantine IX Emperor
Morochazanios *see* John VII Patriarch
Mountanes *see* Niketas Patriarch
Palaiologos *see* Andronikos II, Andronikos III, Andronikos IV, Constantine XI, John V, John VII, John VIII, Manuel II, Michael VIII, Michael IX, Emperors; Demetrios, Theodore I, Theodore II, Thomas, Despots
Philanthropenos *see* Syrgiannes Palaiologos

Phokas *see* Nikephoros II Emperor
Rangabe *see* Michael I Emperor
Sarantenos *see* Manuel I Patriarch
Sikidites *see* Glykas, Michael
Theotokites *see* Leontios Patriarch
Tzimiskes *see* John I Emperor
Xiphilinos *see* George II, John VIII, Patriarchs

Index of Foreign Names

References

Alexander, P J 1958 *The Patriarch Nicephorus of Constantinople. Ecclesiastical policy and image worship in the Byzantine Empire*. Oxford

Angold, M 1975 *A Byzantine government in exile. Government and society under the Laskarids of Nicaea (1204–1261)*. Oxford

Angold, M 1984 *The Byzantine Empire 1025–1204. A political history*. London

Attwater, D 1959 *Saint John Chrysostom, pastor and preacher*. London

Balfour, D 1979 *Politico-historical works of Symeon Archbishop of Thessalonica (1416/17 to 1429)*. Vienna

Bandy, A C (trs and ed) 1983 *Ioannes Lydus on powers, or the magistracies of the Roman State*. Philadelphia

Barker, J W 1966 *Justinian and the Later Roman Empire*. Madison, Wisc.

Barker, J W 1969 *Manuel II Palaeologus (1391–1425). A study in Late Byzantine statesmanship*. New Brunswick, NJ

Barnes, T D 1981 *Constantine and Eusebius*. Cambridge, Mass

Barnes, T D 1982 *The New Empire of Diocletian and Constantine*. Cambridge, Mass.

Barry, J N and **M J Share** et al. (trs and eds) 1975 *Mazaris' Journey to Hades*. Arethusa Monographs V, New York

Baynes, N H 1955 'The Pratum Spirituale.' In N H Baynes *Byzantine studies and other essays*. London: 261–70

Baynes, N H 1972 *Constantine the Great and the Christian Church*. 2nd ed by H Chadwick, Oxford

Beck, H-G 1959 *Kirche und theologische Literatur im Byzantinischen Reich*. Munich

Bekker, I (ed) 1835 *Georgii Pachymeris de Michaele et Andronico Palaeologis*. 2 vols, Bonn

Bekker, I (ed) 1836a *Michaelis Glycae Annales*. Bonn

Bekker, I (ed) 1836b *Ioelis Chronographia Compendiaria*. Bonn

Bekker, I (ed) 1837 *Constantini Manassis Breviarium historiae metricum*. Bonn

Bekker, I (ed) 1838a *Theophanes Continuatus*. Bonn

Bekker, I (ed) 1838b *Georgius Continuatus. In* Bekker *Theophanes Continuatus*. Bonn

Bekker, I (ed) 1838, 1839 *Georgius Cedrenus*. 2 vols, Bonn

Belting, H, C Mango and **D Mouriki** 1978 *The mosaics and frescoes of St Mary Pammakaristos (Fethiye Camii) at Istanbul*. Dumbarton Oaks, Washington DC

Bidez, J and **G C Hansen** (eds) 1960 *Sozomenus Kirchengeschichte*. 2nd ed, Berlin

Bidez, J and **L Parmentier** (eds) 1898 *The Ecclesiastical History of Evagrius with the Scholia*. London

Böhlig, G (ed) 1973 *Ioannis Caminiatae de expugnatione Thessalonicae*. Berlin and New York

Bonis, K 1938 *Ioannes Xiphilinos*. Athens (in Greek)

Boor, C de (ed) 1883 *Theophanis Chronographia*. 2 vols, Leipzig

Boor, C de (ed) 1904 *Georgii Monachi Chronicon*. 2 vols, Leipzig

Bosch, U V 1965 *Kaiser Andronikos III, Palaiologos*. Amsterdam

Bowersock, G W 1978 *Julian the Apostate*. London

Brand, C M 1968 *Byzantium confronts the West, 1180–1204*. Cambridge, Mass.

Brand, C M (trs) 1976 *Deeds of John and Manuel Comnenus by John Kinnamos*. New York

Bright, W (ed) 1878 *Socrates' Eclesiastical History*. Oxford

Brooks, E W 1893 'The Emperor Zenon and the Isaurians.' *English Historical*

Review **VIII**: 209—38

Browning, R 1961 'A new source on Byzantine-Hungarian relations in the twelfth century. The Inaugural Lecture of Michael (of Anchialos).' *Balkan Studies* **II**: 174—214.

Browning, R 1971 *Justinian and Theodora*. London

Browning, R 1975 *The Emperor Julian*. London

Buckler, G 1929 *Anna Comnena: a study*. Oxford

Bury, J B 1923 *History of the Later Roman Empire from the death of Theodosius I to the death of Justinian (395—565)*. 2 vols, London

Cameron, A 1970 *Agathias*. Oxford

Cameron, A 1985 *Procopius and the sixth century*. Berkeley and Los Angeles

Cammelli, G 1941 *I dotti bizantini e le origini dell' umanesimo*, I: *Manuele Crisolora*. Florence

Campenhausen, H von 1963 *The Fathers of the Greek Church*. London

Catanzaro, C J de (trs) 1974 *Nicholas Cabasilas: Life in Christ*. New York

Chalandon, F 1900 *Les Comnènes*, I: *Essai sur le règne d'Alexis I Comnène*. Paris

Chalandon, F 1912 *Les Comnènes*, II: *Jean II Comnène et Manuel I Comnène*. Paris

Charanis, P 1974 *Church and State in the Later Roman Empire: the religious policy of Anastasius I, 491—518*. 2nd ed, Thessaloniki

Cheynet, J-C 1986 'Les Dalassénoi.' *In* J-C Cheynet and J-F Vannier, *Études prosopographiques*. Paris: 75—119

Chrestou, P K (ed) 1962, 1966, 1970 *Works of Gregory Palamas*. 3 vols, Thessaloniki (in Greek)

Chrysostomides, J (ed and trs) 1985 *Manuel II Palaeologus: Funeral Oration on his brother Theodore*. Thessaloniki

Clucas, L 1981 *The trial of John Italos*. Munich

Constantinides, C N 1982 *Higher education in Byzantium in the thirteenth and early fourteenth centuries*. Nicosia

Dagron, G 1974 *Naissance d' une capitale. Constantinople et ses institutions de 330 à 451*. Paris

Dain, A (ed) 1957 *La 'Tactique' de Nicéphore Ouranos*. Paris

Darkó, E (ed) 1922—7 *Laonici Chalcocandylae Historiarum Demonstrationes*. 2 vols, Budapest

Darrouzès, J (ed and trs) 1966—7 *Syméon le Nouveau Théologien: Traités théologiques et ethiques*. 2 vols, Paris (French trs)

Darrouzès, J (ed) 1970 *Georges et Dèmètrios Tornikès: Lettres et Discours*. Paris

Darrouzès, J 1977 *Les regestes des actes du patriarcat*. I: *Les actes des patriarches*. **v**, Paris

Darrouzès, J 1979 *Les regestes des actes du patriarcat*. I: *Les actes des patriarches*. **vi** Paris

Dawes, E and N H Baynes (trs) 1948 *Life of St John the Almsgiver*. *In* Dawes, E and N H Baynes, *Three Byzantine saints*. London: 193—270

Dennis, G T (ed and trs) 1977 *The letters of Manuel II Palaeologus*. Dumbarton Oaks, Washington DC

Dennis, G T (trs) 1984 *Maurice's Strategikon. Handbook of Byzantine military strategy*. Philadelphia

Dewing, H B and G Downey (ed and trs) 1914—40 *Procopius* 8 vols, Loeb Classical Library

Diehl, C 1904 *Théodora, impératrice de Byzance*. Paris

Diehl, C 1906a *Figures byzantines*. Ier série, Paris

Diehl, C 1906b 'Zoé la Porphyrogénète. *In* C Diehl 1906a: 245—90

Dieten, J-A van (ed) 1975 *Nicetae Choniatae Historia*. 2 vols, Berlin, New York

Dindorff, L (ed) 1831 *Ioannis Malalae Chronographia*. Bonn

Dindorff, L (ed) 1871 *Historici Graeci Minores* II, Leipzig

Dölger, F 1931 'Johannes VII. Kaiser der Rhomäer.' *Byzantinische Zeitschrift* **XXXI**: 21–36

Drake, H A (trs) 1967 *In praise of Constantine. A historical study and new translation of Eusebius' Tricennial Orations.* California

Driver, G R and **L Hodgson** (trs) 1925 *Nestorius. The Bazaar of Heracleides. Newly translated from the Syriac.* Oxford

Dvornik, F 1948 *The Photian schism, History and legend.* Cambridge

Dvornik, F 1970 *Byzantine missions among the Slavs. SS Constantine-Cyril and Methodius.* New Brunswick, New Jersey

Eustratiades, S (ed) 1906, 1912 *Michael Glykas: Aporiai.* I, Athens 1906: II, Alexandria 1912 (in Greek)

Failler, A and **V Laurent** (eds and trs) 1984 *Georges Pachymérès Relations Historiques.* Paris (in progress) New ed of Bekker 1835 (French trs)

Fassoulakis, S 1973 *The Byzantine family of Raoul-Ral(l)es.* Athens

Follieri, E (ed) 1980–1 *I calendari in metro innografico di Cristoforo Mitilineo.* Brussels

Frendo, J D (trs) 1975 *Agathias: The Histories.* Berlin

Friedländer, P (ed) 1912 *Johannes von Gaza und Paulus Silentiarius.* Leipzig

Gardner, A 1905 *Theodore of Studium, his life and times.* London

Gardner, A 1912 *The Lascarids of Nicaea. The story of an empire in exile.* London

Gautier, P (ed) 1972 *Michel Italikos: Lettres et Discours.* Paris

Gautier, P (ed) 1975 *Nicephori Bryennii Historiarum libri quattuor.* Brussels

Gautier, P (ed and trs) 1980 *Théophylacte d'Achride: Discours, traités. poésies.* Thessaloniki (French trs)

Gautier, P (ed) 1986 *Théophylacte d'Achride: Lettres.* Thessaloniki (French trs)

Geanakoplos, D J 1959 *Emperor Michael Palaeologus and the West. 1258–1282.* Cambridge, Mass.

Gill, J 1958 *The Council of Florence.* Cambridge

Gill, J 1964 *Personalities of the Council of Florence and other essays.* Oxford

Gonis, D B 1980 *The literary works of the Oecumenical Patriarch Kallistos I.* Athens (in Greek)

Goubert, P 1971 *Byzance avant l'Islam*, I. *Byzance et l'Orient sous les successeurs de Justinien: L'empereur Maurice.* Paris

Gouillard, J (ed) 1967 'Le Synodikon de l'Orthodoxie: édition et commentaire.' *Travaux et Mémoires* **II**: 1–313

Grabar, A and **M Manoussacas** 1979 *L'Illustration du Manuscrit de Skylitzes de la Bibliothéque Nationale de Madrid.* Venice

Grecu, V (ed) 1958 *Ducas: Istoria Turco-Bizantină.* Bucharest

Grecu, V (ed) 1966 *Georgios Sphrantzes Memorii 1401–1477 in anexă Pseudo-Phrantzes: Macarie Melissenos Cronica 1258–1481.* Bucharest

Grosdidier de Matons, J (ed and trs) 1964–81 *Romanos le Mélode: Hymnes.* 5 vols, Paris

Grumel, V 1936 *Les regestes des actes du patriarcat.* I: *Les actes des patriarches.* ii Constantinople

Grumel, V 1947 *Les regestes des actes du patriarcat.* I: *Les actes des patriarches.* iii Constantinople

Grumel, V 1972 *Les regestes des actes du patriarcat.* I: *Les actes des patriarches.* i 2nd ed Paris

Guilland, R 1926 *Essai sur Nicéphore Grégoras. L'homme et l'oeuvre.* Paris

Halecki, O 1930 *Un Empereur de Byzance á Rome.* Warsaw

Hase, C B (ed) 1828 *Leonis Diaconi Caloensis Historiae.* Bonn

Haury, J (ed) 1905–13 *Procopii Caesariensis Opera Omnia.* 3 vols, Leipzig

Hausherr, I and **G Horn** (ed and trs) 1928 *Vie de Syméon le nouveau théologien.* Rome (French trs)

Heisenberg, A (ed) 1903 *Georgii Acropolitae Opera.* I, Leipzig

Heisenberg, A 1973 *Quellen und Studien zur spätbyzantinischen Geschichte.* London

Henry, R (ed and trs) 1959–65 *Photius: Bibliothèque.* 8 vols, Paris (French trs)

Hergenröther, J 1867–9 *Photius: Patriarch von Konstantinopel.* 3 vols, Regensburg

Hero, A C (ed and trs) 1983 *Letters of Gregory Akindyos.* Dumbarton Oaks, Washington DC

Hoeck, J M and R J Loenertz 1965 *Nikolaos-Nektarios von Otrànto Abt von Casole.* Ettal

Honoré, A 1978 *Tribonian.* London

Hunger, H (ed) 1969 *Johannes Chortasmenos. Briefe, Gedichte und kleine Schriften.* Vienna

Hunger, H 1978 *Die hochsprachliche profane Literatur der Byzantiner.* 2 vols, Munich

Hussey, J M 1937 *Church and learning in the Byzantine Empire.* London

Hussey, J M 1986 *The Orthodox Church in the Byzantine Empire.* Oxford

Hussey, J and P McNulty (trs) 1960 *Nicholas Cabasilas: A Commentary on the Divine Liturgy.* London

Janssens, E 1969 *Trébizonde en Colchide.* Brussels

Jeffreys, E, M Jeffreys and R Scott (trs) 1986 *The Chronicle of John Malalas.* Melbourne

Jenkins, R 1966 *Byzantium: the Imperial centuries AD 610–1071.* London

Jenkins, R J H (ed) 1962 *Constantine Porphyrogenitus: De administrando imperio. Commentary.* London

Jenkins, R J H and Gy Moravcsik (ed and trs) 1967 *Constantine Porphyrogenitus: De administrando imperio.* 2nd ed, Dumbarton Oaks, Washington DC

Jenkins, R J H and L G Westerink (ed and trs) 1973 *Nicholas I Patriarch of Constantinople: Letters.* Washington, DC

Joannou, P (ed) 1956 *Ioannes Italos: Quaestiones quodlibetales.* Ettal

Jones, A H M 1964 *The Later Roman Empire. A social, economic and administrative survey.* 3 vols, Oxford

Jurewicz, O 1962 *Andronikos I. Komnenos.* Warsaw (reprinted Amsterdam 1970)

Kaegi, W E 1968 *Byzantium and the decline of Rome.* Princeton, NJ

Kaimakis, D B (ed) 1983 *Philotheos Kokkinos: Dogmatic works.* Thessaloniki (in Greek)

Kambylis, A (ed) 1976 *Symeon Neos Theologos: Hymnen.* Berlin and New York

Karlin-Hayter, P (ed) 1970 *Vita Euthymii Patriarchae.* Brussels

Karpozilos, A D 1973 *The ecclesiastical controversy between the Kingdom of Nicaea and the Principality of Epiros (1217–1233).* Thessaloniki

Karpozilos, A D (ed and trs) 1990 *The letters of Ioannes Mauropous Metropolitan of Euchaita.* Thessaloniki

Kazhdan, A P 1978 'On the authenticity of Kaminiates' "Capture of Thessalonica."' *Byzantinische Zeitschrift* **LXXI**: 301–14

Kazhdan, A P 1984a 'The social views of Michael Attaleiates.' *In* A P Kazhdan and S Franklin (eds) 1984: 23–86

Kazhdan, A P 1984b 'Eustathius of Thessalonica: the life and opinions of a twelfth-century Byzantine rhetor.' *In* A P Kazhdan and S Franklin (eds) 1984: 115–95

Kazhdan, A P 1984c 'Theodore Prodromus: a reappraisal.' *In* A P Kazhdan and S Franklin (eds) 1984: 87–114

Kazhdan, A P and S Franklin (eds) 1984 *Studies on Byzantine literature of the eleventh and twelfth centuries.* Cambridge

Keydell, R (ed) 1967 *Agathiae Myrinaei Historiarum libri quinque.* Berlin

King, N Q 1961 *The Emperor Theodosius and the establishment of Christianity.* London

Kourousis, S I 1975 *The learned Oecumenical Patriarch John XIII Glykys.* Athens (in Greek)

REFERENCES

Krivocheine, B and **J Paramelle** (ed and trs) 1963—5 *Syméon le nouveau théologien, Catéchèses.* 3 vols, Paris (French trs)
Kurtz, E (ed) 1903 *Die Gedichte des Christophoros Mitylenaios.* Leipzig
Laiou, A E 1972 *Constantinople and the Latins. The foreign policy of Andronicus II, 1282—1328.* Cambridge, Massachusetts
Lambros, S P 1879—80 *Michael Akominatos Choniates: The surviving works.* 2 vols, Athens (in Greek)
Lampsides, O (ed) 1958 *Michael Panaretos, Chronicle.* Athens (in Greek)
Lamza, L 1975 *Patriarch Germanos I. von Konstantinopel.* Würzburg
Laurent, V 1971a *Les regestes des actes du patriarcat.* I: *Les actes des patriarches,* iv, Paris
Laurent, V (ed and trs) 1971b *Les mémoires du Grand Écclesiarque de l'Eglise de Constantinople Sylvestre Syropoulos sur le Concile de Florence.* Paris (French trs)
Lawrence, G (trs) 1964 *A study of Gregory Palamas.* London
Leib, B (ed and trs) 1937—45 *Anne Comnène: Alexiade.* 3 vols, Paris (French trs)
Lemerle, P 1965 'Thomas le Slave.' *Travaux et Mémoires* I: 255—97
Lemerle, P *et al.* (eds) 1970—82 *Actes de Lavra,* I—IV (Archives de l'Athos). Paris
Lesmüller-Werner, A and **I Thurn** 1978 *Josephi Genesii Regum libri quattuor.* Berlin and New York
Lippold, A 1968 *Theodosius der Grosse und seine Zeit.* Stuttgart
Loenertz, R-J 1956, 1960 *Démétrius Cydonès: Correspondance.* 2 vols, Vatican City
Maas, P and **C A Trypanis** (eds) 1963 *Sancti Romani Melodi Cantica* I: *Cantica Genuina.* Oxford
Maas, P and **C A Trypanis** (eds) 1970 *Sancti Romani Melodi Cantica* II: *Cantica Dubia.* Berlin
Magoulias, H J (trs) 1975 *Doukas, Decline and fall of Byzantium to the Ottoman Turks.* Detroit
Magoulias, H J (trs) 1984 *O City of Byzantium, Annals of Niketas Choniates.* Detroit
Mango, C 1963 'The Conciliar Edict of 1166.' *Dumbarton Oaks Papers* **XVII**: 315—30
Mango, C (ed and trs) 1990 *Nikephoros Patriarch of Constantinople, Short History, text, translation and commentary.* Dumbarton Oaks, Washington DC
Martini, A (ed) 1900 *Manuelis Philae Carmina Inedita.* Naples
Meineke, A (ed) 1836 *Ioannis Cinnami epitome rerum.* Bonn
Mendelssohn, L (ed) 1887 *Zosimus: Historia Nova.* Leipzig (repr. Hildesheim 1963)
Meyendorff, J (ed) 1959 *Introduction à l'étude de Grégoire Palamas.* Paris
Meyendorff, J (ed and trs) 1973 *Grégoire Palamas: Défense des saints hésychastes.* 2 vols, Louvain (French trs)
Michel, E 1925, 1930 *Humbert und Kerullarios.* 2 vols, Paderborn
Miller, E (ed) 1855, 1857 *Manuelis Philae Carmina.* 2 vols, Paris
Miller, W 1922 'The last Athenian historian: Laonikos Chalkokondyles.' *Journal of Hellenic Studies* XLII: 36—49
Miller, W 1926 *Trebizond. The last Greek Empire.* London
Mohler, L 1923—7, 1942 *Kardinal Bessarion als Theologe, Humanist und Staatsmann.* 3 vols, Paderborn
Moravcsik, Gy 1983 *Byzantinoturcica,* I: *Die byzantinischen Quellen der Geschichte der Türkvölker.* 3rd ed, Berlin
Mosshammer, A (ed) 1984 *Georgios Synkellos; Ecloga chronographica.* Leipzig
Munitiz, J A 1988 *Nikephoros Blemmydes, a partial account. Introduction, translation and notes.* Louvain
Niavis, P E 1987 *The reign of the Byzantine Emperor Nicephorus I (AD 802—811).* Athens
Nicol, D M 1957 *The Despotate of Epiros.* I *(1204—1267).* Oxford

153

Nicol, D M 1968 *The Byzantine family of Kantakouzenos (Cantacuzenus)* ca *1100– 1460. A genealogical and prosopographical study*. Dumbarton Oaks, Washington DC
Nicol, D M 1972 *The last centuries of Byzantium. 1261–1453*. London
Nicol, D M 1979 *Church and society in the last centuries of Byzantium*. Cambridge
Nicol, D M 1984 *The Despotate of Epiros*, II *(1267–1479)*. Cambridge
Noret, J (ed) 1982 *Vitae duae Sancti Athanasii Athonitae*. Louvain
Obolensky, D 1971 *The Byzantine commonwealth. Eastern Europe. 500–1453*. London
Obolensky, D 1988 *Six Byzantine portraits*. Oxford
Oikonomides, N 1986 'The "Peira of Eustathios Rhomaios." An abortive attempt to innovate in Byzantine Law.' *Fontes Minores* (Frankfurt am Main) **VII**: 169–92
Ostrogorsky, G 1968 *History of the Byzantine State*. (trs Joan Hussey), Oxford
Papadakis, A 1983 *Crisis in Byzantium. The* Filioque *Controversy in the Patriarchate of Gregory II of Cyprus (1283–1289)*. New York
Pappadopoulos, J B 1908 *Théodore II Lascaris empereur de Nicée*. Paris
Pertusi, A (ed) 1952 *Costantino Porfirogenito. De thematibus*. Vatican City
Pertusi, A (ed) 1959 *Giorgio di Pisidia, Poemi*, I. *Panegirici epici*. Ettal
Petit, L 1906 'Vie de S. Athanase l'Athonite.' *Analecta Bollandiana* **XXV**: 1–89
Petit, L, X A Siderides and **M Jugie** (eds) 1928–36 *Oeuvres complètes de Gennade Scholarios*. 8 vols, Paris
Philippides, M (trs) 1980 *The fall of the Byzantine Empire. A chronicle by George Sphrantzes, 1401–1477*. Amherst
Pinder, M and **T Büttner-Wobst** (eds) 1841–97 *Ioannis Zonarae Epitome Historiarum*. 3 vols, Bonn
Pinto, E (ed) 1977 *Giovanni Cananos, l'assedio di Costantinopli*. Messina
Pitra, J B (ed) 1891 Demetrios Chomatianos, *Works. In Analecta sacra et classica spicilegio Solesmensi parata*. VI, Rome
Polemis, D I 1968 *The Doukai, A contribution to Byzantine prosopography*. London
Presle, W B and **I Bekker** (eds) 1853 *Michaelis Attaliatae Historia*. Bonn
Psevtongas, B S (ed) 1981 *Philotheos Kokkinos: Speeches and homilies*. Thessaloniki (in Greek)
Quasten, J 1960 *Patrology*. III: *The Golden Age of Greek Patristic Literature. From the Council of Nicaea to the Council of Chalcedon*. Westminster, Maryland
Queller, D E 1977 *The Fourth Crusade. The conquest of Constantinople 1201–1204*. Philadelphia
Reinsch, D R (ed) 1983 *Critobuli Imbriotae Historiae*. Berlin and New York
Reiske, I I (ed) 1829–30 *Constantini Porphyrogeniti imperatoris de cerimoniis aulae byzantinae*. 2 vols, Bonn
Renauld, E (ed and trs) 1926–8 *Michel Psellos: Chronographie*. Paris
Riggs, C T (trs) 1954 *History of Mehmed the Conqueror by Kritovoulos*. Princeton NJ
Ruether, R 1969 *Gregory of Nazianzus: Rhetor and Philosopher*. Oxford
Runciman, S 1929 *The Emperor Romanus Lecapenus and his reign. A study of Tenth-Century Byzantium*. Cambridge
Runciman, S 1951, 1952, 1954 *A history of the Crusades*. 3 vols, Cambridge
Runciman, S 1955 *The Eastern Schism. A study of the Papacy and the Eastern Churches during the XIth and XIIth centuries*. Oxford
Runciman, S 1965 *The fall of Constantinople 1453*. Cambridge
Runciman, S 1978 'The Empress Irene the Athenian.' *In Medieval Women* (=*Studies in Church History*, Subsidia I) Oxford: 101–18
Runciman, S 1980 *Mistra, Byzantine capital of the Peloponnese*. London
Scheidweiler, F (ed) 1954 *Theodorets Kirchengeschichte*. 2nd ed, Berlin
Schlumberger, G 1890 *Un empereur byzantin au Xe siècle: Nicéphore Phocas*. Paris
Schlumberger, G 1900 *L'épopée byzantine à la fin du Xe siècle*. II: *Basile II* (989– 1025). Paris

Schopen, L (ed) 1828–32 *Ioannis Cantacuzeni eximperatoris Historiarum Libri IV*. 3 vols, Bonn

Schopen, L (ed) 1829, 1830, 1955 *Nicephori Gregorae Byzantina Historia*. 3 vols, Bonn

Schwartz, E 1939 *Kyrillos von Skythopolis*. Leipzig

Seibt, W 1976 *Die Skleroi, Eine prosopographisch-sigillographische Studie*. Vienna

Ševčenko, I 1960 (ed and trs) 'Alexios Makrembolites and his "Dialogue between the Rich and the Poor."' *Zbornik Radova Vizantološkog Instituta* **VI**, Belgrade: 187–228

Ševčenko, I 1975 'Theodore Metochites, the Chora and the intellectual trends of his time.' *In* P A Underwood (ed) *The Kariye Diami* **IV**, London: 19–91

Sewter, E R A (trs) 1966 *Fourteen Byzantine rulers: the* Chronographia *of Michael Psellus*. Harmondsworth

Sewter, E R A (trs) 1969 *The Alexiad of Anna Comnena*. Harmondsworth

Speck, P 1978 *Kaiser Konstantin VI*. 2 vols, Munich

Stadtmüller, G 1934 *Michael Choniates, Metropolit von Athen*. Vatican City

Talbot, A-M M 1975 *The correspondence of Athanasius I Patriarch of Constantinople*. Dumbarton Oaks, Washington DC

Tannery, P (ed) 1940 *Le Quadrivium de Georges Pachymère*. Vatican City

Thurn, I (ed) 1973 Ioannis Scylitzes Synopsis Historiarum. Berlin and New York

Tittmann, J A H (ed) 1808 *Iohannis Zonarae Lexikon*. 2 vols, Leipzig

Toynbee, A 1973 *Constantine Porphyrogenitus and his world*. Oxford

Treadgold, W 1988 *The Byzantine Revival 780–842*. Stanford, California

Treu, M (ed) 1890 *Maximi Monachi Planudis Epistulae* Breslau

Tsaras, G (ed) 1958 *Ioannou Anagnostou Diegesis*. Thessaloniki (in Greek)

Tsolakis, E T (ed) 1968 *Skylitzes Continuatus*. Thessaloniki (in Greek)

Tzamis, D G (ed) 1985 *Philotheos Kokkinos: Hagiological works*. Thessaloniki (in Greek)

Vannier, J-F 1975 *Familles byzantines. Les Argyroi (IX–XII Siècles)*. No. 12, Paris

Vasiliev, A A 1950 *Justin the First. An introduction to the epoch of Justinian the Great*. Cambridge, Mass.

Vasiliev, A A 1968 *Byzance et les Arabes*, II, i: *La dynastie Macédonienne*. (trs M Canard), Brussels

Veh, O 1977 *Prokop, Bauten, Paulos Silentiarios, Beschreibung der Hagia Sophia*. Munich

Verpeaux, J 1959 *Nicéphore Choumnos homme d'état et humaniste byzantin (ca 1250/1255–1327)*. Paris

Verpeaux, J (ed) 1966 *Pseudo-Kodinos: Traité des offices*. Paris

Vlasto, A P 1970 *The entry of the Slavs into Christendom*. Cambridge

Vogt, A (ed and trs) 1935–40 *Constantin VII Porphyrogénète. Le livre des cérémonies*. 4 vols in 2, Paris, with French trs.

Vryonis, S 1957 'The Will of a provincial magnate, Eustathios Boilas.' *Dumbarton Oaks Papers* **XI**: 263–77

Wassiliewsky, B and **V Jernstedt** (eds) 1896 *Cecaumeni Strategicon et incerti scriptoris de officiis regis libellus*. St Petersburg

Weiss, G 1969 *Joannes Kantakuzenos – Aristokrat, Staatsmann, Kaiser und Mönch*. Wiesbaden

Weiss, G 1973 'Hohe Richter in Konstantinopel. Eustathios Rhomaios und seine Kollegen.' *Jahrbuch der österreichischen Byzantinistik* **XXII**: 117–43

Westerink, L G (ed and trs) 1981 *Nicholas I Mystikos, Patriarch of Constantinople: Miscellaneous writings*. Washington, DC

Whitby, M 1988 *The Emperor Maurice and his historian*. Oxford

Whitby, M and **M Whitby** 1986 *The* History *of Theophylact Simocatta. An English translation with introduction and notes*. Oxford

Williamson, G A (trs) 1965 *Eusebius: The history of the Church from Christ to*

REFERENCES

    Constantine. Harmondsworth
Williamson, G A (trs) 1966 *Procopius: The Secret History*. Harmondsworth
Wilson, N G 1983 *Scholars of Byzantium*. London
Winkelman, F (ed) 1975 *Eusebius: Werke*. I, Berlin
Wirth, P (ed) 1978 *Georgii Akropolitae Opera, I*. Stuttgart
Wolska, W 1962 *Topographie Chrétienne de Cosmas Indicopleustès. Théologie et science au VIe siècle*. Paris
Wolska-Conus, W (ed) 1968, 1970, 1973 *Cosmas Indicopleustès: Topographie Chrétienne*. Paris
Woodhouse, C M 1986 *Gemistos Plethon. The last of the Hellenes*. Oxford
Zakythinos, D A 1975 *Le despotat grec de Morée*. I, 2nd ed, London